BEHIND THE GLORY
100 YEARS OF THE PFA

JOHN HARDING

BEHIND THE GLORY
100 YEARS OF THE PFA

breedon **books**
PUBLISHING

First published in Great Britain in 2009 by
The Breedon Books Publishing Company Limited
Breedon House, 3 The Parker Centre,
Derby, DE21 4SZ.

Photograph Credits: Copyright PFA except:
Fifpro, 211, 261; Team England, 275; Paul Cousans, 240, 241;
PA Photos, Cover (top left), 9, 223, 245, 246, 248, 259, 260, 269, 271, 272, 276, 277;
Phill Heywood, 264 (top); MEN Syndication, 264 (bottom); Bryan Horsnell, 185.

ISBN 978-1-85983-682-8
Printed and bound by TJ International Ltd, Padstow, Cornwall.

CONTENTS

ACKNOWLEDGEMENTS

There are many people I have to thank for helping me with gathering information for this book: John Litster, Pat Woods and Bob Crampsey provided Scottish facts and figures; Harry Glasper, Sam Rendell, Stewart Beckett, Mr E. Griffiths, Ian Rigby, William Powell, Denis Turner, David Smith, Harry Berry, Mark Skoal, Ron Gould, M.J. Spinks, Phil Tooley, Keith Warsop, Mrs K. Ashcroft, J. McCormick, Miss K. Holdsworth, Duncan Carmichael, T. Waite, R. Shepherd, John Relish, Derek Higton, F.G. Jeavans, Phil Soar, Brian Truscott, Brian Horsnell, Peter Cullen, Andy Ward, Alan Futter, Denis Clarebrough, Dave Goody, Ray Simpson, Paul Trevillion, Ian King, Jim Brown, Peter Jones, Arthur Bower, Gary James, Stuart Basson, Geoff Mitchell, Mike Davage, Julian Pugh, Roger Wash and Nick Fishwick all provided valuable photographs, statistics and player information.

Braham Dabscheck's excellent papers on the PFA and Simon Inglis's official Football League history have been invaluable and essential guides, while Chris Lightbown provided some fascinating insights through his Meltdown Report. I am also especially indebted to Dr Tony Mason for reading through the original manuscript and offering pertinent and constructive advice.

Ex-management committee members have been very helpful: in particular I would like to thank Tony Ingham, Frank and Elsa Broome, Danny Winter, Harry Hough, Jack Campbell, Ian Dargie, Tommy Cummings, Keith Peacock, Maurice Setters, A. Robertson, Jimmy Hill, Terry Neill, Alan Gowling, Steve Coppell, Brian Talbot, Garth Crooks and the late Joe Mercer OBE.

Relatives of ex-management committee men have also kindly contributed photos and memories: in particular, Mrs Hinchcliffe, F. Robbie, Mrs Crooks, Stuart Crooks, Will and Chris Roberts and Christine Kerry, while journalist Dave Caldwell and ex-players Tom Finney OBE and Jack Crayston also contributed fascinating anecdotes.

The late George Davies, PFA solicitor for many years, was both kind and encouraging. David Green, once of the Davies law firm, was extremely helpful in explaining the intricacies of the George Eastham case.

At the PFA offices, I would like to thank Brendon Batson OBE, Micky Burns, Pat Lally, George Berry, Sue Walsh and Mick McGuire for all their time, patience and friendly assistance. Likewise, a special thank you must also go to Carol Brown, Karen Evans, Anne Stephenson, Zoe Holmes, Pat Wilkinson, Judith Marsden and Louise Pearson.

One man in particular deserves special mention — the late Cliff Lloyd. He was most helpful and generous to me with his time and knowledge and I only hope this book will serve in some way as a tribute to the many years he devoted to the association as secretary.

Finally, I must pay tribute to the PFA Chief Executive, Gordon Taylor OBE. Gordon is a keen student of the game's history and without his considerable help, support and advice this book most certainly could not have been written.

PROLOGUE
by John Harding

In January 2007 the Professional Footballer's Association Chief Executive Gordon Taylor launched the association's centenary celebrations in Manchester Town Hall's Great Hall. It was, on the face of it, a surprising venue for such an event. Decorated with murals by the Pre-Raphaelite artist Ford Madox Brown depicting notable events and persons in the history of the city since its Roman beginnings, the hall was intended as a tangible and visible symbol of Manchester's emerging power as an industrial city in the mid-19th century. What place, it might be asked, was there for mere professional footballers in such surroundings? The simple answer would be that the association's formation at the Imperial Hotel opposite Manchester's Piccadilly railway station in 1907 was a defining moment in modern sporting history. Today, the PFA is the world's oldest and by far the most powerful sporting union, with a crucial role to play in the continuing development of the nation's premier sport. Thus, the huge canvas images of Billy Meredith and Bobby Charlton, Arthur Wharton and Ryan Giggs were not quite so out of place alongside tableaux featuring fly shuttle inventor John Kay, theologian John Wycliffe plus assorted scientists, engineers, weavers and soldiers.

In his opening speech that morning, made to an audience including union stalwarts George Eastham and Jimmy Armfield sitting alongside young stars Wayne Rooney and Micah Richards, Taylor struck a decidedly earnest note. Underplaying the glamorous, essentially ephemeral nature of the game, he stressed instead the role the association and its members could and should play in developing football's 'grass roots', in helping deprived communities, in promoting anti-racist and drug-awareness campaigns designed to heal some of the uglier aspects of 21st-century Britain.

Given the association's long and largely penurious history, it was surprising that Taylor should have felt the need to play down its – and many of its members – present robust health. After all, professional football, for most of its history, had been notable for a lack of financial generosity towards its practitioners. For generations a precarious calling, often marred by injury and insecurity, the pro-game guaranteed the majority of players a few years of questionable glory and local celebrity, before it cast them off with little more than a pittance to live on.

Tied to restrictive contracts, receiving poor wages, lacking freedom of speech and beholden to a governing body that treated them like pariahs and an employer who treated them like chattels, professional footballers laboured in a strange netherworld, rather like well-fed animals in a circus. Though the worst of the conditions that once prompted Union chairman Jimmy Guthrie to characterise his members as no better than 'bonded serfs' had disappeared by the 1970s, it still took another 20 years or so before players could consider themselves masters of their own fates.

The PFA's subsequent rise from almost total obscurity to its present eminence is therefore a remarkable success story, and while its transformation has been in some part due to the astonishing riches flowing from television revenues, nevertheless, the association's role in orchestrating and managing the changes the national game has undergone in recent years has been pivotal.

Nonetheless, Gordon Taylor's desire to avoid any undue triumphalism was sensible, given the delicate relationship the footballing public has with its heroes. By dedicating the association's centenary year to a campaign to raise £1 million for a new rehabilitation and physiotherapy unit at the University Children's Hospital, Manchester, he was able to direct our gaze away from the excesses of the modern game and some of its irresponsible millionaires and reconnect with its working class origins. There was a pleasing symmetry to the concept: the world's oldest sporting union reaching out to help the world's oldest children's hospital.

The 'One Goal, One Million' campaign achieved its target, and Taylor's credo, outlined a year earlier in a speech to the Trades Union Congress conference at Brighton, was thus vindicated: 'We have a role to play outside each of our own professions. We want footballers to have social responsibilities. Let us all play our role, not only for ourselves, for our industry but also for the world beyond.'

The late, great Danny Blanchflower always understood that football was much more than just a job. He declared: 'The great fallacy is that the game is first and last about winning. It is nothing of the kind. The game is about glory, it is about doing things in style and with a flourish, about going out and beating the other lot, not waiting for them to die of boredom.'

To be able to realise that ambition, those who play the game at the highest level require protection, guidance and reward. Over the past 100 years, the Professional Footballer's Association has fought and won many crucial battles to secure such essentials for its members. Through its coaching and educational endeavours it has played a significant role in the modern professional footballer's evolution into one of society's most charismatic and compelling entertainers. With its considerable financial muscle it has enabled thousands of ex-players to discover new vocations once their usefulness to football clubs ended. Through its community and charitable programmes it has elevated the practitioners of what was initially considered a sordid vocation into becoming significant members of society, able to positively influence and affect the lives of millions in ways that could only be dreamt of by men like union pioneer Billy Meredith. Meredith once complained: 'The unfortunate thing is that so many players refuse to take things seriously but are content to live a kind of schoolboy life and to do just what they are told ... instead of thinking and acting for himself and his class.'

Thanks in large part to the PFA, that cannot be said today. 'Behind the Glory' is the story of that radical transformation.

FOREWORD

by Sir Bobby Charlton

I joined the Players' Union back in 1956 when I signed on as a professional for Manchester United. As I recall, the great Roger Byrne was Union representative at the club, although in truth I felt at the time that the union was more for lower division players, those who did not receive the 'perks' and better conditions that went with Division One.

My opinion changed on that in 1961 with the campaign led by Jimmy Hill for the removal of the maximum wage. I can still recall the meetings we held – even Stan Matthews came to one! It was an exciting time and I saw then how important the union was to all players. Later on, Cliff Lloyd, who in many ways was the union in those days, invited me to serve on the management committee along with good friends like Terry Venables, Nobby Lawton, Tony Leighton and Terry Neill. We realised then how crucial education was for professional players – in fact, I went on one of the first management courses set up by the Football Association at Lilleshall.

Today the association is recognized as being a key player in football politics. Superbly led by Gordon Taylor, it holds the balance between the Premier League and the Football Association and its views can no longer be ignored.

So I wish the PFA and its official history all the very best of luck!

Sir Bobby Charlton and PFA Chairman Chris Powell at the PFA Centenary launch, January 2007.

INTRODUCTION

by Gordon Taylor OBE

When I first became Secretary of the Professional Footballer's Association in 1981 we were situated across the city of Manchester in offices in the old Corn Exchange – a lovely old building but a little bit antiquated. Indeed, I remember one day coming across a camera crew in the corridor filming an episode of Sherlock Holmes! I knew then that it was time for a move to somewhere that reflected a more modern image of professional football and yet, ironically, by transferring to our new home – a spacious and purpose-built Georgian-style office block off Lower Mosley Street – we were moving back next to the site of the PFA (then the Players' Union) office in 1907, in St Peter's Square. Thus while moving forward, we were retaining our links with the past.

The union has always had strong links with Manchester. My predecessor, Cliff Lloyd, told me of his visit to Welsh wizard Billy Meredith – one of the union's founders – a Manchester City and United player and a true servant of the union right up until his death in 1958. Billy was ill and destitute yet beneath his bed he kept a battered old suitcase filled with caps and medals, his only reward after an incredible career that spanned 30 years. 'Always remind your members that those caps and medals didn't look after me in my old age', he said. The difference between what Billy was left with at the end of his career and what the vast majority of today's players at all levels can look forward to when they retire is a measure of the great strides the association and the profession have made.

Looking through the papers that came to light during the move, I was struck by the way the battles of long ago so closely mirrored those of recent years. Back in the early 1900s the union that was so dear to Billy Meredith's heart was trying to prove itself as an organization with credibility and respectability, that looked to advance not just the status of players but the overall interests and health of the game as well. It is ironic that Meredith in his opening statement to the Press at that first meeting said how one day he hoped players would be part of the FA Council making decisions which would affect their lives. It has taken us exactly 100 years!

On a personal note, I have witnessed many of the significant milestones along that journey. When I achieved my boyhood dream of joining Bolton Wanderers in 1960 I was well aware of the glory of the profession but not its inadequacies, with its ceiling on wages and its draconian restrictions on contracts and players' rights. A year later, in 1961, Jimmy Hill and Cliff Lloyd led the campaign to reform conditions and achieved a notable victory on wages. In 1963, the year I made my first-team debut, there came the momentous victory in the courts by George Eastham, supported by the PFA, against the retain-and-transfer system.

Following in the footsteps of my father, who was a branch secretary for the Amalgamated Union of Engineering Workers, I took over as Bolton's union delegate from the England international goalkeeper, Eddie Hopkinson. In 1971 I joined the management committee and in 1978 became chairman. After retiring from playing in 1980 I accepted an invitation from Cliff Lloyd to join the PFA full-time and on his retirement in 1981 I took over as secretary. However, I did not dare envisage that I would still be at the helm when we reached our centenary!

We built our centenary celebrations around a 'One Goal, One Million' campaign dedicated to raising £1 million for the new Manchester Children's Hospital. I believe Billy Meredith and the union's founding fathers would have been proud of our achievement, which fully demonstrated the good work that football does for those less fortunate than ourselves. On the day itself, Sunday 2 December 2007, we staged an international football match – England versus the Rest of the World – involving some of football's greats, including Terry Venables, Sven Goran Eriksson, Alan Shearer, Gianfraco Zola and many more. This was followed by a tremendous Gala Dinner in central Manchester attended by dignitaries from the world of football including four of the greatest football knights – Sir Bobby Charlton, Sir Bobby Robson, Sir Tom Finney and Sir Alex Ferguson! The icing on the cake of the centenary year was the award of an OBE to myself, which, in truth, was recognition of the PFA's role throughout these 100 years in establishing football as the greatest participant and spectator sport in the world.

The PFA is today one of the strongest unions in the world with an incredibly loyal membership. It has pioneered football's links with the wider community, has led the way in fighting the scourge of racism and is ever active in promoting better health and education through its involvement in a score of charities and initiatives both here and abroad. It is no exaggeration to say that it has become a fourth force in the governance of the English game and through its membership of FIFPro, the International Association of Football Players' Unions, it plays a vital role in developing the game worldwide.

These achievements are a testimony to the work of PFA officials, management committee members, delegates and players down the century. It has been a long, long journey from the Imperial Hotel to where we are today! It was to document that journey as fully as possible that we commissioned John Harding, biographer of Billy Meredith, to produce this extensive history. John has worked closely not only with myself, but also with the late Cliff Lloyd, like Meredith, a great servant of the union, and many other PFA notables. We hope the results will not only inform and educate but also – in the best traditions of professional football – entertain.

PART ONE

MEREDITH'S BIG IDEA
1897–1909

1. A Profession in Chains 1888–1900

In 1885 professionalism in football was reluctantly 'legalised' by the game's ruling body, the Football Association, a group of men drawn from the upper echelons of British society – honourable men but, as Percy Young has written: 'Men of prejudice, seeing themselves as patricians, heirs to the doctrine of "leadership" and so law-givers by at least semi-divine right.'

Three years later the Football League was founded by a group of very different men – shopkeepers, minor government officials, small businessmen – not for the purpose of encouraging football but, as a journalist of the period put it, 'so that allied clubs may make more money than they already do…'

William McGregor, the architect of the League, had seen that professional football as a commercial venture was in danger of destroying itself. Clubs were too concerned to compete on individual terms – to lure the best players, to attract the best crowds – with no concern as to the economic fate of opponents.

Fixtures were haphazard, with smaller clubs often finding games cancelled at the last moment because a larger club had arranged what was likely to be a more profitable match. With the FA Cup – the only national, prestigious competition – being organised on a knockout basis, eliminated clubs often had nothing more exciting than county cups to offer their patrons. In short, there was no pattern and, increasingly, no credibility to competition.

The League simply repackaged in a clever and novel way a potentially lucrative product and it was immediately successful, growing rapidly from 12 teams in 1888 to 36 in 1900. From being a predominantly North/Midlands organisation, it soon embraced all areas of the country until no football club of substance or ambition could afford to remain outside it.

Membership brought with it many benefits: a regular flow of income derived from a guaranteed number of fixtures; sustained competition that kept interest high throughout the season, thereby attracting large crowds; plus rules and regulations designed to bind members together for their own protection. It was a cartel, which rapidly assumed monopoly powers; only the Southern League offered any sort of competition over the years but even that was eventually absorbed.

For the newly recognised professional player the rise of the League proved to be both a blessing and a curse. Not that players were against the establishment of the League system, far from it, the League was seen at the outset as being of great benefit.

Pro-players increasingly desired security of employment, regular pay and a good working environment. The League appeared to produce all these. Indeed, without it professional football might not have survived into the 20th century.

In 1885, however, the player had been as free as the next man to sell his labour to the highest bidder; yet by 1900 he was being described as a bonded slave, a chattel, no better than a piece of merchandise. In rescuing the professional game from financial ruin, the founders of the Football League had created a category of workman like no other before or since.

League administrators would argue down the years that the success of the League depended on balance – teams of near-equal ability in competition; the outcome of games uncertain; the entertainment factor consequently high, resulting in large, enthusiastic crowds. However, with the rapid growth of the League in centres of large population, imbalances appeared. Small town clubs, no matter how successful on the pitch, could never earn as much as big town clubs at the turnstile. Unable to pay sufficiently high wages to attract the best players, they seemed doomed to struggle, facing dwindling crowds and eventually the spectre of bankruptcy.

'Survival of the fittest', although the law of the business world, was nevertheless anathema to League philosophy because the folding of smaller clubs, it was contended, would destroy the essential balance. It might even lead to a Super League which, in turn, would mean less variety and smaller and smaller attendances.

Therefore, almost from the start of their phenomenally successful competition, the founders and administrators of the League saw the maintenance of the shape and size of the League as one of the principal tasks.

The obvious method of achieving this was the sharing of gate-money. A club situated in the centre of a large population was merely fortunate; playing no better football than a team from a smaller town, it could earn three, four times as much – yet it depended on the small town team for competition. Both, it was argued, should share in the financial results.

Yet from the outset this idea (favoured by William McGregor) was resisted by a majority of clubs, for the earning of massive amounts of money and building of an edifice to one's own memory was more appealing to directors and owners than the less tangible concept of brotherly love. The only realistic alternative to pooling, therefore, was to control (and share) the raw material of the game – the players.

If clubs – especially smaller clubs – could be certain of keeping their players from season to season instead of having them snatched by bigger, wealthier clubs, then talent would remain equally spread and thus no team could dominate the competition. But how to secure such control? Fortunately for the League, the FA had, unwittingly, created a perfect mechanism.

The amateur-professional split was a profound one, reflecting deeply held class prejudices. Certain key members of the FA were extremely disturbed by professionalism in sport and had only accepted it if they could somehow 'control' it and, in their view, safeguard the principles essential to 'true' sport.

In the eyes of the FA football would always be a sport, never a business, while those who played it would always be 'sportsmen', never workmen. That the pro-player was a workman with a legal contract and recognised as such (after a struggle) by the law of the land would make no practical difference. For the FA, football was a world within a world, and they were its rulers.

To ensure that pro-players remained under the FA's control a regulation was passed that compelled all pro-players to register annually. No player was allowed to play until he was registered, nor was he free to change clubs during the same season without the FA's permission.

Clearly the FA intended that once the season was over players could move on if they wished. The League, however, quickly realised that to achieve the necessary control it had to go one step further. Thus it insisted that any pro-player who had signed for a particular club and wished to move on to another had to obtain the permission of his present club.

More controversial still, however, was the League rule that, once signed, a player was tied to his club for as long as the club wanted him (and even beyond that point). Thus, the season would end, the player might refuse to sign a new contract, but he could sign for no one else unless the club gave permission.

The smaller clubs, it was argued, could thus be sure of keeping their 'assets'; if a larger club wanted a particular player, then it would have to compensate the smaller club by offering money with which the latter might buy a replacement or service its debt. Although, admittedly, it was not the man who was being bought, merely his registration, the point was a technical one. Within a year or two of the League's formation, men were being bought and sold. The retain-and-transfer system had been created.

In years to come this uncomfortable truth would be justified on many grounds, not least the insistence that the chaos of pre-League days had been caused by the players and their excessive financial demands; that clubs, fearful of losing 'star' players, had been blackmailed into paying whatever had been demanded; that many clubs had bankrupted themselves in the process while the players had moved on to pastures new.

This was, of course, a convenient fiction. Some men certainly had behaved unscrupulously, but it had been the club managements that had created the atmosphere in which such 'mercenaries' had been able to flourish. Clubs – or their directorates – in their anxiety to fill grounds and make money had broken whatever rules had then existed and in the process had reduced the game to a shambles. Nevertheless, the myth of the greedy, grasping player would prove a powerful and convenient one.

From 1893, therefore, players in the Football League were not free to negotiate a new contract on anything like equal terms with their employers. In fact, if a player wanted to leave a League club he could be prevented from doing so; to continue playing in League football he would have to sign a new contract with his original club – hardly a situation in which a player could make demands for better conditions.

In effect, the Football League abolished the free market where players wages and conditions were concerned; indeed, once the question of retention had been settled, it was not long before clubs began clamouring for an 'equal' wage – a maximum that a player, any player, might be able to earn.

At first the situation did not look too grim for players. During the early 1890s the Football League, though growing fast, was also wracked by controversy and dissent which appeared to herald its demise. Furthermore, imitation leagues sprang up all over the country (and in Scotland and Ireland).

Thus, there were 'escape routes' to clubs and countries where a player could ply his trade freely and earn a reasonable (indeed, where some Southern League clubs were concerned, highly lucrative) wage. However, as the League expanded, or struck up deals with these rival leagues, that freedom began to disappear.

It was then that professional players began to think of protecting themselves, of speaking out to suggest alternative methods of running League football. During the late 1890s there was lively debate as to the future of professional League football in England. It was in order that players could participate effectively in such discussions and to clarify their position in a rapidly changing 'industry' that the first players' organisation was formed.

2. The Old Union

The first players' union, called The Association Football Players' Union, came into existence in 1897 as various top players from Liverpool, Everton and the Glasgow giants Celtic and Rangers set out to forge a negotiating link based on equality of status with the Football League and the FA.

The *Lancashire Daily Post* of 22 December 1897 announced: 'Football Professionals Form a Union. An Ambitious Scheme Floated.' Its sudden appearance came as a surprise to many observers. There had been little advance publicity and no circulars to leading players. Yet the men involved were all 'stars' and the authoritative sports paper *Cricket and Football Field* was certainly impressed, commenting in the same month, 'They are representative in every way and men who would do credit to any organisation as its champions.'

Champions they undoubtedly were. They included Bob Holmes and Jimmy Ross of Preston North End; John Devey of Aston Villa; John Somerville of Bolton Wanderers; Jack Bell of Everton; Hugh McNeill of Sunderland and Harry Wood of Wolverhampton Wanderers.

Holmes was almost ever-present in the England team during the early 1890s while both he and Ross had been members of the 'Invincibles', that classic Preston side that had won the double. Jack Bell would win 10 caps for Scotland between 1890 and 1900, while Wood and Dave Calderhead (another committee member) were both respected internationals. John Devey was Aston Villa's captain and there was no more powerful team than Villa during the 1890s – five times League champions between 1894 and

John Devey Chairman Old Players' Union 1897

John Devey was present at the start of the first-ever Players' Union, formed in December 1897. It was not a militant union, however, and Devey declared at the outset: 'We're not taking up the question of wages and we are not taking any strike business.' He had signed for Aston Villa in March 1891 and for eight years was captain, during which time they won the League Championship five times between 1894 and 1900 and the FA Cup twice. The crowning triumph of his career, however, came in 1897 when Villa emulated the example of Preston North End and carried off the English Cup and the League Championship in the same season. He retired in April 1902 and was an Aston Villa director for the next 32 years. He owned a sports outfitters at Lozells, Birmingham, and later joined forces with Harry Hampton, another famous Villa star, to form the Winson Green Picture House Company, opening a 1,500-seat cinema in 1915. When he died in 1940 he left an estate worth £2,000.

Jack Bell Chairman Old Players' Union 1897–98

John Devey shared the chair with Jack Bell, whose long career took in Dumbarton, Everton, Celtic, New Brighton Tower, Everton again and, finally, Preston North End. A right-winger, he won 10 Scottish caps and scored five goals in the process, as well as winning the Scottish League Championship with Dumbarton. He was also on the losing side for Everton in the 1897 Cup Final, beaten by John Devey's Aston Villa. He was considered an exciting but 'rough' player. Bell served on various Players' Union committees and played in the first-ever fund-raising match between the English and Scottish Players' Unions in April 1898. In July 1898 he left Everton hoping to sign for Tottenham Hotspur but spent a season with Celtic instead, eventually returning to Liverpool where he had a small cycle business. As captain-coach of Preston North End he helped revive that great club, leading them to promotion to Division One in 1905, then to a runners-up spot in 1906. On 2 December 1907 he was present at the first meeting of the new union (later the PFA) at the Imperial Hotel, Manchester.

Charlie Saer Secretary Old Players' Union 1897–98

A fine goalkeeper, his pro-career would be moderate but respectable. After three years as an amateur with Fleetwood Rangers, a non-League side, he turned professional with Stockport County. He then moved to First Division Blackburn Rovers and towards the end of 1897–98 to Second Division Leicester City. It was while playing for Blackburn that he became an active member of the Old Players' Union and was elected secretary to fight for better conditions of employment and a reformed transfer system. He devised a new system of compensation intended to replace the existing transfer system that would have rewarded the selling club as well as allowing the player some sort of freedom to choose where he went. In 1898, when renewing his teaching appointment, his Education Authority insisted he undertake no other paid occupation, so he decided to give up the game completely. It was a financial sacrifice. At the time he was earning £85 per year as a senior teacher, much less than his wage from football, but it was probably a greater loss to the players' cause.

---

1 If a club offers a player no terms for the ensuing season, no fee shall be charged for his transfer. An offer of less than £1 a week – £52 a year – shall not be considered a bona-fide one.

2 If a club offers a player a sum exceeding £52 a year then should he refuse, half the difference between £52 and the sum offered shall be the maximum fee chargeable for his transfer.

The following table shows at a glance how the maximum transfer fee is arrived at in the cases of players offered various weekly wages:

Player	Weekly salary offered Winter 35 weeks £	Summer 17 weeks £	Total annual salary £	Less £52 £	Half the difference or max. transfer fee £
A	–	–	–	S	–
B	1	1	52	–	–
C	2	–	70	18	9
D	2	2	104	52	26.10
E	3	2	139	87	43.10
F	3	3	155	104	52
G	4	4	208	156	78
H	5	5	260	208	104

Charlie Saer's transfer system. *Lancashire Daily Post,* October 1898.

1900. McNeill was a member of the Sunderland 'Team of all the Talents' – three times champions in four years between 1892 and 1895.

These were men who had been at the top of the profession for almost as long as the League had been in existence. They saw the sense in some kind of 'transfer' system, but felt that a better, more just arrangement could be devised to prevent players being traded like cigarette cards with little say in their own destinies.

Bob Holmes Chairman Old Players' Union 1898–1900

Bob Holmes made his full League debut for Preston North End in the Football League's inaugural season in 1888 and eventually became captain. As a key member of the famous 'Invincibles' he helped the team to win the first FA Cup and League double in 1889 as well as a second League Championship in 1890. Bob was a one-club player making some 300 appearances at full-back for Preston and 35 FA Cup appearances. It was said of him: 'Few more judicious backs than Holmes have ever been identified with the game.' Bob took over as Players' Union chair from Jack Bell in 1898 and presided over the old union's first AGM. With just 400 members and a cash balance of £132 8s 10d, matters looked grim. Bob, however, emphasised the grass roots work that had already been done: money sent to the relatives of players who had died; a recruitment campaign and a significant victory in a court case brought against Notts County forcing the club to pay a player wages and expenses after he had undergone treatment for an injury received while playing. Bob's basic idea as to how the Union should operate: building slowly and carefully, putting in place solid insurance schemes, providing legal assistance and seeking to maximise membership would prove the way ahead.

John Cameron Secretary Old Players' Union 1898–99

An amateur player who represented Scotland in 1896, he worked as a clerk for the shipping line Cunard while playing for Queen's Park. He then spent two seasons with Everton, much of the time in the reserves. Towards the end of the 1897–98 season he established himself in the Everton side and, as an astute ball-playing inside-forward, was on the point of signing professional forms when he found himself on the transfer list. He moved south to Tottenham Hotspur, and Charlie Saer took over as union secretary to replace him. In an eight-year period initially as player then as manager, John succeeded in building Spurs into the first truly great professional side in southern England. They won the Southern League Championship in 1899–1900 and the FA Cup in 1901. He returned to Scotland, became a journalist and coach and was working in Germany at the outbreak of World War One when he was interned. He managed Ayr United on his return in 1919. One of the most talented and intelligent of football administrators.

From the start the new unionists adopted a deliberately non-controversial (that is, non-political) stance. John Devey announced: 'We're not taking up the question of wages and we are not taking any strike business'. The players involved clearly believed that reason and the British sense of fair play would prevail. Not for the last time the players were mistaken.

At the outset they were encouraged in their attempts to change existing transfer arrangements by the fact that many members of the Football Association thought the idea of men being bought and sold like chattels was repugnant. Unfortunately, many members of that same Football Association also thought that paying men to play football was equally distasteful, and so preferred to keep professional players (whom they distrusted) under tight control. Some FA members even refused to accept that professional players were actually bona fide workmen with concomitant legal rights.

Although Charlie Saer, the secretary of the new organisation, put forward an imaginative alternative transfer scheme that would have rewarded the selling club as well as allowing the player some freedom to choose where he went, progress was non-existent as the Football League refused to talk.

The early optimism soon faded and various prominent members of the union either retired from the game or became managers and coaches. Charlie Saer was forced out of the game and went abroad to work as a teacher.

Lancashire Daily Post, 23 December 1899.

"My boy," said the lady (Football Association), "I don't like to see that kind of bird being sold. You'll let them go, to please me, won't you?"
"Yes, lady," said the boy (Football League) "course I will." (M'yes! Lot's of it!)

The union's last secretary, John Cameron, moved south to manage Tottenham Hotspur and in 1901 he guided them to their first FA Cup win. In that same year the first Players' Union folded.

3. The New Union

In 1900 the FA and the Football League combined to enforce a maximum wage on professional players. Set at £4 a week, it meant that no player, no matter how talented or experienced, was free to negotiate with his club to earn more, whether by way of bonuses or signing-on fees.

The secretary of the old Players' Union, John Cameron, interviewed in *Football Chat*, expressed his surprise and dismay:

> In my opinion, the FA haven't acted with their usual discretion over the wages question. Surely the matter of wages is for club legislation alone? Every club knows, or ought to know, what it can afford to pay and if they go above their means I should certainly call it bad management and the club who does that deserves to be stranded. I noticed with a little amusement that it was those clubs that had paid more than they could afford that fought hard to carry the new measures through. Now look here, how would any man in business like to have his wages reduced by 25 per cent if his employers could well afford better terms?

Some clubs could afford 'better terms' and were determined to pay them, particularly those with ambitions to establish themselves in the top echelon. At least seven clubs were investigated and punished for 'financial irregularities' (paying players 'under-the-counter' wages) in the period between 1901 and 1911. Many other clubs were thought to have been guilty but escaped punishment, having successfully disguised the money as 'presents' or extra duties.

Some clubs were less fortunate. Middlesbrough, for instance, had been elected to the League in 1899 and reached Division One in 1902. A year later they opened one of the finest grounds in the country, Ayresome Park. The enormous £10,000 expenditure stretched the club so much that a few years later it was struggling with reduced gates, heavy losses and poor form. Desperate measures were undertaken, but in November 1905 Middlesbrough's directors admitted to making illegal payments worth some £400 over the previous two seasons and creating fictitious accounts to conceal their actions. The FA fined them £250 and 11 of the 12 directors were suspended until 1 January 1908.

However, it would be the fate of Manchester City FC that would have the most significant effect on football politics and which led, indirectly, to the formation of a new players' union.

Billy Meredith
Founder of the Players' Union

Meredith was the first great player for both Manchester clubs, winning the FA Cup with City, and two League Championships and the FA Cup with United. He was also a record-breaker. His last competitive match was an FA Cup semi-final in 1923 against Newcastle, when he was a couple of months short of his 50th birthday! In 1914 he bought a public house, the Church Hotel in Longsight, and in the 1920s and 30s he managed a second public house, the Stretford Hotel on Stretford Road, Manchester. In 1926 he starred in a feature film, The Ball of Fortune, as well as a number of short coaching films. He also appeared on stage in cinemas showing his films and answered questions from the audience. He was friends with many music hall stars of the pre-World War One period, including George Robey and Harry Weldon (who played 'Stiffy the Goalkeeper' in a Fred Karno sketch that also featured Charlie Chaplin). The catchphrase 'Meredith, We're In!' from another pre-World War One Karno sketch was said to have been inspired by Meredith. During his retirement he lived in Manchester. He died on 19 April 1958 and is buried in Southern Cemetery, Manchester.

City, like Middlesbrough, was a club in a hurry. Entering the League as Ardwick in 1892, they struggled for a decade to establish themselves in the top flight, were promoted to the First Division for the second time in 1903, won the FA Cup the following season and looked all set to storm the League in 1905. Years later, Billy Meredith, City's captain during those years, was blunt in his explanation of their success:

'What was the secret of the success of the Manchester City team? In my opinion, the fact that the club put aside the rule that no player should receive more than four pounds a week…The team delivered the goods, the club paid for the goods delivered and both sides were satisfied.'

The following season City's strong ch ge for the League title ended disappointingly: needing to beat Aston Villa in their last match (in the hope that Newcastle might drop a point at lowly Middlesbrough), City tried hard but lost 3–2. The match was marred by fighting among the players both during and after the game and, following as it did some ugly incidents in an earlier match City played against Everton, the FA felt obliged to investigate.

The subsequent enquiry revealed startling and totally unexpected evidence of attempted bribery involving Billy Meredith who, despite his protestations of innocence, was suspended for a year, banned from City's ground and heavily fined.

More sensational revelations were to follow as Meredith, angered by the attitude of Manchester City's officials, pestered the club for financial recompense. This led to yet more official investigations with Meredith ultimately turning 'King's Evidence' admitting to illegal payments and thus bringing down the whole pack of cards City had so carefully constructed.

So outraged was the FA by what had been uncovered that it virtually dismembered the City club. The complete Cup-winning side of 1903 was suspended and banned from ever playing for City again; club directors (including Joshua Parlby, one of the original Football League founding members) were banned for life and the club was fined to within an inch of survival.

Billy Meredith eventually moved on to Manchester United and resumed his glittering career, but he was a changed man. The traumatic events of 1905–06 turned a taciturn but essentially contented man into a bitterly aggressive critic of a system he felt had robbed him, not only of his dignity, but also of the financial rewards he considered were rightfully his. Moreover, for a few horrific months he had been an outcast, with no prospect of employment in football and facing bankruptcy: no benefit, heavy fines to pay, his career in ruins.

A more cynical man might have shrugged his shoulders and awaited developments. After all, it was a cynical game. However, the year and a half he had been out of the game had left him with time on his hands to contemplate exactly what had happened, not only to him, but also colleagues at Middlesbrough, at Sunderland, at clubs both high and low.

Within six months of his return to the game Meredith was chairing the inaugural meeting of the newly reformed Players' Union at the Imperial Hotel, Manchester.

****

William Henry Meredith was born on 29 July 1874 at The Wharf, Chirk, Denbighshire, the ninth of 10 children of mining engine winder Henry Meredith and wife Jane.

Meredith attended the local Chirk school until the age of 12, when he obtained work at the nearby Black Park Colliery. He was a pony driver and 'hutcher' before later becoming a boiler-firer, his ambition then being to become a mining-engineer. He was also a precocious footballer.

By the age of 15 he was playing for Chirk reserves and by 18 was a first-team member, winning a Welsh Cup Medal in 1894. Uncertainty in the mining industry in 1893 led him to follow the example of his brother Sam, then a professional with Stoke City, to play semi-professionally for Northwich Victoria of the Second Division of the Football League. In September 1894 he signed professional forms for Manchester City, also in the Second Division, and in January 1895 he finally gave up his job at Black Park. He would remain a full-time footballer until 1924 when he retired from the game aged 50 years old. In his first 10 years with Manchester City he captained the club to promotion to the First Division and, in 1904, to the club's first significant trophy, the FA Cup, scoring the only goal in a 1–0 victory over Bristol City at Crystal Palace.

Like many professional footballers, then and now, Billy Meredith appeared profoundly indifferent to organised politics. He was said to be an admirer of Lloyd George, perhaps understandable for a proud Welshman, but overt political ideology

The Stepping Stone.
International Association player: 'Come on boys; it's an easy jump from here.'

Manchester Evening News.

The Resurrection.

Willie Meredith endeavours to revive the Players' Union.

Manchester Evening News cartoon.

would seem to have played no part in his personal philosophy. Meredith can not have been totally immune to mainstream political action, however. Along with his father and brothers who were also miners, he had been pitched into the national coal dispute of 1894 that had seen local North Welsh mining communities reduced to near starvation and engaged in bitter disputes among themselves over strike-breaking. He thus had 'hands-on' experience of organisation and struggle and would regularly extol the merits of 'united action'.

What is more, during his early years at Manchester City Meredith had witnessed the way local and national politicians used the club to promote their careers. A.J. Balfour had been a celebrity guest at Hyde Road (Meredith shook hands with him on the centre-circle) while City director John Chapman cajoled players into canvassing for his local council ward candidacy.

Once the union was launched, however, Meredith's sharp wit, combined with a sometimes withering sarcasm, would be put to good use in a regular newspaper column he produced for the popular *Weekly News*. His no-nonsense approach can be seen in the following assessment of his playing colleagues:

> They (the players) are, as a whole, an over-generous careless race who do not heed the morrow or prepare for a rainy day as wise men would. This trait in the character of the players has been taken advantage of over and over again by club secretaries in England. Many a lad has been tricked into signing on by vague verbal promises deliberately made to be forgotten once the ink was dry on the form. It is only recently that with steady improvement in the class of men playing the game as professionals the players have seen the folly of the careless life and have realised that they have too long put up with indifferences and injustices of many kinds. The only way to alter this state of things was by united action hence the formation and success of the Players' Union…

＊＊＊＊＊＊＊＊＊＊＊＊＊

Whether Meredith had taken any part in the running of the old Players' Union is hard to establish but it would have been difficult for him to avoid hearing about it as at least two of his close friends and playing partners during his early Manchester City days, Joe Cassidy and Jimmy Ross, had been Players' Union Management Committee members.

However, one senses that Meredith's initial impulse was deeply personal. When he told a reporter in 1907 that 'the player of today realises the serious side of football more than the player of five or six years ago', he was clearly speaking from bitter personal experience. Although he would always declare his love for football (and would continue playing at the highest level until he was 50 years of age) he now appeared increasingly impatient with what he called the 'sentimental' reasoning which had created regulations that had punished and branded him an outlaw and forced him to sit in front of committees of 'gentlemen' who had treated him no better than a common thief.

The appearance of the new union in December 1907 can have taken no one by surprise. Its formation had been discussed at length for some months prior to the inaugural meeting and Meredith appears to have been interviewed on at least three or four occasions. His views and aims met with little opposition from football's authorities. Indeed, almost everyone seemed to be in favour of it.

John Lewis, referee, founder of Blackburn Rovers and Football League committee member commented in his *Athletic News* column: 'It is the duty of all professional players to at least hear what can be said in favour of the union,' while the newspaper itself declared in an editorial: 'We cannot conceive of any player with a grain of sense refusing to support the establishment of a body for the protection of his own interests.'

Doubts were nevertheless expressed elsewhere concerning the amount of support Meredith would receive. Another authoritative journal, the *Bolton Cricket and Football Field*, commented:

From past experience, though, of the apathy of the player towards anything of the kind we confess to being sceptical as to the success of the scheme. We may be wrong and if so we are sorry but at the same time we feel that we should not like the task of collecting the Union subs. We sincerely hope that the players will prove these views are pessimistic but we remember the last Players' Union meeting called at Birmingham when not a single player put in an appearance.

New Welsh Revival.
Meredith: 'Friends, countrymen, players, lend me your ears!'

Manchester Evening News cartoon.

Meredith was enthusiastic, however, and from the outset placed his own experience at the forefront of his argument for the union, particularly where wages were concerned: 'What is more reasonable than our plea that a footballer with his uncertain career should have the best money that he can earn? If I can earn £7 a week, why should I be debarred from receiving it?'

Where the transfer system was concerned player opinion seemed to have softened. While still irked by the system, Meredith seemed keener to amend it to include the player in any possible benefits it might bring. It was a key difference between the old and new unions reflecting the changed circumstances of the football industry.

One thing, however, had not changed. The new union was also inclining to the FA for help: 'Meredith hopes to see the day when the players have direct representation on the ruling body. He says there are many matters that ought to be brought to the attention of the FA and he is convinced that the members of that body do not realise some of the conditions under which players labour.' Little would Billy Meredith realise that it would take almost exactly 100 years for this to happen!

The first meeting of the new body was held on 2 December at the Imperial Hotel, Manchester. Among those present were no less than seven Manchester United players: Meredith, Charlie Roberts, 'Sandy' Turnbull, Herbert Broomfield, Alec Downie, Charlie Sagar and Herbert Burgess. There were two Manchester City players, Johnny McMahon and Irvine Thornley, plus Andrew McCombie of Newcastle United; C.J. Craig of Bradford City; A.J. Evans of West Bromwich Albion; Harry Mainman from Notts County; Bert Lipsham of Sheffield United and Walter Bull of Tottenham Hotspur. Jack Bell, now of Preston North End, provided a link with the old union, and application in writing was made for John Cameron's account books.

Many Famous Players are Writing Special

FOOTBALL ARTICLES

FOR

THOMSON'S WEEKLY NEWS

AMONG OTHERS

COLIN VEITCH
WILLIAM MEREDITH
JAMES LAWRENCE
BILLY HOGG
JACK RUTHERFORD
CHRIS DUFFY
TOM NIBLO

Look out for these up-to-date articles EVERY WEEK

On Sale Every Thursday.   Price 1d

Vice-presidents of the union were appointed. They made impressive reading: John Davies chairman of Manchester United, John Cameron of Newcastle United, plus the chairmen of Spurs and Bradford City. Jimmy Catton, *Athletic News* editor, was also proposed and in the following weeks H.G. Norris of Fulham and John McKenna of the Football League Management Committee were also asked to join. A solicitor was taken

The Imperial Hotel, Manchester, demolished in 1997.

on (who just happened to be Manchester City director W.A. Wilkinson) and a bank account opened.

Two weeks later, in London at the Charterhouse Hotel, Meredith chaired the southern section meeting and an entrance fee of 5s plus subs of 6d a week were confirmed. A week later, a third meeting at the Maypole in Nottingham saw Herbert Broomfield officially appointed as secretary.

Finally, in January 1908, the first management committee met: Mainman, Bull, McCombie, Meredith, Roberts, Lipsham, Craig and Broomfield. A request was made to the FA for a fund-raising match; the request was granted. It was a painless, one might almost say, euphoric beginning and within weeks it was claimed that the majority of players in League football had joined.

****

The new union, though staffed mainly by 'star' players, was devoted to the interests of all players high and low. Meredith's original title for the union had been the Players' Union and Benefit Society and although this soon became the Association Football Players Union the aim of the organisation was clear.

According to its press release its first objective was:

> To promote and protect the interests of the members by endeavouring to come to amicable arrangements with the governing football authorities with a view to abolishing all restrictions which affect the social and financial position of players and to safeguard their rights at all times.

Other objectives were to provide members with legal advice and assistance; to help transfer-listed or disengaged players to find employment; to provide temporary financial assistance for members and their families if and when necessary; to generally regulate relations between professional football players and their employers; and to do all things necessary to help advance and promote the interests of members.

A typical World War One player's contract.

RULES TO BE OBSERVED BY PLAYERS.

1. Players must attend the ground on Tuesday, Wednesday and Thursday of each week from 10 to 12 a.m. and 2 to 4 p.m. and on any other day when required to do so, due notice of which will be given.

2. During training times the players are required to follow exactly the trainer's orders, who will report daily to the Manager the attendance of the players and their exercises.

3. Teams will be posted as selected, and on the field of play players must be subject to the officials and the Captain, the latter being selected by the Directors.

4. Any player or players having grievances or complaints are requested to lodge the same in writing with the Manager.

5. Players may not absent themselves from training without having permission from the Manager, or sufficiency of excuse, such as illness, etc.

6. Any player or players neglecting or breaking any of the foregoing rules will become liable to be dealt with as the Directors may think fit and proper.

It is expected that players will recognise the value of temperance in matter of language, action and drink, as any grave breaches in these matters will be summarily dealt with.

Rules found on the back of the contract.

Within a few months of being established the union began operating like a friendly society, pressing clubs with compensation claims for injured players and arranging money for families of men who had passed away leaving no adequate provision. The Sheffield United player Frank Levich had died in just such circumstances, whereupon the union sent £20 to his mother and wrote to the Sheffield club to request that the amount paid out would equal a season's wages. They also wrote to the FA to ask for a grant from the FA's Benevolent Fund.

The union also began a series of investigations into broken player contracts and case work, secure in the knowledge that the newly passed Workman's Compensation Act provided legal backing for such activity. Ironically, it would be this work, rather than the potentially more explosive issues of wages and transfers, that would eventually bring the union into head-on collision with football's authorities.

Inevitably, though, it was the question of wages that consumed most of the newsprint devoted to the union in the second part of 1908. Specifically, it was asked, how should the maximum wage be altered or amended, given that it was not being adhered to by many clubs? And how might the new union come to influence the debate?

In May the Players' Union Management Committee met in Manchester at the Midland Hotel to discuss alternative pay schemes but there was little prospect of any idea coming to fruition. The Southern League had set its face against the idea of bonuses as suggested in the new Football League scheme and had indicated that it would block any such innovation. Having waited patiently to see whether real change was a possibility, the union finally declared at its AGM in December: 'For the policy of limitations and restrictions that has failed after a trial of seven seasons, the Players' Union begs leave to offer a policy of mutual arrangements based on free bargaining in all matters affecting the services of players and their clubs.'

As for the transfer system, the union suggested that: 'clubs and players should be encouraged to enter into arrangements for periods of two seasons and upwards'.

The resolution was accompanied by this pointed observation: 'Free bargaining between clubs and players would do something more than merely bring to an end the generally admitted inequalities of remuneration; it would cause the scandal of suspensions to cease and save gentlemen of high social standing the humiliation of being pilloried in the public press.'

In August 1908 new offices were opened in St Peter's Square, Manchester, and newly appointed secretary Herbert Broomfield was granted a salary of £156 per annum plus an assistant at 30s a week. The union rules were printed on strong card and sent to all clubs that had members to be hung on dressing room walls. A union badge was suggested and designs were being considered, while a union journal was also in preparation to secure a direct line of communication to members.

Not that the union was finding it difficult to find press outlets for its views. With the rapid growth of football papers – almost every town had at least one evening paper that carried football news and results and most local papers now produced 'specials' or carried pages devoted to the game – the opportunities to be interviewed or to contribute articles were numerous.

One paper in particular, *Thomson's Weekly News*, a penny weekly appearing on a Thursday and selling well over 300,000 copies a week, announced in November 1908 that Colin Veitch, Billy Meredith, Jimmy Lawrence and many other 'popular, prominent players' would be writing special football articles.

From that point on the *Weekly News* would continue to offer players – particularly union members and officials – a regular platform from which to hold forth in unprecedented fashion. This freedom to voice their ideas and reactions, to criticise openly Football League and FA officials and their actions, would significantly alter the nature and climate of the struggle between football's administrators and the men they sought to control.

The year 1908 had thus seen a new union, confident and outspoken, establish itself at the heart of football's affairs. At the Ye Old Royal restaurant in Birmingham, Herbert Broomfield declared that 'a trying ordeal has been pursued successfully' and that the union had been successful in stirring the FA into action. Changes, Broomfield predicted, were on the horizon. He could not have known just how close those changes were.

4. The Approaching Storm

In December 1908 C.E. Sutcliffe, a prominent member of the Football League Management Committee, vigorously attacked the Players' Union's 'amazing proposals'. They were, he said, 'but the outward and visible sign of their inward greed…' The union's resolutions were 'contemptible clap-trap'; 'immoderate and unreasonable', to grant them would be 'suicide' for football and would lead back to the days 'when such a spirit of selfishness was ruining the game and the clubs'.

Just why Sutcliffe should have responded in such a way at such a point appeared a mystery to many. The union's opposition to the maximum wage was shared by the FA and a majority of First Division clubs. Thus, in attacking the union in such contemptuous terms Sutcliffe was behaving, on the face of it, rather oddly.

However, Sutcliffe had a clear vision of the way the Football League system should operate. The continual arguing, lobbying and pressure by the bigger clubs for wage reform irked him. Talk of a possible 'super-league' of bigger clubs was both unsettling and distasteful to him. His own club, Burnley, would not feature in such a breakaway; it was too small and vulnerable and was already struggling financially. Thus the idea of players being free to demand more money for their services must have been genuinely disturbing.

Response to his outburst was at first muted. Within days Colin Veitch, Newcastle captain and a future union chairman, took him to task in his *Weekly News* column, pointing out the obvious – that the union was not alone in advocating abolition of the wage limit and that changes to the present system would be welcomed if that was all that could be expected. However, Veitch was more concerned to answer Sutcliffe's more serious charge – that professional players could not be trusted, that they were not to be regarded with the respect that professional men might automatically deserve. For this, one senses, was the real issue – the status of professional players and their right to stand as equals alongside administrators, managers, directors, etc. and to have a voice in their own affairs.

Sutcliffe clearly preferred to see the players as they had supposedly been in the 1880s: mercenaries, 'pirates', racing from club to club grabbing whatever they could. Veitch was adamant that those days had gone: 'The type of man in the professional ranks of today is of another stamp altogether to the professional of twenty years ago and you must not saddle the misdeeds of his predecessors upon his shoulders…'

Veitch concluded by pointing to where the union could prove its value:

> The players are joined in brotherhood through the agency of the Players' Union and I am quite at one with him [Sutcliffe] that the Union should take strong measures with any member found guilty of offences detrimental to the true interests of the game and incidentally harmful to the rest of the professionals by the same process…It is the duty of the present-day professional to vindicate himself in the eyes of everyone, even those whose prejudices prove a formidable barrier to understanding, and the Players' Union can help in the manner suggested.

Sutcliffe's prejudices, however, would prove formidable. Within days he had returned to the fray in an *Athletic News* article entitled: 'Who Shall Be the Masters – Players or Clubs?' Events would gradually move his way.

The old union had been practically strangled at birth by the Football Association's insistence that recourse to the courts to settle disputes between clubs and players could only happen with their permission. However, that had been before the passing of the Workman's Compensation Act in 1906 – a piece of legislation that offered all working men the chance to obtain compensation for injury at work.

Once it had been established that a player was a working man (something that could only be decided upon in court, hence the union's determination to push certain cases through in order to establish casework) the League clubs had decided to band together in an insurance federation. Therefore the union was anxious to establish proper machinery to deal efficiently with claims. After all, this was one of the reasons it had come into existence.

The long-winded procedure of clubs referring individual cases to the FA and then waiting until the latter came to a decision (while charging the player £1 for the privilege!) was, the union felt, being exploited by the clubs as a delaying device. Broomfield saw

The Cut Direct.
Broomfield (to Meredith): 'Pooh! Who wants the old frump to recognise us?'

Manchester Evening News cartoon.

The Conspirators or the Guy Fawkes of the Football Chamber.
The Football Association and the Football League, who are to meet in
conference shortly on the subject of players wages and bonuses, are
promised a bombshell from the Players' Union.

Manchester Evening News cartoon.

the possibility of a claims board being set up consisting of union members and club representatives, perhaps with some FA representation as well.

It turned out that such good sense was far too progressive for the majority of clubs. The spectre of the law of the land intruding into sport was already causing alarm bells to ring in boardrooms up and down the country and the FA, urged on by club directors peeved and resentful at the union's 'litigious' approach, decided that it would not be pressured into anything.

In late January 1909 the Players' Union Management Committee decided to take Reading FC to court on behalf of one of its players seeking compensation under the Workman's Compensation Act. The player had injured himself while playing cricket during pre-season training and had claimed that the club was liable. The judge disagreed and turned the claim down but the union immediately announced that it would be taking more such cases to court.

In mid-February the union was flatly told by the FA: 'All such disputes must be adjudicated by it [the FA] and not taken to a court of law.' Broomfield responded: 'The management committee of the Association Football Players' Union are not convinced that they are expected to regard seriously the opinion that a football player forfeits a common legal right on entering a professional engagement with a football club.' He referred to union rules (which had been approved by the FA) that provided for legal assistance to be offered and insisted they would continue to provide that assistance. The FA retorted that Broomfield was being 'bombastic' and a fortnight later, on 8 March, abruptly withdrew its recognition of the union.

This sudden 'crisis' had not, however, occurred in a legalistic vacuum. The court case at Reading and the moves by the union to institute proceedings at Rotherham and Croydon County Courts on behalf of more players had rapidly altered attitudes.

C.E. Sutcliffe was now no longer alone in criticising the union. In the *Athletic News* slighting references to the union being little more than a 'debt-collecting agency' and to its 'fighting, antagonistic attitude' were becoming more frequent, while elsewhere in the sporting press rumours were spreading that the union was contemplating the unthinkable – a strike.

Billy Meredith was probably the cause of this new development. Some time in January 1909 he had penned an article entitled 'If the Pros Struck' – purportedly a light-hearted account of a dream he had had. Sutcliffe wasted no time in separating fact from fantasy: 'When I read this wonderful dream I thought it was a rich joke but I was solemnly and publicly assured last Wednesday by a member of the PU that they are all laying their plans for a strike three years hence…'

J.J. Bentley, a prominent League official and journalist and sometime supporter of the union, was also moved to protest: 'The very suggestion of a strike of footballers shows the meanness of the motives behind it and in my judgment cannot be too strongly condemned.' The FA, he went on, 'would stand no nonsense of that sort…The union are making the pace too hot to last…they seem to have the idea that they are the people and everybody else must take a back seat. But they will have their knuckles rapped.'

Despite protestations from the union that nothing of the kind was contemplated, the feverish speculation continued. There was also a rapid closing of ranks on behalf of large and small League clubs. A year earlier, in the summer of 1908, anxious to rid itself of involvement in the squabbles regarding club finances and the responsibility to prosecute clubs breaking the rules, it had offered the clubs an 'amnesty' whereby all past misdemeanours such as the paying of illegal wages and bonuses would be forgotten. The clubs would reaffirm their loyalty to the FA and its laws, and with the decks thus cleared a final settlement regarding wages could be reached. In February a majority of clubs voted to accept the 'amnesty' offer.

According to Sutcliffe this dramatically altered the 'balance of power'. The clubs, he wrote, had previously been afraid of upsetting the players (and thus their union) because of the danger of players turning 'King's Evidence' – as Meredith had done – and revealing all to the FA: 'But the FA offered a free pardon to the clubs if they would cease to be dictated to by the players; if they would refuse to pay players sums of money in violation of the rules. The clubs consented to be honest and started with a clean slate. The players have lost their power, they ceased to be the real master!'

Within a week of its refusal to recognise the union the FA demanded that every player sign a 'loyalty' pledge to the FA to be inserted in his agreement for the new season. From that moment on the union was, as its motto states, on the defensive, having to react to events rather than initiate them. They insisted that face to face negotiations with the FA would sort out all 'misunderstandings' and they continued to work quietly to bring about such a meeting. To those members unhappy with what they were reading in the press and fearing their careers would be ruined, Broomfield wrote:

> With regard to professionals suffering, in my opinion, the suggestions appearing in the press regarding suspension of players are all bluff. The members of the union need have no fear of suspension. If anyone were to suffer in that way it would be the management committee and myself, not the players. But there is little likelihood of even that. Everything will be done for the benefit of the professionals without jeopardising their means of livelihood.

Through committee member Jimmy Ashcroft, Broomfield did indeed meet FA committee member John Lewis (as the latter walked between main stations in Manchester on his way south!) to talk over a possible arbitration meeting. According to Ashcroft, who had also talked at length to Lewis, the FA was 'sympathetic' to the union's demands; it simply wanted to know what the union required: 'He was much impressed by what I said and his personal opinion was that we shall be refused nothing by the FA.'

Unfortunately, nothing of substance was agreed upon – certainly no invitation to the next important FA meeting on 2 April just prior to the England-Scotland international, a meeting that might have avoided much of the ensuing strife. Instead, towards the end of March all this delicate behind-the-scenes diplomacy was replaced by some remarkable front-page drama, the popular press once again setting the pace with rumours that certain England players were thinking of refusing to play in the forthcoming international. A *Daily Sketch* report claimed that the England selectors were 'haunted by the fear of a strike during their deliberations…'

Who the players were and exactly why they were threatening to strike remained obscure and largely irrelevant – the 'strike' bogy was refusing to lie down. At this crucial moment Broomfield made a decision that seemed to fly in the face of all the union's denials that a strike was being contemplated. It was announced that on the Friday prior to the international, Broomfield would be meeting with officials of the General Federation of Trade Unions, as well as talking to the England players.

The GFTU's role in the ensuing dispute would be something of a puzzle. It was a body independent of the TUC and had been formed in 1899 to work for

Harry Mainman Chairman 1907–10

Harry Mainman played for Burton Swifts, Reading and later Notts County in a career stretching from the late-1890s to 1911. He captained Reading for five years and eventually retired there as a publican in 1911. Unlike many of the prestigious players on the union Management Committee, Harry met with little tangible success on the field during his own playing career but was considered a fine player. It was written of him at the time: 'He tackles fearlessly and skilfully and renders every assistance to the forward line, whilst in defence he is a tower of strength, using his head with capital effect.' Oddly enough, this assessment could also serve as a suitable commentary on his career with the union.

industrial peace and to seek to prevent strikes and lockouts, particularly those involving smaller unions. Thus, it would seem to have been the perfect organisation to act as mediator between the FA and the Players' Union. However, there had been no indication either in letters or in union minutes that the management committee had ever contemplated involving the mainstream union movement.

Despite vigorous denials by Broomfield that such a move was contemplated, pictures of him in the *Daily Sketch* in consultation with GFTU officials on the eve of the international beneath the caption 'The Crisis Over' suggested otherwise. What is more, the *Sketch* reported that the GFTU had advised the union to 'grin and bear it', and that the 'smoother way out of the difficulty for the present was to lie low until the season proper starts.' One GFTU official was even quoted as saying: 'A strike at the fag end of the season would be suicidal for the great body of pro-footballers.'

It was all very mystifying and was made worse by the fact that there appeared to be no clear union line. Anonymous union spokesmen were quoted setting a needlessly belligerent tone, such as the 'well-known captain' quoted in the *Sketch* on the fateful Friday declaring that 'the climax had been reached…come when it may there is to be a war and the battle will eventually go to the players.'

As for the England players themselves confusion reigned. The *Athletic News* claimed that Broomfield had been turned away from the England hotel: 'What did he want? The team had no need of any advice from him and we hear that they strongly resented his intrusion. An England eleven can surely battle their bravest for England without the emissary of a union to stimulate them?'

The players were said to have drawn up a statement after the game (which England won 2–0) stating that 'there was never the slightest doubt as to our determination to play our hardest and do our best to accomplish a victory for England against Scotland'. Suggestions to the contrary were dubbed 'an insult'.

Bob Crompton, England's captain, was said by the *Bolton Cricket and Football Field* to have used the traditional after-match dinner speech to 'expose the impudent assumption of the Players' Union' and that he 'gave voice to his indignation in no uncertain terms'.

For the many 'loyalists' it was an opportunity to display the patriotism that had gradually entered the argument – the implication that unions and strikes were somehow 'un-English'. The England-Scotland match was then the pinnacle of the season, being the oldest such fixture in history and a royal occasion.

To be selected was akin to being called up and certain players looked at it in just such a way. Thus, when Billy Wedlock, Bristol City's captain and England centre-half, had been asked if he would play: '…the little wonder turned abruptly and with withering scorn in his voice he said, "I am chosen, am I not?"'

Billy Meredith later claimed in his *Weekly News* column that there was no truth at all in the assertion that Broomfield had been trying to bring the England players out. He blamed the London press for whipping the whole thing up. Whatever the truth there can be little doubt that the incident was a publicity disaster for the union, losing the organisation a great deal of credibility in the eyes of players ambivalent towards the union as well as shocking many of the union's supporters among the club directors. It also afforded the union's enemies a field day as they poured scorn on Broomfield and the union idea in general. Clear evidence that the union realised that it had made a mistake was the decision a few days after the England international to 'defer the question of joining the GFTU until August' and to continue the original course of obtaining a meeting with the FA.

April was a nervous month. The management committee sought legal opinion on the rules of the FA and the so-called 'loyalty' clause to be inserted into each professional's contract. They also pressed on with a compensation case against Crystal Palace in Croydon Crown Court but in doing so they lost a valuable ally. The union solicitor and Manchester City director Wilkinson decided he could no longer continue acting for the union and resigned. It was an ill wind, however – the solicitor who took over the case, Thomas Hinchcliffe, was destined to become one of the union's greatest friends and would play a part in its affairs for over 50 years.

From the FA's point of view life continued as normal, the George Parsonage case being a perfect example of what Billy Meredith called the 'autocratic' nature of the governing body.

George Parsonage, a Fulham player, had been asked by his manager to talk to the manager of Chesterfield who was interested in signing him. Parsonage had no desire to leave Fulham but was prevailed upon to meet Mr Swift who made the customary offer of a £10 signing-on fee and £4 a week. Parsonage reiterated the fact that he did not want to be transferred but, in his own words, 'I became tired of Mr Swift's endeavours to persuade me to transfer my services from Fulham to Chesterfield. I asked him, in what I regarded as jocular mood and only with the idea of getting rid of the matter, for £50…'

Swift promptly reported Parsonage to the FA. An enquiry followed and Parsonage was suspended from football for life. No wonder, then, that when the

FA and the union finally met at the end of April Harry Mainman, union chairman, would say to Charles Clegg, Chairman of the FA, 'We look upon the clubs as the enemies of the players.'

The meeting had been the union's main hope. Broomfield and Mainman for the union, Charles Clegg and Secretary Frederick Wall for the FA all talked over a number of union proposals: a claims board with equal representation for the FA and Players' Union to decide on players' claims against clubs; a national compensation fund with compulsory contributions jointly administered; plus the dropping of the £1 fee demanded of players who wished to make a claim against their clubs. All were rejected. It was a disaster.

The meeting over, the FA wasted no time in issuing another ultimatum stating that officials of the union who did not give an undertaking before 17 May that they would in future act in accordance with the rules of the FA would be suspended from taking any part in football or football management.

The FA also claimed that AFPU members had not been fully consulted and called for a special general meeting at which union members could express their opinions upon the policy of the committee. It was clear that the FA had decided that Broomfield and Mainman did not represent the bulk of the players and that they alone were responsible for much of the trouble that had occurred.

Finally, the FA pointed out that unless the AFPU complied with FA rules: 'It will be necessary for players to withdraw from membership of the union if they desire to continue their connection with the FA.'

Events now moved swiftly towards total breakdown. On 7 May the union Management Committee decided to resign except for Mainman and Broomfield who, being non-players, would not be affected by the threatened ban from football.

Early in June came yet another ultimatum. In order to hasten the inevitable the FA ordered all players to cease their membership of the union, the deadline being set at 1 July. If they did not do so their registrations as professionals would be cancelled.

On 1 July, as an opening shot in the coming hostilities, the union officially affiliated with the GFTU.

5. The Outcasts

Once the union Management Committee had resigned in early May and chairman Harry Mainman had left to spend the summer in his Reading home, Herbert Broomfield was very much alone in the union office. Indeed, for all practical purposes he was the union: dealing with all correspondence, advising players on a range of problems, sending out information to the press, setting up meetings, paying bills, as well as taking all the key strategic decisions in the propaganda war with the FA.

His union activities were to prove a considerable emotional burden – nor did he receive a great deal of thanks or even support for shouldering it. At one stage in late

July he travelled down to London, back up to Newcastle and then across to Manchester in the course of three days to speak at three crucial meetings, exhorting players to stand firm and not to resign from the union.

In London he was simply rebuffed; in Newcastle he was at first supported, but no sooner had he returned to Manchester than the Newcastle players, led by Colin Veitch, had second thoughts and wrote to say they were resigning after all; only in Manchester did players declare their determination to hold on, although a few weeks later they too were writing in secret to say that if no one else came out to support them they would also have to throw in the towel. Broomfield managed to persuade them to stick it out but one would have sympathised with him had he simply closed the office and settled down in London for he was newly married.

Nor was Broomfield cashing in directly. For instance, when *Truth* magazine offered him a fee of two guineas for an article on the dispute he only agreed if the fee was donated to the Fresh Air Fund, which was set up in 1892 to provide impoverished children from London's East End with a day in the country. He also refused to supply a picture of himself.

He appears to have been driven by a genuine radical zeal, although where he stood in conventional political terms would be difficult to determine. Like the majority of Players' Union representatives over the years, he gave little away.

For all Broomfield's enthusiasm, however, there can be no doubt that the indifference, not to say downright hostility, of many of the rank and file players

Herbert Broomfield Secretary 1908–10

Broomfield had been a pro-footballer for some years, but by 1909 was on the verge of giving up the game. His career had been interrupted by injury although he was, in truth, more of a reserve player than a first-team regular. He played a handful of games for Manchester United before transferring to Manchester City in 1908, where he managed no more than four first-team appearances. Indeed, had union affairs not sprung into such prominence in 1909 it is more than likely he would have left football to concentrate on his new business, setting up his own manufacturing company to produce revolutionary rubberised footballs. Broomfield was not a typical professional footballer. Well-educated (having passed civil service exams), he was a part-time oil painter as well as the proprietor of his own painting and decorating business in Northwich where he lived. He was also a theatre goer and concert lover. As Billy Meredith said, 'He is too clever and industrious a man to depend on football.'

towards his campaign took its toll on him. At one point Broomfield appeared close to resigning:

> 'The constant strain, the worry, the publicity and the criticism is not to my liking. I would much prefer to cultivate the social side of life which I have sadly neglected through my desire to obtain the emancipation of professional footballers.'

He did not resign and Mainman apologised, as well he might. Without Broomfield's presence in Manchester it is clear the union would have collapsed. No one else would risk their careers by taking over his job; he was all the union had.

His basic strategy was quite simple: to prevent the new football season commencing in August and thus pressurise the League clubs into leaning on the FA to back down in its threat to destroy the union. It was a propaganda war, the FA claiming that the union had already been deserted by its members, the union claiming that players would return in August and rejoin. Figures were regularly bandied about but only when pre-season training began would it be possible to draw firm conclusions.

The Outcasts FC: J. Picken, W. Corbett, R. Holden, H. Burgess, J. Clough, W. Meredith, G. Boswell, G. Wall, A. Turnbull, C. Roberts (Captain), T. Coleman, R. Duckworth. (H. Moger not in picture).

Broomfield's day-to-day tactics, therefore, once he had secured affiliation to the GFTU and was certain of the defiance of the Manchester United men, was to broadcast these facts as loudly and as often as he could to anyone who might be interested; to emphasise in letters and at meetings that there was something to fight for, that the union still existed and was not fighting alone; and to stress that the GFTU, not to mention the union movement in general, would ensure that men who stayed with the union would not suffer financially if it came to an all-out strike.

The trade union movement did indeed appear to be genuinely sympathetic. Broomfield addressed numerous union meetings and received many individual letters of support from rank and file members. By late August a number of unions had declared themselves solidly behind the Players' Union's struggle for recognition and in September the whole issue was debated at the TUC's Annual Conference in Ipswich.

The Yorkshire and District Trades and Labour Council, the Lancashire and Cheshire Federation of Trades Unions, the National Union of Railwaymen, the Sheffield ILP – all wrote to offer support while the *Sheffield Guardian,* the *Railway Review* and the *Clarion,* a socialist weekly established by Robert Blatchford in 1890, among others, printed sympathetic articles.

There was reason to suppose that Broomfield's approach was not looked upon with favour by quite a number of players. However, this is not to say that they did not want the union to survive; just that they felt, like Veitch, that 'confrontation' and wider union links were provocative and liable to be counterproductive. Fear was part of the reason for such timidity.

Many men were faced that summer with painful choices. Most simply resigned from the union, signed a new contract with their clubs and went on holiday. Others, however, agonised over what to do and many wrote to Broomfield apologising for resigning from the union. Some wrote defiantly one week, yet sent in their resignation the next.

All of which made the Manchester United men's decision to stick by their union membership, after a preliminary wobble, all the more remarkable, their sacrifice all the more real.

Charlie Roberts had been the first to hear that he and his team were to be suspended for publicly stating that they would not resign from the union. He read about it in the evening papers delivered to his newsagent's shop: 'I had a benefit due with a guarantee of £500 at the time and if the sentence was not removed I would lose that also, besides my wages, so that it was quite a serious matter for me.'

The club had told him nothing, however, so he and the rest of the United team turned up as usual at the ground the following Friday to see whether they would receive any summer pay. No one was prepared to talk to them except an office boy who told them there was no money. Roberts recalled that Sandy Turnbull, United's centre-forward, was the first to react:

'"Well, something will have to be done," said Sandy Turnbull as he took a picture off the wall and walked out of the office with it under his arm. The rest of the boys followed suit, and looking glasses, hairbrushes and several other things were for sale a few minutes later at a little hostelry at the corner of the ground. I stayed behind a while with the office boy who was in a terrible state over the players taking things away and he was most anxious to get them back before the manager arrived. "Come along with me and I will get them for you," I said. "It's only one of their little jokes." I soon recovered the lost property for him. But it was funny to see those players walking off the ground with pictures, etc. under their arms.'

Being barred from the ground, the Manchester men decided to continue their pre-season training at Fallowfield, the Manchester Athletic Club ground, secured for them by Broomfield. This turned out to be a publicity coup for the union as reporters and photographers arrived to interview and photograph the famous 'rebels'. During one such session Roberts had the happy inspiration that helped create a legend:

'After training a day or two a photographer came along to take a photo of us and we willingly obliged him. While the boys were being arranged I obtained a piece of wood and wrote on it, "Outcasts Football Club 1909" and sat down with it in front of me to be photographed. The next day the photograph had a front page of a newspaper, much to our enjoyment and the disgust of several of our enemies.'

The Manchester men's defiance was admired by almost everyone, even J.J. Bentley, the Manchester United chairman, who made plain his disagreement with his players over the question of unions and strikes (to the point of resigning from the club in late 1909) yet who still expressed admiration for their honesty.

As August began, however, and men started to drift back from their holidays to prepare for pre-season training, the growing uncertainty as to exactly how many men would refuse to abide by the FA's edict and rejoin the union began to have the desired effect.

On 4 August the FA suddenly and surprisingly requested a meeting with the GFTU in order, as it explained, to outline its own case. It was reported in the *Manchester Evening News* that the meeting 'left a good deal to be desired. There was less frankness than there ought to have been. The Federation will be quite unable to bring about a settlement unless both sides are ready to discuss all that is on their minds.'

The GFTU officials – Pete Curran MP, Alderman Allen Gee of Huddersfield and W.A. Appleton of the GFTU executive – then went back to the union and began to work out a list of demands.

Broomfield travelled to Newcastle to talk to Veitch and Jimmy Lawrence and on 11 August it was announced that Newcastle United had come out in support of the

Manchester United men. They were swiftly joined by players at Oldham, Liverpool, Everton and Sunderland. As the pressure mounted the FA took yet another significant step. On 18 August it met the Players' Union 'executive' for the first time since its 'abolition' to discuss the latter's demands.

6. Recognition

Colin Veitch had now entered the picture as a union spokesman and Broomfield's influence on events consequently began to diminish, though his campaign had succeeded in securing the key concession – recognition of the union's existence. The three-hour meeting, which the GFTU attended as intermediary, was declared a success from the union's point of view but a week later at a second meeting the optimism was beginning to fade.

Putting aside relatively minor problems such as finding an appropriately worded formula, the FA and the union essentially reached agreement on four issues. First, the union agreed to observe the FA's rules regarding resorting to law until they were changed in return for the FA agreeing to recognise the union and lifting the suspension of the 'striking' players; second, the FA sanctioned the union pursuing legal cases on behalf of its members against League clubs after the FA had first had a reasonable amount of time to resolve the dispute; third, the FA would pursue the abolition of the maximum wage and the retain-and-transfer system at future meetings; and fourth, the FA would continue to give its consent to an annual match to be played for the benefit of union funds.

The issue on which the second meeting of 24 August ultimately foundered was the payment of the lost summer wages to the players who had refused to resign from the union. The union representatives were adamant that the players should receive the £38 owing to them. The FA representatives voted by four votes to three against such payment and the conferences broke up leaving the dispute unresolved.

According to Billy Meredith the refusal to pay the back-pay gave the FA a way out of a deal it secretly disliked. He wrote: 'As a matter of fact, I believe that the FA, believing that they would have the clubs with them…did not want a settlement…There is no doubt in my mind that the FA and the clubs believed that, if put to the test, the players would not fight. And it is not half a test that the players have to go through. The club officials are working for the FA all the time, the players are talked to unceasingly, invited to dinners, and all that kind of thing. It needs strong men to stand by the union under such circumstances but I hope to see the players prove their worth to the public and earn the respect of all who like to see men fight.'

Now began a process of intense lobbying, meetings and headcounts. On 27 August the GFTU strongly advised all professionals to refuse to attend any meeting or conference not officially arranged through the Players' Union. The following day the FA met representatives of all the League clubs to ask for their unqualified support.

Meanwhile, all players were advised by the union to tell their clubs that they were willing to play, that they recognised the binding character of their contracts and that they were 'quite willing to fulfil their part and play football when and where directed'.

The clubs, of course, were obliged to suspend any players rejoining the union. The rank and file's stance on this was not unanimous. The Aston Villa team, for instance, signed a declaration that they had not rejoined the Players' Union and would not do so until it was sanctioned by the FA. Such defections served to encourage the FA in its obduracy.

In fact, despite a last minute plea by Arthur Henderson, the chairman of the Labour Party, who offered to arbitrate in the dispute, the FA appeared determined to follow a course that appeared to mark a return to its earlier attempt to divide the union members from those who led them. To this end it announced that it was willing to assist the players in forming another organisation to promote their affairs, advised and financed by the FA itself.

The FA had a shrewd idea as to the nature of the men over whom it held such total sway. It had played a game of brinkmanship and now, with barely a day left before the season was scheduled to commence, it would gamble on its powers of persuasion combined with the overwhelming desire of most players to stop all the arguing and get back to playing. The FA's gamble would pay off.

The Birmingham meeting on 31 August 1909 must be regarded as a landmark in professional football politics. For the first time ordinary players had the opportunity to meet, talk to and even argue with the men who effectively ruled their lives. At the outset the FA's insistence that the meeting was for non-union players only was swiftly rendered null and void. Of the couple of hundred who turned up at the hall, at least 50 per cent were either members or ex-members of the union. However, Charlie Roberts, Billy Meredith, Herbert Broomfield and representatives of the GFTU had not been invited.

Charles Clegg spoke first, the gist of his opening remarks being that the present trouble 'had arisen out of the action of certain parties who have been acting on behalf of the Players' Union'. The FA, he claimed, had been all in favour of the union but the union had broken its own rules by not trying to come to 'amicable' agreements with the governing bodies. He then warned that players were 'ill-advised to think that because they had signed for their clubs that a court of law would uphold their claim to wages. I am not mentioning this at all with the idea of deterring you from doing anything that you want. I am just mentioning it…' He continued: 'Even if the courts did decide that you were entitled to this year's wages, what about next season? This is a serious question, is it not?' He went on to say that he hoped players would not place money too high on their agenda because that would be bad for the sport and he finished by suggesting that the FA would like to fund an alternative union: 'We are not wanting you to form a union that shall be under the finger of the association but we don't want a union in constant opposition to us. Surely we are entitled to ask for that?'

He sat down to ringing applause. He was followed by Charles Crump (another prominent FA committee man), the main thrust of whose speech appeared to be that 'there is a desire in certain directions that the game be dominated by trade unions.' Clubs were not profit-making organisations, he explained, and the players ought to realise this: 'There are a great many men whose interests in sport had led them to invest very considerable sums in the clubs. They were anxious that the game should go on. He asked the players to pause before they turned their back on those whose friendship they had tried…'

The whole slant of the FA's argument was that football was not an industry, that too much emphasis on money threatened to ruin it as a 'sport', that unions had no part to play in the game and that the players had been led astray by certain elements on the management committee of the union.

The players' response was revealing. Instead of talking in high-sounding generalities, those who spoke immediately got down to the realities of the FA's rule. Why, it was asked, had the Manchester United men been suspended? Why had George Parsonage been so abominably treated? 'Ginger' Lyons, late of Manchester City and one of those punished by the FA during the Meredith scandal of 1905, took the opportunity to put his own case, claiming that he had been denied a personal hearing at the time of his suspension.

The Kick-Off.
The football season opened yesterday with every prospect of the dispute being finally settled.

Daily Dispatch, 1 September 1909.

The key intervention was made by Colin Veitch who made two simple points: first, that the existing union should continue, it being too much trouble to create a new one, and second, that the Manchester United players should receive their back-pay and have their suspensions lifted: 'That is the chief trouble that is standing in our way. We all wish to conform to the rules of the FA but we also wish that this question of arrears of wages might be conceded by the association…The wages are the only bar.'

Veitch ended by declaring that he personally would try to secure a settlement along those lines. Clegg and Crump were not immediately receptive, however, to Veitch's suggestion. Could he guarantee that the suspended men would promise to abide by the rules of the FA? Clegg also suggested that all the trouble had been caused at earlier negotiations by the presence of a 'third party', the GFTU. He claimed that it would have been so much better if it had been left to themselves (the FA) and the players to sort things out.

Veitch said he would try to contact the missing Manchester United players that very day by telegraph but Clegg quickly seized his opportunity saying: 'We cannot possibly get the thing in order to formally consider it and Mr Veitch has suggested the readiest way of getting at it. We had better conclude this conference and follow the matter up through Mr Veitch and his friends…'

There followed a string of platitudes: 'We must not expect to have it all our own way'; 'Life is a compromise'; 'Nobody gets his own way'; 'There must be give and take by both parties' etc, but when the final resolution was drafted the FA had achieved largely what it had set out to do. There was to be a 'truce'. Football would commence immediately. The Players' Union's proposals would 'be considered'.

A cartoon adorning the report of the conference that appeared in the *Daily Dispatch* the next day depicted a player joyfully booting a football labelled 'discord' out of the ground. For the majority of players that appeared to sum everything up – the trouble was all over now and they could get back to playing football.

In a sense, the players were right. The critical moment had passed; the possibility of halting the soccer season (the only way in which the powers that be would ever be brought to the negotiating table) had gone and the unique combination of circumstances that had created such a situation would not occur again.

For Herbert Broomfield, architect of that supreme moment of truth, the 'victory' claimed by some was no victory at all. He wrote: 'I am not overjoyed, though everyone else seems satisfied…because there is something sad about the whole business, to think that athletes should be so devoid of moral courage is not a pleasing thought and if you knew my experience the afternoon of the conference you would feel as I do.'

Billy Meredith, interviewed a day later in the *Clarion* newspaper, seemed equally adamant that no victory had been achieved. On being told by the reporter that the FA had recognised the union he replied: 'Yes, provided the players observe the rules and practice of the FA. What's the good of belonging to a union if one fetters one's hands like that?'

Colin Veitch, on the other hand, was full of hope. 'Peace With Honour' was the headline above his *Weekly News* article in which he claimed that the Birmingham conference had brought a complete settlement one step nearer: 'Step, did I say?…A gigantic leap is more accurate in description of the space covered!'

Veitch's famous conciliatory nature, his determination to press on with negotiations, confident that the FA had the best of intentions, would, however, be sorely tried.

Putting a brave face on things, the Manchester United team, wearing their new Players' Union armbands, ran out for their first match to resounding cheers. Within a month the armbands would be prohibited by the League. Their back-wages would take almost six months to be paid, Charlie Roberts's benefit match against Newcastle United would be refused and it would take the intervention of both Veitch and Broomfield to persuade the United men not to go back on strike.

As the weeks passed into months, and with Veitch now taking a leading role in the discussions, the elusive settlement seemed further off than ever. With no deadline set the football authorities felt free to linger, to prevaricate, to change their grounds – in particular to demand that the union disaffiliate from the GFTU.

The simple fact that the law of the land guaranteed any man or woman the right to strike, whether affiliated to the GFTU or the TUC, made no difference to the game's rulers. The FA was seeking a declaration of principle from the players; an acknowledgement that they were different, that football was a special world governed by men possessing ancient and benevolent wisdom. They would get their way.

In mid-October the union relented. It agreed to hold a ballot of all members to decide whether to remain affiliated to the GFTU. The vote was decisively against: 470–172. The union thus passed a resolution thanking the GFTU for all its help. The FA lifted its 'suspension' of the Manchester players and paid them their money.

Charlie Roberts, however, declared himself disgusted with the result: 'As far as I am concerned, I would have seen the FA in Jericho before I would have resigned membership of that body, because it was our strength and right arm, but I was only one member of the Players' Union. To the shame of the majority they voted the only power they had away from themselves and the FA knew it.'

Meredith was equally despairing of his fellow players. In his *Weekly News* column he wrote: 'The unfortunate thing is that so many players refuse to take things seriously but are content to live a kind of schoolboy life and to do just what they are told…instead of thinking and acting for himself and his class'.

For Herbert Broomfield it was the final straw. In December he tendered his resignation; anxious as he was to turn his full attention to his business, he would remain close to the union for some time and even resume the secretaryship for a period in 1913 when the position fell vacant.

So the painful year 1909 ended, a year destined to remain etched on the memories of those who took part. As Charlie Roberts would write some years later: 'I shall never forget the summer of 1909 as long as I have breath in my body…'

PART TWO

LIVING FROM HAND TO MOUTH
1909-45

1. Kingaby and after 1910-39

Justice, or the lack of it, was a persistent theme running through players' newspaper articles during the post-1909 years: whether it was the arbitrary treatment men received at the hands of FA disciplinary tribunals or the grossly unfair manipulation by clubs of the 'signing-on' process at the end of each season, there was always some cause célèbre to exercise the mind – and the Players' Union felt increasingly drawn to intervene.

For the union the law of the land remained the great hope, yet there were obvious risks involved. It was one thing to take cases to county courts under the Workman's Compensation Act in order to claim compensation for injury, loss of back-wages, etc. It was another thing entirely, however, to engage eminent legal counsels and mount a major challenge in the High Court to question the legality either of the transfer system or the maximum wage. This would involve major expense, with no firm guarantee of

TRUCE DECLARED IN THE FOOTBALL WAR.

Birmingham again held the attention of the football world yesterday, while the conference, which ended in a truce being called, was in progress at the Grand Hotel. The snapshots were secured outside the hotel. On the left: Mr J.T. Jones (of the Municipal Employee's Association), Roberts, Thornley and Mr. Boswell (assistant secretary to the Players' Union) on picket duty; in the middle, Mr. J.J. Bentley (president of the Football League) leaving the hotel; on the right, three who have been leading the players' movement, Messrs Veitch, Lawrence and Bridgett. *Daily Dispatch,* 1 September 1909.

eventual success. The union, in the years following the 1909 confrontation, was plucking up courage. In a sense it appeared to be the next logical step. It had been established to bring about major reforms. It had survived a massive assault by football's rulers; it might not survive another. Meanwhile the Football League was growing more and more powerful and the FA less and less inclined or able to help professional players. The union had no power to change things from without – having cut itself off from the Trade Union movement, it had no industrial 'muscle'. Thus it had to change the legal ground rules – and it would be the retain-and-transfer system that would be its principal target.

By mid-1910 the union was busy consulting lawyers in London about the legality or otherwise of the transfer system and by September it had compiled a shortlist of possible test cases to take to trial. In September 1910 the name Herbert Kingaby appears for the first time in the union minutes.

It was ironic in some ways that it had been a court case that had led, albeit indirectly, to the contractual restrictions under which players presently laboured. In June 1890 Nottingham Forest sought an injunction to prevent Henry Campbell from playing for Blackburn Rovers. In March of that year Campbell, then a Blackburn player, had signed a contract committing him to play for Nottingham Forest in the 1890–91 season. However, following his involvement in Blackburn's historic 7-1 FA Cup Final victory over Sheffield Wednesday that April, he proceeded to sign another contract with Blackburn Rovers, apparently unilaterally tearing up his agreement with Forest.

The application for an injunction was refused in the first instance but Forest were not to be denied and took their case to the Court of Appeal, where the case was heard by no less a personage than the Master of the Rolls, Lord Esher. The short report of his judgment is instructive:

> It was not in every case in which a man was about to break his contract that an injunction should be granted restraining him from doing so. What was there at stake in the present case? There was no question of character or of property except that it was said there would be a diminution in gate-money. But the real point was the pride of the club; they wanted to win their games, and in order to do so they had engaged these professionals. Ought the solemn machinery of the Court in granting an injunction to be invoked in order to satisfy their pride in winning their matches? If the defendant broke his agreement an action would lie against him, and it might be even that an action would lie against the other club for enticing him to do so. But it was unnecessary to decide that now; all that needed to be said was that Mr Justice North (at first instance) was right and that this was not a proper case for granting an injunction.

The player had won but Lord Esher's contempt for the sport, in particular for professionalism and the clubs' obsession with 'winning their games', is evident

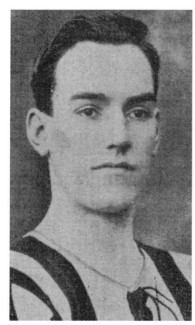

Colin Veitch Chairman 1911–18

A strong, thoughtful half-back, cool and steady and very much a tactician (he pioneered team talks at half-time while at Newcastle). He captained Newcastle United on many occasions, turning out for the club 321 times during his 15 years with them. During this time they were League champions three times (1905, 1907 and 1909) and Cup winners five times (1905, 1906, 1908, 1910 and 1911). He also won six England caps. He served for over two years in France during World War One, being commissioned as a lieutenant in the Royal Garrison Artillery. After demobilization he returned to football as reserve team coach at Newcastle where he established one of the first nursery teams, Newcastle Swifts, with the aim of spotting and developing local footballing talent. The ensuing depression led to economies, the Swifts were disbanded and he was sacked in 1926. He then managed Bradford City for two years before turning to journalism full-time. He had written articles for both the local and national press while still a player, and in July 1929 he joined the Newcastle Evening Chronicle group of newspapers as a sports reporter. A multi-talented man, he was a socialist, playwright, theatrical producer, composer and actor of some merit, being a star of the Newcastle Operatic Society, an amateur society which he joined in 1901. In the 1920s Veitch was twice asked to stand as the prospective Labour candidate for the Newcastle East parliamentary constituency, but on each occasion he refused. In June 1938 he was taken ill and travelled to Switzerland to recuperate but pneumonia caused complications and he died at Bern on 26 August 1938. On the following day, the first of the 1938–39 football season, the crowd before United's home match with Plymouth stood silently for two minutes in memory of a footballer and a man who was out of the ordinary. Greta Veitch died in March 1968 and left the bulk of her £19,000 estate for a Burke-Veitch scholarship intended to enable a woman or girl born in Northumberland or Durham to study at the Royal College of Dramatic Art.

Acknowledgements to Dr Tony Mason.

from the judgment. The subtext was: the Court ought not to involve itself with something so trivial as football.

As sports law expert David McArdle has said, 'One can only speculate whether the player registration provisions would have developed differently if Radford had been decided in Forest's favour.' However, it appears that the Campbell case, among others, was instrumental in persuading Football League officials that restrictions had to be placed on the richer clubs' ability to tempt players into joining them, in order to ensure an equal spread of talent and to keep the League competitive. They thus took the registration scheme through which the Football Association had regulated professionalism since 1885 and adapted it to suit their own requirements. From the start of the 1893–94 season a player had to be registered with the club he intended playing for and, once he had registered, he could play for no other club unless the club gave its permission.

The limited degree of freedom of movement granted to professionals by the original FA registration scheme was enough to prevent it being considered an unlawful restraint of trade. The more stringent restrictions on player movement inherent in the Football League's scheme's were quite probably unlawful. The League, however, appeared unconcerned. If the Radford case demonstrated anything, it was the law's indifference to professional football. Sadly, the players and their advisers misread the signs.

Herbert 'Rabbit' Kingaby.

Herbert Kingaby

Herbert 'Rabbit' Kingaby had had a colourful though not particularly untypical career, complicated only by the fact that he worked for a woollen manufacturer in London and thus was only free to play on Saturdays and bank holidays. He played for Clapham Orient at outside-right until 1906 when Aston Villa spotted him, bought him for £300 and paid him the maximum wage of £4 a week for his Saturday game. After two months, however, Villa decided they no longer wanted him and offered him back to the Orient for £150. Orient could not, or would not, pay the fee so Kingaby went on to Villa's 'retained' list with no contract and no wages.

During the close season of 1906 he received an offer of £3 10s a week from

Fulham who were then in the Southern League and thus not covered by the League's regulations. He went to Craven Cottage and when Villa tried to lure him back, offering him £4 a week, he refused. Villa appealed to the FA but they decided Kingaby was justified in accepting Fulham's offer so he stayed at Fulham until 1908 when he moved to Leyton Orient.

In 1910 the Football League and the Southern League reached an agreement regarding registration and transfers, part of which closed the loophole that had allowed disaffected Football League players to join Southern League clubs. Kingaby, under the complicated terms of that agreement, found himself re-registered as an Aston Villa player and thus was unable to play for Leyton Orient or any other team unless Villa agreed to transfer him! Villa, for reasons known only to themselves, then slapped a £350 fee on his head, a ridiculous sum given Kingaby's age and talents but the League Management Committee could only see its way to reducing it to £300. Kingaby was, to all intents and purposes, out of football for life. When a non-League club called Croydon Common said they were prepared to pay him £2 a week he asked for a free transfer from Villa, but Villa initially refused.

On paper it looked like the perfect case for the Players' Union to bring to court. Kingaby, however, being very much his own man insisted on instituting legal proceedings privately; only after the case had begun did he approach the union and ask for assistance. The union advised him to place the case in the hands of Thomas Hinchcliffe, the union solicitor, but Kingaby refused.

In December 1910, however, Harry Mainman was authorised by the management committee to go to London with £50 as a contribution towards Kingaby's costs on the strict understanding that he press on with the case and not drop it. However, it transpired that Aston Villa had offered Kingaby the free transfer he had asked for and that the player, having now obtained a contract with Peterborough City at 30s a week, was declaring himself satisfied.

This was not quite true. Kingaby then approached the union with an offer. If it conceded 'certain terms' to him he said would continue with the action, presumably in the hope of winning damages, but Colin Veitch commented: 'To those terms, no one on earth would have agreed.' The union decided to look for another test case, but Kingaby's solicitors then threatened to take the union to court over possible libel of their client!

The union was now caught in a legal web, a situation that appears to have induced both parties to join forces once again. In January 1912, therefore, the case was back on course and on 30 March, before a special jury of the King's Bench Division in London, the case of Aston Villa versus Kingaby opened.

The trial

For what would prove such a momentous case for the union, this strange prelude was hardly the best preparation. Acting for the defence would be Montague Shearman KG, an Oxford Rugby Blue and champion sprinter. A short time previously he had given his opinion to the union that the players contract was 'contrary to law'. He now appeared to think the opposite.

KC for Kingaby would be Mr F.J.P. Rawlinson who had played in goal for both Corinthians and Old Etonians, appearing in three Cup Finals for the latter in the 1880s. He had also been capped for England. Described as a 'sound, cool custodian, although the coolness seemed at times to border on casualness', it was the latter quality that characterised his performance in court.

Rawlinson immediately made what would turn out to be a fundamental error. He set out to attack Aston Villa's motives in setting a prohibitive fee on Kingaby's head, rather than attacking the transfer system itself. He contended the club had acted maliciously and had used the retain-and-transfer system to stymie Kingaby's career in an act of revenge for his deeming to leave them without their permission. He thus sought damages for breach of contract, conspiracy and for maliciously procuring breaches of contract and an injunction. He made no attempt to prove that the system holding Kingaby was an 'unreasonable restraint of trade'. The subsequent debate therefore took for granted its 'legality'.

Mr A.S. Owen, the Leicester Fosse amateur and secretary of the Players' Union, conferring with the assistant secretary, Mr Brett, on the now famous Kingaby case.

Aston Villa's motives, however, were irrelevant because, according to the law, even the most malicious or capricious of motives could not render a lawful act unlawful. The club had no case to answer said Mr Justice Lawrence, declaring that there were no grounds for challenging the transfer system itself as it was simply a necessary registration system to prevent clubs filching players from one another. Costs were awarded against the union, resulting in its near-bankruptcy and ruinously adverse publicity. As for the clubs of the Football League, the retain-and-transfer system would remain the key to their power over every aspect of players' lives for the next half a century or more.

The aftermath

In 1920 C.E. Sutcliffe wrote: 'The Football League is not yet ripe for freedom of contract and until the true League spirit of mutual respect and help has permeated every club and its management, I am bound to regard freedom of contract as mischievous and a misfortune to the game.'

Players might receive a share of any fee – with a ceiling fixed at £650 at about this time – but abolition was never contemplated, no matter how many abuses of the system might be highlighted. Clubs remained free to use the retention clause to block a player's movement, to discipline him – even to save on wages.

In 1924, for instance, Tommy Hamilton of Preston North End – a full-back who had been with the club four seasons and played over 120 matches – suddenly found himself on the transfer list: 'At the close of the season I was asked to make arrangements to be photographed as I was going on the tour to Belgium and a photo would be required for my passport. But a few days later that was all knocked on the head. I found my name on the open-to-transfer list! And the fee opposite my name was £4,000! Who can afford to pay that these days?'

The fee was reduced on appeal to £2,000, but it was still too much for a player like Hamilton and, although Everton expressed an interest, he remained on the list throughout the close season, receiving no pay. He found a job in a shop and turned out for a Lancashire Combination club before Preston eventually offered him another contract and Hamilton resumed his career, playing another five seasons. The Preston club had therefore saved money on his wages for a short while, with Hamilton having no way of protesting or claiming recompense. Such a case might not appear particularly scandalous as it had a 'happy' ending, but the sense of helplessness that men felt where their careers were concerned was oppressive and helped to inculcate a fatalism and cynicism about their calling that marked the profession for almost a century.

The only way out for those players willing to take the risk was to go to a country where the long arm of the League could not reach them. In the 1920s the United States saw a pro Soccer League established and scores of British players broke their existing contracts to 'go West'.

Enough men of quality made the break to cause some startling headlines: 'Is American Football Menace Real?'; 'US Agents On The Prowl'; 'Menace of American Football', etc. Scottish clubs in particular suffered. Men from Aberdeen, Partick Thistle, even Rangers left for clubs in Boston, Brooklyn and New York. Tom Muirhead, Scots international, signed for Brooklyn for two years; McIntyre of Morton joined Boston for a good job and $2,400 a year; Mick Hamill, Irish international, spent some years with Boston. English clubs also lost players: Gillespie from Preston, Mitchell from Notts County and Sam Chedgzoy of Everton were prominent captures, while Bill Harper, Arsenal's Scottish international goalkeeper, also fled to the US for a number of years.

For a time the lure of the Yankee dollar unsettled the football rulers in Britain – particularly when the threat to decamp to the US was used as a bargaining counter at signing-on time. It was known that Jack Hill, Burnley captain and England centre-half, threatened to go to the US if his terms were not substantially improved by the club, while Joe Cassidy of Celtic played cat-and-mouse for some weeks before finally resigning from the Glasgow club. It was case of the 'biter bit'.

In 1928 it was even announced that the New York Giants, a baseball club which also ran a soccer team, had offered Dixie Dean – who had just completed his record 60-goal season to bring Everton the League title – £25 a week to play for them. He was Britain's most famous player at that stage and being sought by Arsenal. Whether he seriously considered the US offer is not known. Had he gone, who knows what the consequences might have been?

Nonetheless, the American experience (and in the 1930s, the newly professional French League as well) suggested there was another way of doing things, one that seemed

Scottish players in the US. Scottish football circles were much perturbed when some of their best-known players succumbed to the blandishments of agents of the 'Almighty Dollar', and went off to join Boston in the U.S.A. Any English or Scottish League Club would be pleased to have this trio for their half-back line (left to right): Jock McIntyre (late Greenock Morton), Micky Hamill (Irish international and once of both Manchester League clubs) and Tom Muirhead (Scottish international and late of Glasgow Rangers). These players are the pioneers of a movement which looks like rivalling baseball in the States. *Sports Pictures,* 27 December 1924.

more equitable, that rewarded celebrity and skill and entertainment value. For a while the tedious and repetitive justifications of League officials, allied with the constant cries of poverty from club directors, could not, on the face of it, be contradicted, but the idea that this was the inevitable order of things was being challenged. It was a frustrating business for the union, however.

In November 1929, for instance, the union Management Committee requested a meeting with the League Management Committee 'to discuss the adjustment of certain rules which are considered not to be in keeping with the times' i.e. the retain-and-transfer system.

The union then spent some months working on various proposals to put to the proposed meeting. However, in April 1930, they received a letter from League secretary Tom Charnley baldly stating that 'after careful consideration of the suggestions made, the management committee were not prepared to suggest to the clubs that any alterations of rules and regulations be made. It would, therefore, be useless to arrange for any deputation…'

At the union AGM of that year a resolution was sent to the FA protesting at the 'harsh and unfair treatment which many of its members are made to suffer each year under Rule 31 (Retaining Fee)', but this too resulted in nothing but silence. The League Management Committee's refusal to meet and talk suggested that the pointless cycle of supplication and rejection would go on indefinitely.

In fact, it would be another decade before anything like a serious challenge would be mounted by the union and only the advent of World War Two saved the football authorities from having to make a stark choice: free the players or face outright rebellion.

2. Struggling to Survive 1911–39

Money would be the principal problem for the union; where ready cash was concerned for administrative purposes, it would remain at the mercy of the FA and to a lesser extent the Football League. The annual benefit match to raise ready cash had to be sanctioned by both bodies and, after a good start in 1910, this crucial fixture would be shamelessly manipulated by football authorities in order to twist and bend the union in whatever direction was required.

Yet the years leading up to World War One were optimistic, as men from the top League clubs continued to take a hand in running the union and membership remained relatively healthy.

The summer union sports festivals of 1911, 1912 and 1913 were ambitious, sometimes chaotically organised affairs run on shoestring budgets and reliant on the endless energy of men like secretary Syd Owen (who made himself ill running the Old Trafford festival of 1911), Harry Newbould, Colin Veitch, plus scores of unpaid helpers drawn from a variety of club officials and players. Club supporters came from all over the country to cheer their own men on – a crowd of 15,000 attended the 1911 Festival.

There were place-kick and 'dribbling' competitions, sprints and half-mile runs, strangely, no five-a-side competitions. The FA refused to give its permission for these.

Prizes were small – except for the magnificent cup presented by the *Athletic News* and awarded for the fastest sprinter among pro-footballers. In 1912 the union invited professional track runners from all over the world to compete for prizes of up to £100 but Harry Wright of Derby County would be its first winner.

Ostensibly to raise money for the union's Benevolent Fund (and to help players get fit for the coming season), the sports festivals were a brave attempt to establish the union as an independent organisation capable of looking after itself. Sadly, the

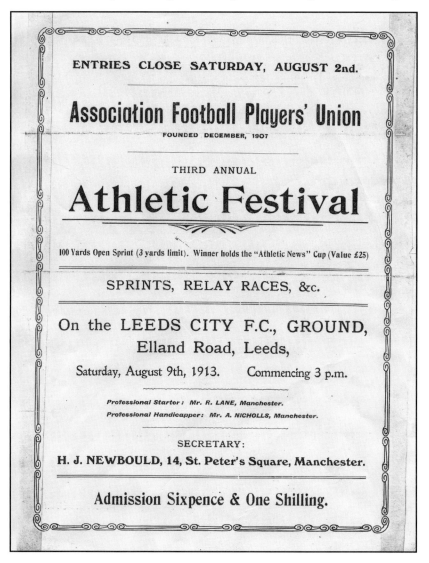

Evelyn Lintott Chairman 1910–11

'Never flags from start to finish. Adept with either foot, clever in obtaining the ball but the use he makes of it to his forwards is his strong point.' A left-back, he went to Guilford Grammar School and later qualified as a teacher at Exeter Training College. With Woking he captained the side to a Surrey Senior Charity Shield in 1904 and represented Surrey in county matches. Evelyn was a teacher in Willesden while playing for Queen's Park Rangers. In 1908 he won an England amateur cap against Ireland and went on to win seven full England caps. He later turned out for Bradford City and Leeds City. He joined the 15th Battalion West Yorks (The 'Leeds Pals') and was the first professional footballer to hold a commission. He was killed in action on the first morning of the Somme offensive.

hoped-for profits were not forthcoming – only the Old Trafford festival made any money (£150) and that had to be dragged from the Manchester United club via a writ!

The Players' Union magazine was a well-produced and generally well-written publication. Edited by Evelyn Lintott of Queen's Park Rangers and later by Harry Newbould, it devoted its pages to discussions of standards of conduct on the field, union news and training tips. It also opened its pages to referees and club managers. It undoubtedly lost money but there was no other publication of its kind attempting to draw together clubs and players in dialogue. Neither the FA nor the League with their more considerable financial means ever attempted such an enterprise. In that, as in many other things, the Players' Union was ahead of its time.

However, it was the day-to-day benevolent work that would prove to be the union's most solid achievement. The business of distributing sums of money to

Thomson's Weekly News. From left to right: Charlie Roberts, Arthur Bridgett, Colin Veitch and A.S. Owen, Secretary of the Players' Union.

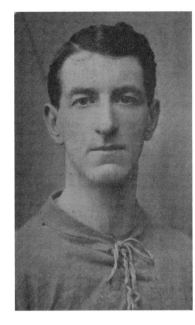

Syd Owen Secretary 1910–13
Syd was a chartered accountant and initially served as the union's membership auditor for three years. He had played for both Stoke City and Leicester Fosse as an amateur but by 1910 was with Northern Nomads. Syd represented England at amateur level with the English Wanderers and was once a reserve to the full England side against Wales. Having played football in Russia, Sweden, Denmark, Holland and Germany, he would eventually go abroad as a coach. Syd Owen would prove to be a perfect replacement for Broomfield – an energetic, enthusiastic organizer with a firm belief in principles. Only his temper would eventually let him down.

players fallen on hard times or to the families and dependants of players who had died continued apace. Between 1908 and 1914 the numbers of men and women the union assisted ran into hundreds, the amount of money disbursed into thousands.

Widows automatically received a £10 grant (raised via a levy of all members) plus any other expenses deemed necessary. Management committee members spent a great deal of their free time travelling up and down the country looking into individual cases, investigating appeals, handing out small but crucial sums, paying funeral expenses, removal costs, bailing men out of prison, replacing hocked furniture or paying hospital fees.

Billy Meredith contrasted the union's endeavours with those of the FA. In the *Thomson's Weekly News* of February 1913, in an article entitled: 'Ever Heard of the Benevolent Fund?' he wrote, 'Judging by the constant applications to the Players' Union for assistance from players suffering from misfortune, the FA Benevolent Fund, whatever else it does, does very little for players…'

The Players' Union, by contrast, being prepared to knock on people's doors and make on-the-spot assessments, not to mention immediate payments, filled a pressing need. Even with the advent of the Workman's Compensation Act and the establishment by the Football League of the Football Mutual Insurance Federation, the legal casework of the union increased dramatically in the first few years of its existence.

Cases concerning clubs failing to pay arrears of wages, clubs not paying wages in full, clubs refusing to honour contractual agreements or not offering players agreements at all – year by year the work of Thomas Hinchcliffe, union solicitor, became more and more an integral part of union affairs.

It was during these years that the union also established itself as an unofficial employment agency, a clearing house for players desperate to find a new club but possessing no knowledge of possible openings or opportunities. Clubs often put men on their 'retained list' but failed to circulate the information to other clubs. In 1910 this vast pool of unused labour became such a scandal that the League, urged on by the Players' Union, issued an instruction to clubs to release players after a certain period if they had no more use for them. In general, hard information – even the price the club had placed on a man's head – was hard to come by and the union served a useful purpose by bringing players and clubs together.

Harry Newbould Secretary 1913–28

A qualified accountant, Harry Newbould played for Derby St Lukes and Sheffield Wednesday before being appointed assistant secretary of Derby County FC in 1896. He was promoted to secretary some years later and became the first manager of the club in 1900. In July 1906 he moved to Manchester City as secretary-manager and helped rebuild the club following the bribery scandal of 1905. Harry became secretary of PFA in 1913 and remained in the post until his death in 1928. In his youth he was a fine sprinter, an attribute that equipped him well as a right-winger. Harry was one of the unsung heroes of the players' struggle, serving 16 years on and off and sacrificing a great deal of his own time and money. He was a tireless organiser, playing a significant role in the organising of the summer sports festivals of 1911, 1912 and 1913 as well as editing, unpaid, the union magazine before World War One. In 1919, when the union was revived, he was granted £7 a week, plus £1 a week rental for the union office that was situated in his home. He was also granted £100 for his war work on the union's behalf (to compensate for earnings lost as a travelling salesman). He pressed for Henry Leddy to take his broken contract case to court, thus achieving the first significant breakthrough for the union in its battle for justice. He regularly upbraided players during the 1920s for not supporting their organisation. In 1924 he declared, 'The player today is reaping the benefit of that history and until such times as he needs the help and assistance of the Union is prepared to let others bear the burden. Shame, I say.' He died in 1928 after a long, debilitating illness and was sorely missed by the union.

THE ASSOCIATION FOOTBALL PLAYERS' UNION, MANCHESTER.

Balance Sheet, August 4th, 1913.

LIABILITIES.

	£	s.	d.	£	s.	d.
To Sundry Creditors				121	5	7
,, Funds as per Abstract of Income & Expenditure :—						
General Fund ...	49	15	8			
Benevolent Fund	222	2	7			
				271	18	3
				£393	3	10

NOTE.—There is a further liability for Law Costs in connection with the Kingaby Case of £725.

ASSETS.

	£	s.	d.	£	s.	d.
By Cash :—						
At Bankers ...	259	9	8			
In Hand ...	0	0	5			
				259	10	1
,, Office Fittings, Fixtures and Furniture (at cost) ...	51	5	0			
,, Magazine Account	32	8	9			
,, Arrears of Subscriptions ...	50	0	0			
				£393	3	10

We have examined the above Balance Sheet with the Books, Vouchers, etc., of the Union, and find same to be duly correct, and in accordance therewith.

(Signed) ASPELL & BARNES, C.A.
Leicester,

Players' Union Balance Sheet.

Unfortunately, the heavy financial cost of the Kingaby case would be a burden for many years to come. What made matters worse for the union was its inability to raise the money it owed in legal costs. What was more, by taking the plunge and pursuing the case to the bitter end the union had incurred the deep displeasure of the FA.

Ever since 1910 when the Kingaby case had first been mooted, ominous signals had come from FA headquarters – in particular, the refusal to allow the union to hold its apparently automatic benefit fund match in 1911. The FA's reason for refusing had been that the union already had enough money in its benevolent fund.

Anxious to raise money to clear its debts, in early 1912 the union asked permission to hold a benefit match between the English Players' Union and the newly formed Scottish branch. The Football League raised objections, ostensibly that players were needed by clubs for important matches.

The proposed match was thus shelved until the new season but now it was the turn of the FA to cause problems, suggesting that Players' Union secretary, Owen, was misusing the union's Benevolent Fund cash. Owen then penned an angry letter to the *Sporting Chronicle* accusing the FA of breaking its word concerning the granting of the match:

I venture to suggest that the have clearly shown that they are desirous of handicapping the Players' Union in every way they can…Of all the high-handed, intolerable things Mr Grump and his colleagues at the FA have ever done, this act of breaking faith with the players, of failing to keep a promise and of advancing for doing so the extraordinary reason that the Players' Management Committee refuse to allow the FA to dictate how the union funds shall be spent, is the king of them all. It is regrettable because it is stupid, and because it is clear evidence of a vindictive spirit…

Owen's outburst would cost him his job. The FA decided to make an issue of the letter and demanded an apology. Owen refused to give it, nor would he give the FA the undertaking it required regarding the benevolent fund. If he had counted on the support of his colleagues on the management committee, however, he was to be mistaken.

In October management committee members Charlie Roberts, Jesse Pennington and Jimmy Fay were invited to meet Football League officials after a League Management Committee meeting 'to have a chat over the trouble'. According to a journalist, 'Friendly advice was offered by the President of the League and others…'

Subsequently, the management committee decided that it could not endorse the contents of Owen's letter which had, they conceded, been 'ill-conceived, hastily written, full of tactless remarks and random insults'. In December Owen was formally censured by the committee which also assured the FA that all its conditions regarding the benevolent fund would be met. Owen had, by now, had enough. He announced in January that he had secured a job as a coach in Budapest and resigned as secretary of the union. The union had thus allowed its secretary to be hounded out of the game, a disgraceful episode and one that could do it no good in the eyes of its members, whatever their opinions on the matter.

Although Harry Broomfield returned as secretary 'pro term', his main task was a mournful one – attempting to prevent the Scottish branch from withdrawing from the union. He failed. In March 1913 the union appointed Harry Newbould, ex-Derby County and ex-Manchester City manager, as secretary. No firebrand, he announced in the union newsletter:

I am sure that our members realise that we must have a governing body and that the rules and regulations of these authorities must be observed. This is absolutely necessary for the proper conducting of our great national winter pastime…

In late 1913 the union offices in St Peter's Square in the heart of Manchester were removed to a back room in Newbould's house at Longsight in Manchester's south-eastern suburbs. Charlie Roberts was appalled by the lack of interest shown by his fellow professionals: 'Shame on you!' he wrote in an article in the Players' Union magazine in

March 1914, pointing out that, of an estimated 4,740 professional players engaged by some 158 clubs in England and Wales, only 700-odd were members of the union. Prestigious clubs such as Aston Villa, Tottenham Hotspur, Chelsea, Blackburn Rovers, Sheffield Wednesday and Middlesborough were among those without a single member. Roberts continued:

> I know no class of working people who are less able to look after themselves than footballers; they are like a lot of sheep…They cannot think for themselves and as for taking care for themselves, it makes me smile. The work has been left to a handful of us but I am telling you now that I have just about had enough of trying to raise the status of the professional footballer. It takes up time that I now cannot afford to spare and unless the players next season take a greater interest in the union I for one am going to leave them to it…

****

Charlie Roberts's threats to leave the union would be overtaken by events. The outbreak of war in 1914 saw professional players first have their wages cut (about which they were not consulted) and then have their contracts dissolved indefinitely. The Players' Union attempted to gain assurances that the contracts would eventually be honoured but their representations were brushed aside. The following season, 1914–15, just prior to the League competition being abandoned in its traditional form, plans were drawn up by the football authorities to scrap summer wages entirely and pay players no more than £2 a week. Semi-pro North and South competitions took the place of the regular League competitions.

Men were simply expected to enlist in the forces – and they did in droves, including many Players' Union committee-men. In fact, it was an ex-chairman of the union, Evelyn Lintott, who would be the first pro-footballer to earn a commission. Colin Veitch – despite earlier pacifist leanings – joined the Royal Garrison Artillery as a private, applied for a commission and became a lieutenant. Other union committee-men to join up were Everton's Tim Coleman (who joined the Footballers' Regiment, along with Joe Mercer's father) plus Manchester United's Sandy Turnbull, who was to die on the Somme. Charlie Roberts made repeated attempts to join but was refused on medical grounds, while Billy Meredith, being well into his 40s, was ineligible.

In October 1915 the union Management Committee held its last ANNUAL GENERAL MEETING of the 'pre-war' period at the Old Swan Hotel, Pool Street, Manchester. Its liabilities over its assets were £478, with a bank overdraft of £48. Secretary Newbould had by then resigned but agreed to act in a voluntary capacity while not demanding rent for the union offices.

The union, in fact, was almost non-existent. In April the union minutes summed up the air of gloom:

Expressions of regret were made at the lack of interest shown by the majority of players in their own welfare and the hope expressed that they would come forward and support the union in its endeavours to right matters ere the position of the professional players become hopeless.

The many pro-players who played on during the war years had no way of voicing their feelings at the precarious position they found themselves in, with many clubs paying little or nothing for their services. It is difficult to know how many of them agreed with the two Liverpool men who, late in 1916, tried to present a petition to F.J. Wall of the FA asking that players be paid £1 a match, but the *Thomson's Weekly News* reporter wrote: 'You can take my word for it that from what I know the petition was presented echoes the sentiment of every player with whom I've come in contact.'

Charlie Roberts, writing in the *Saturday Post* in August 1916, was typically forthright:

> The players have now put in a full season without pay and are being asked to do the same for the forthcoming season. We can but admire those who are anxious to help another make ends meet but if he keeps helping until he himself cannot make ends meet then he must be classed as a fool. I'm strongly of the opinion that players should receive pay for playing. If a player is ineligible for the army or working on munitions he should not be debarred from picking up a few shillings extra because one or two members of the FA (who are very comfortable thank you) think that professionalism in war-time is 'all wrong'. The hypocrisy of the whole thing stinks in the nostrils.
>
> I hear the clubs are saying 'We won't forget you.' I've been at the game too long to take any notice of such piffle and I hope others will take the same view of it. We've had some! I do feel that the player has been the MUG too long. Some are only earning now about 3s a week instead of their £4–£5 a week. Food too is twice as dear and yet the FA ask the footballer to give them more 'thank you football'…Players, come along and show your British pluck – for heavens sake, stick up for your rights!

War ended in November 1918 – and within days arguments were raging as to when professional football might recommence. On 23 November the Football League announced that professional players could receive £1 a week – consisting of two shillings and six pence for training twice a week and 15 shillings expenses per game. League spokesman C.E. Sutcliffe explained:

> 'Before clubs can pay normal wages they must get back to normal gates and normal players and until they arrive at something like normal conditions it is impossible to get back to the old order of things when they paid what one could regard as generous wages to players…At the same time they were bound to remember they had a number of players who had been loyal to the

clubs and played the game, and they must not forget they had a large number of players who had been loyal to the country and played the "Greater Game".

The decision clearly disappointed the vast majority of players. They had agreed to the suspension of their contracts for the duration of the hostilities; the war had now ended but the emergency regulations were to continue. More worrying was the suspicion that many clubs were quite happy to let players continue playing as semi-pros (or rather, poorly paid amateurs) indefinitely. It was this that finally sparked off the first rebellious move on behalf of the players.

On 16 December the *Sporting Chronicle* reported that a meeting had been held at the Memorial Hall in Farringdon, London. H.W.T. Hardinge, the Arsenal and England international, had presided over a meeting of 'former professionals' (60 in all, representing the majority of clubs in the London Football Combination) who had decided to form a union to be known as 'The Professional Football Players' and Trainers' Union'.

Among those present had been 'old' union men Frank Bradshaw, Tommy Elliot and Harold Halse, plus Charlie Rance of Spurs, Danny Shea of Fulham and eight Spurs and Arsenal men. The 'niggardliness' of the £1 allowance was mentioned, but what was distinctive about the meeting was the presence of bona fide trade union officials: W. Wells, London District Secretary of the Electrical Trade Union; S. Bradley, London District Secretary of the Amalgamated Society of Engineers; and Mr Mulhearn of the Boilermakers Union. Mulhearn was elected secretary of the new organisation.

Wells declared that there was only one way in which pro-footballers could ensure their livelihood and that was by becoming members of a bona fide trade union. Bradley, who had previously helped Colin Veitch draw up the constitution of the 'late Players' Union', assured players of trade union support in the case of a dispute, while on a more traditional note Frank Bradshaw suggested a deputation should meet with the London Football Combination to urge that body to ask the FA to increase allowances.

Hardinge then bitterly attacked the transfer system and the meeting closed after arranging a future session when a constitution would be drawn up. The new Players' Union certainly galvanised the Football League into action. When a series of demands were drawn up, including a £6 a week minimum wage, yearly contracts and an end to the transfer system, the League Management Committee responded by convening a meeting in the second week of January to which it invited a representative of every League club plus two players per club. As Sutcliffe put it: 'This is an innovation in football but the needs of the time demand the change.'

By the time the meeting began, Charlie Roberts – present now as one of Oldham Athletic's players – had been elected as 'spokesman' for the players. It would be a strange turnaround. In 1909 Roberts had been the radical locked

Harold Thomas William 'Wally' Hardinge 1919

An individualistic, tricky, inside-forward, he flourished at Sheffield United scoring nearly 50 goals in just under 150 League matches. He played for the 'Blades' for eight years, served as a chief petty officer in the Royal Navy in World War One and ended his career with Arsenal in 1921. Harry gained an England cap in 1910 but was also a cricket international and played for Kent from 1902 to 1933, scoring over 33,000 runs. By profession he was an employee of the sports goods retailer John Wisden, doing occasional stints as a coach in the US and in Spain.

outside while declaring his allegiance to the wider union movement; now he would be very much on the inside, the moderate declaring that the Players' Union should be run on constitutional lines with League and FA approval. In that sense he appeared to be at odds with the newly formed 'London' Union.

The League's spokesman, C.E. Sutcliffe, started out by responding to that organisation's proposals and spent a great deal of time juggling charts, statistics and bank balances to demonstrate that the demand for £6 a week was an 'impossibility', that most clubs were deep in debt and that, if pushed, only a third of them could afford just £3 a week. Nevertheless there was a definite feeling that more money could be paid. Henry Norris, chairman of Fulham FC, announced that his club could pay its men more and would be asking the League for permission to do so.

It was at this crucial point in the proceedings that Jesse Pennington rose to ask whether if there was an amalgamation of the 'old' and the 'new' unions the League would meet their representative and negotiate accordingly.

John McKenna, Football League president, replied: 'So long as you are organising along trade union lines the League cannot meet your representatives. We never refused to meet the representatives of the old Players' Union but there was a vast difference between football players and trade unionists ('hear hear'). We will not accept a players' union on trades union principles and whose strength lies in the strike clause.'

Sutcliffe went further stating that what the League objected to was 'men who were officials of trades union and who knew nothing at all about the management of football coming to interfere with those who had managed football all their lives'.

It was the old issue: men 'outside football' seeking to drag the players into conflict with the clubs.

Charlie Roberts then announced that the 'old' union was, in fact, still in existence and would be prepared to deal with the League on proper constitutional lines and perhaps to renunciate 'traditional' union methods and links with the wider union movement.

The Delinquent
by Alfred Leete
Topical Times 8 November 1919

Hasher Smith, of the Dare-Devil Rovers, appears before the F.A. for rough and ungentlemanly conduct on the field.

There followed a hurried meeting between both players' organisations before Hardinge returned to announce that the players concerned who represented the London clubs 'had unanimously decided to join hands with the old Players' Union and by doing so had dropped forthwith the old trades-union influence in the London movement.'

Famous footballers and their families.

Charlie Roberts wrote later that it had taken the London men a mere 10 minutes to decide to give up their organisation and hand over their books to him. With everything happening so quickly, the two union sides had clearly not had time to meet prior to the conference, and knowing what would please the League officials and also judging that strike threats were simply not on Roberts had decided to bargain away what he had once called 'our strength and right arm' in order to break the deadlock. Along with the announcement that traditional trade unions had been discarded he made a request for a doubling of the £1 'allowance' currently being paid to players. The response was swift. Players and press were asked to leave the room while the clubs talked it over.

Within half an hour the players were called back. The £2 was theirs. For Charlie Roberts it was a moment to savour: 'Nothing I have done has pleased me better,' he wrote afterwards, adding that he had surprised even himself at how persuasive he had proved to be, especially with the London men who had been 'seething with discontent'.

He then returned to Manchester, assumed the mantle of chairman in Veitch's absence and set about formulating plans for the election of a new management committee. There would also be a request to the FA for a benefit match to raise funds.

It was an odd episode in many ways. The union was now up and running again, but very much beholden to the League and the FA. It would be another 25 years or so before it could begin to behave as a proper trades union.

Chairman Roberts

Where the football industry was concerned, the gloom and depression of the war years were shaken off with almost indecent haste. Within two years of the armistice the Football League had expanded to four divisions and by 1923 the pre-war complement of 40 teams had risen to 88. The bulk of the Southern League had been 'lifted' to form the Third Division South, thus the Football League reigned supreme in England and Wales and for a year or so made more money than it knew what to do with.

Inflation played its part, of course. Admission fees went up from 6d to 1s but attendances were now massive as men flocked back into 'civvy street', repossessing the factories and the towns they had temporarily handed over to their women-folk. Football was the immediate beneficiary of this return to normal, although within a year or so other entertainments would begin to compete with a vengeance.

For Charlie Roberts, chairman of the union between 1919 and 1921, it was a period of great hope: union membership grew rapidly; funds swiftly moved into the black; and the status of professional players looked set to rise. Roberts himself worked tirelessly during his period in charge, travelling the country and speaking at numerous meetings. His was a blunt, no-nonsense approach, as suggested by his various writings exhorting men to join the union for their own good. He did not attempt to persuade but rather to shame players into working for their own benefit.

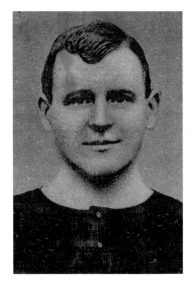

Charlie Roberts Chairman 1919–21

Charlie Roberts was one of Manchester United's greatest captains, leading them to both their first League Championship and their first FA Cup Final win in 1908. He left elementary school at the age of 12 in 1895 and for six years worked as a mill furnaceman in a local ironworks. Signed by Manchester United from Grimsby Town for £400 in April 1904 while only 20, he was an attacking centre-half and, despite his pale appearance which earned him the nickname of 'The Ghost in Boots', he went straight into United's League side. His immense stamina he attributed to summers spent working on east coast trawlers. Noted for his shaven head and short shorts (at a time when the FA ordered that 'players should cover their knees'), he was highly skilled and quick-thinking and could run 100 yards in 11 seconds at a time when the world record stood at 9.6 seconds. Because of his sympathies for the players' cause, and partly because Bristol City's Billy Wedlock was firmly established as England's centre-half, Roberts gained only three England caps. In August 1913 he signed for Oldham Athletic. He retired during the war but at a conference with the Football League in January 1919, attended by players from all over the country, Charlie took charge and announced that the 'old' union was still in existence. He then became the first post-war chairman, stepping down in July 1921 to become Oldham manager. To mark his departure the management committee presented him with £53, a gold watch and an illuminated address. Although a union 'radical' his politics were solidly Conservative and in the 1920s he stood as a Conservative in local Manchester by-elections. He held the Oldham job for 18 months before resigning, confessing that he could not stand the strain of watching. Charlie was also an astute businessman, establishing a wholesale tobacconists company in Manchester that traded until the 1990s. He died just before World War Two, aged 56.

Robert's early 'radical' days when he had seemed to be more aggressive and overtly political than the genuine socialist Colin Veitch were now over. By the late 1920s he was standing as a Conservative in local Manchester by-elections. Yet in comparison to many of the men who would serve on the management committee during the inter-war years, Roberts would always appear a firebrand – outspoken, given to impatient outbursts, a genuine product of the more optimistic, hearty Edwardian days.

Charles Buchan (1891–1960)
Chairman 1920s

Charles Buchan was a tall, elegant inside-forward, a true great of English football. After serving an apprenticeship with Leyton Orient he moved to Sunderland in 1911 where he became the Black Cats' all-time record League scorer with 209 League goals to his credit. After serving with distinction in World War One in the Grenadier Guards, he continued to play with Sunderland and was their leading scorer in 1923 with 30 goals. In 1925 Herbert Chapman caused a sensation by bringing Charles to Arsenal for a £4,000 fee that was considered a gamble for a 33-year-old player. He captained Arsenal to their first-ever Cup Final in 1927 but was on the losing side as Cardiff City beat the Gunners 1–0. He finally retired at the end of 1927–28, having scored 16 League goals that season despite being 36 years of age. In the immediate post-World War One years he was a stalwart of the Players' Union, serving on the management committee and taking the chair on occasions. On retirement he became a journalist and football commentator and, in 1947, along with three others, he formed the Football Writers' Association. It was Charles who suggested that an award should be given 'to the professional player who by precept and example is considered by a ballot of members to be the Footballer of the Year'. If that was not enough in 1951 he noticed that there was no paper or magazine devoted exclusively to the game. In 1951, in a bid to fill this gap, he started Charles Buchan's Football Monthly, the world's first such soccer magazine. His total of 257 goals makes him the Football League's sixth-top goalscorer of all time. He also earned six full England caps, scoring four goals.

After its return north the union swiftly reorganised itself, although its offices were to remain for some time a room in secretary Newbould's house in Longsight, just a short stroll from Billy Meredith's successful public house, the Church Hotel.

In March 1919 its bank balance stood at less than £50 and membership under 300. In May a benefit match was played at South Shields – the Players' Union against South Shields and District. Great players such as Charles Buchan, Billy McCracken, Clem Stephenson, Fanny Walden, Ted Vizard, Eli Fletcher and Sam Hardy took part and the match raised over £500.

At the ninth ANNUAL GENERAL MEETING in Manchester in August 1919, the entrance fee to the union was raised to 1 shilling and Newbould was given a rise to

£7 a week, plus £1 a week rental. He was also granted £100 for his war work on the union's behalf.

By August 1920, at the 10th AGM, the general account had soared to over £2,000 and membership had risen to the highest-ever figure – well over 1,000. In November, to cope with the flood of correspondence at the office, a typist was taken on at £2.50 a week. By September 1921 union funds had risen to such an extent that the management committee was able to invest £2,500 in corporation stock – the start of a sensible policy of salting away assets. Such a buoyant financial situation, unheard of in the union's short history, merely reflected the sudden relative prosperity of professional footballers in general.

However, it was at the harsher end of the game that the union was now doing its most effective work. Legal casework had begun before World War One but with bureaucracy increasing in day-to-day post-war life, and with new insurance acts on the statute book and income tax being levied on benefits, plus the massive increase in membership due to the expansion of professional football, the union found itself called upon to do more and more.

The union's solicitors fought scores of cases where the sums of money at stake ranged from £40 to £300. Smaller clubs such as Leadgate FC, Aberdare, Pontypridd and Newport Association FC, where rules and regulations regarding contracts often went largely unrecognised but where men were still attempting to make a living by playing football, were chased, badgered and harried into paying money that might otherwise have been refused.

It was not just small clubs that were involved: Sheffield Wednesday, Norwich City, Crystal Palace and Manchester City all found themselves fighting compensation, injury and insurance claims, or being forced by the union to recognise decisions taken by the League management committee that they would rather have ignored.

Nevertheless, there continued to be frustration expressed at the lowly social status of the professional footballer, brought about in a large part by the attitude towards them taken by football's ruling bodies. Players were gagged from 1921 onward where talking to the press was concerned; they were refused a representative on the National War Fund, set up to disburse money among relatives of players killed during the war (raised by players themselves); they were barred from being elected on to boards of football clubs (The FA commented, 'There must be no sinister motive or ulterior reason for seeking to assist in the governing of clubs…'); not to mention being restrained and restricted by their contracts in ways that could hardly be conceived by workers in other walks of life.

For Charlie Roberts, presiding over his last AGM in September of that year, the solution was simple:

> 'If you will tell me how players are going to get anything unless they organise I would like to meet that man. You must all appreciate that the day has arrived for collective bargaining.'

Yet how to bring such a situation about without recourse to traditional union methods? It was a conundrum to which Roberts had no solution, except to berate and exhort his fellow players:

> 'Some of you boys no doubt do not fully recognise the difficulty we have in trying to get the smallest concession for you. The League and the FA are very funny people to deal with and we shall never be able to get much for you unless you stand loyally by us.'

Harry Newbould added, in his address to players at the 1921 AGM, that loyalty was not always forthcoming:

> 'I hope there will be far more real enthusiasm next year. Further, I regret to say that there was a great lack of interest by members even in their own Benevolent Fund match. They let us down shamefully at South Shields. The same regrettable apathy occurred in connection with the revival of the Union Athletics Festival. Gentlemen, this is not worthy of the players, and I feel sure you will agree with me. Surely he is a strange man who cannot help himself?'

For Charlie Roberts, however, such considerations were about to end. Having been appointed manager of Oldham Athletic, he was obliged to retire from the union. To mark his passing the management committee presented him with £53, a gold watch and an illuminated address.

He was clearly moved ('You don't know how I feel here today…' he said at the commencement of his farewell speech). For 14 years he had been at the centre of the players' struggle, had more than once put his own financial future on the line and had almost certainly sacrificed his international career through his outspoken support for the union.

His final words as chairman summed up the man and his achievements:

> 'I like to think to myself that in the future I can say, "Charlie, you have done your duty to your fellow players…"'

The Leddy Case

Roberts's departure in December 1922 was a severe blow to the union. His qualities of tough leadership would never be more essential than in the six months following his resignation when the union found itself in the midst of a wages crisis that would lose it much of its new found prestige, not to mention its precious membership. Jimmy Fay took over the chairmanship and provided some continuity, although he too, was close to giving up the game and taking his benefit. Fay, in fact, could claim to be one of the union 'originals', having joined in 1907 and been elected to the management committee in 1912. He assumed his new post at a crucial turning point in the union's history. In

Henry Leddy.

1922 there were rumours that clubs were facing a crisis. The massive increases in attendance that had occurred so suddenly after 1919 now went into reverse. Clubs which had committed themselves to expensive extensions and improvements found themselves running into large debts as gate money declined. Large and small clubs faced losses ranging from hundreds to many thousands of pounds. Clubs situated in areas particularly hard hit by the trade recession suffered most: Durham City registered a loss in 1922 of almost £2,000, Grimsby of £3,000, Bristol City approaching £4,000.

The first straw in the wind for the union had come in late 1921 in a letter from League secretary Tom Charnley refusing the union permission to organise a benefit match '…in view of the bad times generally caused by the trade recession…'

Nevertheless, the unilateral decision to cut wages, taken in April 1922 at an emergency meeting of the League Management Committee, came as a bolt out of the blue. Although the Players' Union committee had been called in to a meeting just prior to the decision being taken they were accorded opportunity for meaningful consultation.

When asked by John McKenna, League president, for alternative suggestions to help the poorer clubs, the union members were nonplussed. They had been given no time to prepare proposals and were also unconvinced that such a drastic move was justified – after all, Spurs had just made a profit of some £17,000 and Liverpool of £6,000.

When asked for the figures upon which the proposed need for wage cuts had been based, McKenna replied that he did not have them. In fact, where the question of hard facts was concerned, the League officials would remain vague. This simply fuelled the union's suspicion that the calculations had been based upon a crude maximum wage multiplied by the number of first-team players.

The truth was that only a certain percentage of men received the maximum: most were either below it or only earning it when in the first team. What the union called for was a calculation based on an average wage – a more exact guide as to what clubs were spending on wages. Arguments over figures, however, were irrelevant. The League had decided on a crude across the board cut to £8 a week maximum in season and £6 a week during the summer. For some men it meant a loss of wages of up to £80 a year. McKenna's argument that men below the maximum would not be affected merely demonstrated the man's ignorance. The union pointed to cases where pay had been cut from £6 a week to £5; not only that, men on the point of moving up the scale were pegged. Thus it was a combined wage-cut-cum-wage-freeze.

For the union, however, the question was not so much that of the fine details of how much and for whom but of what their response should be. At the first meeting called by the union to discuss the issue, representatives from some 69 clubs attended – a groundswell of indignation that could have been harvested to some effect.

Instead, the union Management Committee decided it would obtain legal opinion concerning men who had signed contracts before the cut was announced. Surely, it argued, there was a chance here for victory in the courts? It was also decided to circularise the clubs in an attempt to persuade them to reconsider the cuts at their ANNUAL GENERAL MEETING in May – there had, after all, been plenty of evidence that some clubs had not wanted to cut wages at all. Finally, union members were advised to hold off signing new contracts until the League clubs' meeting in May.

It was the old question of persuading men to gamble with their summer wages – and many men were not union members anyway. As one delegate put it:

> 'They all know that often players get two or three days in which to make up their minds about signing. A man was probably approached at some railway station and asked if he was going to sign the form or not. The man would sign and the union would be beaten by their own member.'

In fact, committee member Jesse Pennington advised anyone who was asked should sign and thus secure his summer pay. Pennington, however, was simply being realistic. In May the clubs confirmed the cuts and, despite some defiant words (the Huddersfield Town side declared they would stand out if asked to, and one delegate declared that it was not so much a question of wages but an attempt to smash the union), the management committee ultimately decided to advise members to sign 'under protest'.

In a sense the union could not win. If it called a strike, as some men demanded, it would probably have been destroyed. By May a majority of men were thought to have signed on and were already away on their vacations. On the other hand, if the union failed to call for radical action then those looking for a lead would (and many indeed did) feel that the union had nothing to offer.

Instead, the union decided that its only constructive move would be to mount a test case to question the legality of the League's decision. Hinchcliffe felt that the League, in altering rule seven to introduce a new maximum wage, had forced clubs into breaching a number of contracts.

As secretary Harry Newbould said in a letter to *Athletic News*:

> It is common knowledge that this rule was practically forced on the clubs, that they had no opportunity to consider it and that many of them voted for it only under strong pressure and with great reluctance. It is also common knowledge that the rule was introduced on the eve of signing-on time. In other words it was a pistol levelled at the players' heads without reasonable consideration by the clubs or players.

The union ultimately decided to finance the case of Henry Leddy, a Dubliner, centre-half and captain of Chesterfield, who had previously played for Tranmere Rovers and Everton in the First Division. Leddy had signed his contract in March 1922 guaranteeing him £9 a week all year round until May 1923. The League resolution had come a month later, thus Leddy had refused to sign a new contract and had, it was announced, 'brought his action to contest the right of the club or the Football League to break his contract under the common law of the land'.

Although considered a 'union' action, the truth was that the union had had to ask the FA for permission to help Leddy take the case to court. As the *Athletic News* put it: 'It was obvious that the FA would not be prepared to give the union as a union such consent because that would be the full recognition of the union as an agent for the player and that the FA has always rigidly avoided.'

The application, therefore, had to come from Leddy himself. The case dealt with the question of whether the League had the power retrospectively to alter contracts already agreed and signed between a player and a club. In signing a contract both parties bound themselves to abide by the rules of the League, the League in effect being a third party to the contract. A section of League rule 12 stated that the League had power 'to cancel agreements with players which are contrary to the rules of the League'. The nub of the argument was which rules? Those in force when the contract was signed, or the new rules as amended in April by the League to cut the maximum wage?

The judge at Chesterfield Crown Court appeared unwilling to accept that the contract between Leddy and Chesterfield could not be subsequently altered because, he felt, both parties had agreed to abide by 'the current rules, or the rules from time to time existing of the Football League'. As things stood, therefore, no contract could remain inviolable. The League could change the terms at any point. Judgement was for Chesterfield, with costs. It seemed the Players' Union had suffered yet another legal body blow.

Unlike the Kingaby case of 1912, however, when the union had had no money to proceed with an appeal, this time it had several thousand pounds salted away in stocks to draw upon. The union's lawyer, Thomas Hinchcliffe, urged an appeal. On 8 May 1923 (just a few weeks after Wembley staged its first chaotic Cup Final) at the Royal Court of Justice in the Strand, Mr Justice Lush and Mr Justice Salter allowed the union's appeal and awarded Leddy his back-pay and costs for both hearings. The League declined to take the matter further and abandoned the action. Leddy and the Players' Union had won.

An ecstatic Harry Newbould declared:

> 'The result of this case has far-reaching importance to your association and the members thereof, and was indeed a great victory which, as you are aware, was proclaimed in the press throughout the land. It was, of course, a fight for principle and it proved that the courts will not allow the breaking of players' agreements either by clubs, Leagues or Associations…'

The Leddy case would prove to be a turning point in the Players' Union's thus far troubled history. Though it did nothing to stem the outward flow of members and had no effect on players' immediate financial situations, it marked a halt in the relentless grinding down of players in the legal sense. Had the case gone the other way there might well have been no real point in the players' body attempting to stand independently. The League could have continued to act with total impunity, making a mockery of the professionals' legal rights. A line in the sand had been drawn.

Jimmy Fay

The wage cuts and the lack of overt union action to fight them caused the union much damage. Membership plummeted: in August 1923 it was down from almost 2,000 to 500 while the 1925 ANNUAL GENERAL MEETING was attended by just eight delegates representing a little over 100 members.

It was, however, by no means a moribund organisation. Income and investment remained reasonably healthy and the union's solicitor continued fighting case after case for individual members, winning many thousands of pounds in compensation. This provided a ready source of upbeat news to boost the morale of those men still keen enough to persist in the soul-destroying work of seeking out and collecting subscriptions from indifferent colleagues.

With the union effectively locked out of wage negotiations on any level, its role was thus increasingly that of watchdog for those players sensible or aware enough to use the union solicitor when in trouble. Jimmy Fay knew, however, that only when players clinging tenuously onto a career in the game could see that the union might make a difference to their lives would they bother to pay their 1/- a week. For now, however, his hopes of establishing a proper players' insurance scheme and a provident fund were pipe dreams. All that the union could contemplate in the mid-1920s was an improved death levy of £100. There has probably never been a time, before or since, when the union had such a low profile. Its affairs were rarely reported in the national press. Its magazine, though competently produced, was poorly distributed and made a loss.

Gradually, however, changes were occurring. Harry Newbould's sad death in April 1928 after a long debilitating illness resulted in Jimmy Fay being appointed secretary. For so long a reluctant chairman, he was now unanimously chosen – and immediately asked for a rise in salary. He felt that £416 per annum plus expenses was poor recompense for a job that he had, for a year or more, virtually been doing for free, travelling regularly from Southport where he had an outfitters' shop to Newbould's house in Longsight where the union office had been situated.

Charlie Roberts, however, still on board as union vice-president, felt that the salary was sufficient until such time as Fay produced 'results'. Fay thus set about organising a membership recruitment drive. He also moved the union office back into the centre of Manchester. It was a symbolic step. For the next 50 years – apart from a five year sojourn above Jimmy Fay's shop in Southport during World War Two – the Old Corn Exchange Buildings at Hanging Ditch would be the union's home.

Fay's membership drive, which began in earnest in 1929, was based on the belief that pro-footballers, like union members in general, need chasing before they will pay their membership 'subs'. The fact that during the inter-war years the union movement in

Jimmy Fay
Chairman 1921–29, Secretary 1929–53

Jimmy Fay's remarkable playing career stretched across 20 years. He made his professional debut in 1903 for Chorley at the age of 19, earning just 10s a week before being snapped up in 1905 by Oldham Athletic. He would go on to play 100 consecutive games for the Latics during which time Oldham rose from Lancashire Combination level to the First Division of the League. Upon asking for a rise to 30s a week, however, he was promptly sold for £750 to Bolton Wanderers where he stayed for 10 years, finally moving to Southport General in 1921.

Primarily a half-back, Jimmy was a cultured, intelligent player, never a hard man: in fact he earned himself the nickname 'Gentleman Jim'. Remarkably consistent, he missed only one first-team game in six seasons for Oldham from 1905 to 1911 and went on to make 128 for Bolton Wanderers between 1911 and 1921. In 1919, at the age of 35, he gained his third Football League representative cap against the Scottish League. When he hung up his boots he opened a sports outfitters in Southport, although the Players' Union would come to dominate the rest of his life.

One of the union 'originals', having joined in 1907 and been elected to the management committee in 1912, he took over the chairmanship in 1922 on the departure of Charlie Roberts, providing much needed continuity and experience at a crucial moment in the union's history. In 1929 he reluctantly took over the role of secretary on the death of Harry Newbould and, incredibly, Jimmy would serve the union in this capacity until 1953! No one else in the union's history served for so long and many of the early achievements such as the Players Provident Fund were down to Jimmy's selfless endeavour and perseverance. He was a true champion of the player's cause.

general lost members due to mass unemployment could only have had a peripheral bearing on Players' Union activities. Throughout this same period no football club of note folded and few footballers were thrown permanently on to the unemployment scrap heap. Club rosters remained extremely large and, while there was a great deal of cost-cutting at the margins with wages being squeezed, most clubs had on their books the equivalent of three full sides. Thus, as a labour market, pro-football remained relatively unaffected by general industrial trends.

What was more, union membership at certain clubs was often wildly erratic. One season upwards of 40 men might be signed on paying 'subs'; the next, absolutely no one. The problem was that a season's good work could be wiped out at one fell swoop with the untimely transfer of a good collector. The regular movement of men from club to club created an unsettling, ever-changing pattern that made long-term planning

ASSOCIATION FOOTBALL PLAYERS' AND TRAINERS' UNION.

JOIN THE UNION!

REGISTERED OFFICE,
133 CORN EXCHANGE BUILDINGS,
HANGING DITCH,
MANCHESTER.

TO ALL PROFESSIONAL FOOTBALL PLAYERS.

This Pamphlet is issued with a twofold object :—

(1) for the information of Players who are already members, showing the many advantages obtainable by membership of the Union.

(2) to invite Players who are not members of the Union to become members, and to support an organization which has done so much for the whole of the Professional Football Players throughout the country.

Objects and Advantages of Membership.

To organise the whole of the Professional Football Players throughout the country.

All Cases between Clubs and Players.—To promote and protect the interests of the members by endeavouring to come to amicable arrangements with the governing Football Authorities with a view to the abolition of all restrictions which affect the social and financial positions of players, and to safeguard their rights at all times.

Workmen's Compensation Act.—By winning the case of "Walker and Roberts v. the Crystal Palace F.C." the Union succeeded in proving the professional footballer a workman within the meaning of Act of 1906.

Union leaflet.

Howard Matthews Chairman 1929–30

The son of a well-known amateur goalkeeper, Howard was of comparatively light build for the position, especially when one considers the aggressively physical nature of the game then. However, he was a fine player and a model professional on and off the field. A civil servant by profession and a life-long teetotaller and non-smoker, he was probably the oldest player in League football when playing for Halifax in his 45th year. A professional with Burslem Port Vale, Burton United, Oldham Athletic, Port Vale, Halifax Town and Chester, his finest moment came in 1913 when Oldham reached the FA Cup semi-finals, being beaten 1–0 by Aston Villa. The Oldham Chronicle commented, 'One cannot blame Matthews for the goal and his work throughout the game was perfect.'

extremely difficult. The key was to find sufficient men of ability and tenacity to make the effort. This was where management men like Len Davies of Cardiff were worth their weight in gold.

From 1922 until the early 1930s, Cardiff City's membership total was more than healthy. When Davies left to become player-manager of Bangor the tradition was carried on for a season or so by E. Jenkins, but ultimately fell away. Meanwhile, Davies succeeded in 'unionising' little Bangor.

Bury was another unlikely team regularly turning in membership figures in excess of 30 per season, all of which was due to their captain and future union chairman, Dave Robbie, who had built up the numbers almost from scratch. Even Clapton Orient, one of the few clubs in the League to face closure during this period and which survived largely through the efforts of the local community, turned in good union figures due to the presence of committee-man Arthur Wood.

The pattern was repeated at a score or more 'unfashionable' clubs: Archie Rawlings at Preston North End; Jack Hacking at Oldham; Henry Leddy at Grimsby; Harry Goslin at Bristol City; Joe Edelston at Fulham. These collectors and delegates built up membership rolls that would put to shame some of their larger club contemporaries.

Where the bigger League clubs were concerned the pattern of membership was not always consistent or logical. The two clubs with the greatest traditions in union terms – Manchester United and Manchester City – were almost always unionised. City, with the continued presence of Meredith as player and later as coach well into the 1920s, was a union bulwark right through the inter-war period, with men like Sam Sharp, Eli Fletcher, Sam Cowan and Eric Brook proving valuable union servants.

UNION AGM REPORT by Thomas Hinchcliffe

Alf Widdowson

The Union Case: v Coventry City FC

This is a compensation case out of the ordinary run of the many submitted to me by you for attention. Widdowson was injured while playing for his Club [Coventry City] against Newport County on the 27th day of October, 1928, sustaining a twisted joint of the left knee. He consulted you, and you in turn instructed me to do all that was necessary in the matter to see that he obtained his full legal rights, and his interests were protected. This we did and with highly satisfactory results. The Club treated Widdowson very well indeed, not only paying him full weekly wage during his agreement for service, but weekly compensation. He subsequently underwent an operation in the Coventry and Warwickshire Hospital on the 8th day of April last, and although incapacitated the Club have signed him on for the ensuing season paying him £4 per week during the close season, and full wage when playing, and he consequently does not desire any proceedings to be taken, and is well pleased at the treatment received by him from the Club. We have not been able to recover any costs in this matter, and there will be a small bill of costs to be paid by your Union, but nothing calling for any comment.

His career:

Nottingham-born inside-forward Alf Widdowson is more remembered for his feats at Notts County than Coventry City. He made 157 appearances for County and scored 46 goals, many of them in the First Division. He signed for Coventry in March 1928 in a double signing with Norman Dinsdale for £500. In four seasons he made 73 League and Cup appearances, scoring 17 goals. His City career was disrupted by injury and for the last 18 months he was a fringe player in the reserves. Alf only missed three games after the Newport game referred to above but played only a further five games that season, the last on the 29 December 1928. He was back in the first team for the second game of the following season. He was released in the summer of 1932 and joined Newark Town, later playing for Heanor Town.

UNION AGM REPORT by Thomas Hinchcliffe

Arthur George Davis

The Union Case: v Crystal Palace FC

Arthur George Davis received injury while playing for his Club against Torquay United on the 29th September, 1928, sustaining injury to his left leg. Acting upon your esteemed instructions the usual proceedings were taken, liability admitted by the Club, and full weekly compensation of 30/- has, and is being regularly paid to him. Davis, on or about the 15th July ultimo, underwent an operation at the Southshields Nursing Home, Nottingham, in which town he resides, and he is doing very nicely indeed. The cartilage has been removed and also two hard substances attached thereto. We are in touch with the Federation's solicitors with a view to obtaining lump sum payment, but it will take some time to conclude negotiations, as the ultimate result of the operation is doubtful. A further report will be furnished later.

His career:

Birmingham-born Davis began his career with Handsworth Old Boys and played as an amateur with Leicester City and Coventry City before signing in 1919 for Aston Villa. An inside-left, after six appearances in three years he moved to Queen's Park Rangers (62 League appearances and 21 goals) and thence to Notts County (140 League appearances and 51 goals). Signed for Crystal Palace in the summer of 1928, he made his first-team debut on 25 August 1928 against Watford at home. Palace won 3–0 and Davis scored one of the goals. His last game was the one in which he was injured on 29 September 1928 against Torquay United at home. A newspaper report in December 1928 said that his knee trouble was proving very obstinate and would need some time. So it proved. He never played again, his Palace career totalling just five League games and two goals.

The north-eastern giants, Newcastle United and Sunderland, were generally solid with just the occasional year when membership slumped. Jimmy Low and Jesse Carver, at either end of the inter-war period, proved worthy successors to Colin Veitch and Jimmy Lawrence at Newcastle, but Sunderland proved more erratic, missing the years 1935–38 totally for some unexplained reason.

Dave Robbie Chairman 1931–35

Dave Robbie was the archetypal one-club man, joining Second Division Bury from Scotland in 1921 and staying with the 'Shakers' for the next 14 years. As a player Robbie was a speedy right-winger although, at over five feet ten, a little tall for the position. In all he made 421 appearances for Bury and scored 101 goals during that time. When he stepped down from chair in 1935 he was presented with an inscribed gold wristlet watch costing £10 as a tribute to his hard work. Dave eventually went into business as a private physiotherapist. A confirmed bachelor, he lived with his mother throughout his playing career.

More difficult to explain, however, was the poor record of the Merseyside clubs, Everton and Liverpool. From being pioneers at the turn of the century these proud clubs were completely non-unionised when Fay took over as secretary and remained so for four years before McPherson, Hansen and later Matt Busby took on the role of collectors and returned Liverpool to full strength.

Everton, however, remained a non-union club until the 1937–38 season when Joe Mercer, Cliff Britton and Charlie Sagar picked up the banner. It has been said that the Everton board discouraged players from involving themselves in union activities. It was no coincidence that the club chairman throughout the inter-war period was Will Cuff, a dictatorial, 'hard as nails' character who would become League vice-president in 1936 and president in 1938. Cuff was known to enter the dressing room on occasions and tell the team how to play. He was also prone to silencing League Management Committee members if they were saying something that irked him. Perhaps his influence was significant but there is little hard evidence.

Jimmy Fay's missionary work was to take him to every club in the League and within a remarkably short time membership rose well above the thousand mark – well short of 100 per cent but approaching respectability. It was clear, however, that without the larger clubs and the prestigious players the union would remain unsung and largely unnoticed.

Fay's strategy, once he had managed to hoist membership back into respectable figures, was to confront the problem head on: he took to naming the 'guilty' clubs in his AGM report, even releasing such information to the press. Thus Arsenal,

Everton and Chelsea were regularly upbraided, while in 1933 he added Leeds United, Middlesborough, Sunderland, Sheffield Wednesday, Sheffield United and nine other Second and Third Division teams to the sorry list of clubs that could boast of no members at all.

Top players were immune to such tactics, however. Alex James's view of the game and his own position in it would always be unashamedly commercial. As he stated during his famous 'strike' to obtain a better contract with Arsenal in 1933:

> 'I haven't the slightest intention of posing either as a martyr or as a crusader fighting to right the wrongs of the oppressed brothers of my profession. In football – off the field, of course – it must always be each man for himself. And professional footballers didn't invent that rule.'

Militancy was not an option for Fay. However, as the Depression started to bite and clubs began to feel the financial pinch, there were plenty of areas where union action was becoming essential.

By 1932 the number of players being forced to seek unemployment benefit had dramatically increased, not because there were fewer positions for them at clubs, but because clubs were holding more and more men on their retain-and-transfer lists, determined to make something from their departure, and thus keeping a pool of free labour at their disposal. With many clubs unable to afford big fees, the retained men remained out of work and thus had to sign on the 'dole'.

The union had already expanded its unemployment bureau considerably by regularly circularising clubs with lists of available players, their names, positions, and vice versa. Now it took upon itself the job of collating information regarding the newly professionalised French clubs where opportunities for British players were becoming available. While the headlines of the popular press blared out concerns about the 'menace' to British football posed by new professional leagues beyond its shores, the union was arranging for its members to travel to France for trials on good

---

Albert 'Syd' Barrett Chairman 1936

An England Schoolboy international and England amateur international, he earned his one full England cap in 1930. A left-wing half and later a left-back, he was nicknamed 'Snowball' by some because of his very blond, almost white, hair. He was a cool, stylish, unflappable player and as an amateur he assisted the famous touring side, Middlesex Wanderers, as well as featuring for Leytonestone, West Ham, Southampton and Fulham. He won one full England cap against Ireland in 1930 and in 10 seasons with Fulham made over 400 appearances. He continued working as an accountant after turning pro and, following the war, was secretary of a Romford wholesale firm.

UNION AGM REPORT by Thomas Hinchcliffe

Len Bayliss

The Union Case: v Southend United F.C

Your member, Leonard Richard Bayliss, met with an injury on the 23rd day of September, 1925, while playing for the above named Club, as a result of which he received injury to the ligaments of his knee joint, and subsequent removal of cartilage. Liability admitted by the Club, weekly compensation paid, and then lump sum settlement arrived at on the 24th November, 1929. Amount paid over to Bayliss in full settlement was £300, with weekly compensation in addition of £1 17, making a net settlement of £4 17. Our costs have also been paid in addition, and we have no charges against you in respect thereof. Bayliss was more than pleased with his settlement.

His career:

The match in question was Len Bayliss's Southend United debut, and the only game he played that season. He made seven appearances the following season for Southend, but that was the extent of his career with the club. He was born in Alfreton on 28 April 1899, and played for Alfreton Town, Luton Town, Mansfield Town and Southend United before becoming coach, chief scout and finally manager of Coventry City. During the big freeze of 1947 he made a night-time drive from Southend to Coventry but became ill during the trip and subsequently died of kidney failure.

the union approached the Ministry of Labour to complain about 'alien' players coming to Britain and taking British players' jobs. It had been agreed at this point that players had to achieve a two-year residency period before they could be signed as a pro-footballer.

The sudden increase of players on the dole, however, soon caused another headache for Fay – and another opportunity for action. When the Department of Labour ruled that professional footballers were 'seasonal workers' and thus not entitled to unemployment pay, Fay arranged a meeting with the relevant government officials in order that he might mount an appeal on their behalf. As he explained in the report to the 1932 AGM:

After correspondence with the Parliamentary Secretary to the Ministry of Labour I was advised to send in writing a full statement of the case of Professional Footballers to the Umpire for his consideration in connection with the appeals now before him.

In July Fay went to see the umpire at the ministry accompanied by F.J. Wall of the FA, and answered detailed questions. Fay impressed the umpire and sometime afterwards he learned that his efforts had been successful – players could now receive their benefit. As the 1930s progressed Fay would find himself increasingly involved with government departments and civil servants, taking on problems basic to the interests of members – members who were now joining in ever-increasing numbers.

Gradually, professional players were emerging from their netherworld of subservience and dependence into something approaching the 20th century. In 1929 an important resolution was passed at the FA's ANNUAL GENERAL MEETING – despite opposition from the Football League – regarding a player's right to attend an enquiry into his own conduct. Not only could a player now attend; he could now cross-examine witnesses and call for rebutting evidence. As E.J. Scott of Herts FA put it:

'I am quite aware your rules permit a player to ask permission to be heard in person but what is the good if you decline to see him? The most democratic game in the world should not be governed by the autocratic system now in force.'

By 1934 the union had managed to acquire a modern office, duplicators, a salaried secretary and typist, more than £10,000 invested and close on 1,500 members. Yet so much remained the same: the transfer system appeared even more unjust than before the war; the maximum wage had not been raised for a decade. Even Billy Meredith remained on the door, as he would continue to do for the next 20 years, checking members in, keeping strangers out.

Moving towards militancy

No sooner had Fay dealt with the problem of unemployed players being listed as 'seasonal' workers then he was faced with the question of whether players were still classed as 'manual workers'. At stake were various benefits under Health and Insurance Acts passed since the war. The union was asked by the Ministry of Health if it wished to take a test case to court; and on 23 April 1934 Justice Roach decided that pro-players could no longer be considered 'manual workers' if earning more than £250 per annum.

As this affected players' insurance cover there was a great deal of worry, not helped by the attitude of the Football League. At first the League Mutual Insurance Federation let it be known that it would continue to treat all players, no matter how much they earned, in a similar fashion when it came to the question of compensation. Within a few months however, changes to the basic player/club contract were mooted that made such an assurance sound extremely hollow. If adopted they would threaten the financial security of any badly injured player.

At the Players' Union AGM in August 1934 Jimmy Fay announced that the meeting had before it 'a question of a more serious nature than the union has dealt with for many years'. The League had proposed an addition to players' agreements that read as follows:

> That if at any time during the period of agreement the player shall be prevented by illness or accident from performing his duties, he shall receive during the first month, fortnight or any shorter period of such incapacity, the salary mentioned in the agreement and during the second consecutive period at the option of the club, one half of the same salary.
>
> If he shall be so incapacitated during a longer period, then the salary shall at the like option cease to be payable during such longer period without prejudice either to the club's right to transfer fee or to the player's right to compensation (if any) under the Workman's Compensation Act.

Players' Union solicitor, Thomas Hinchcliffe.

The outrageousness of such a proposal brought from the union a swift and determined response. With the press present the union Management Committee issued the following statement:

That the Football League Management Committee, for reasons best known to themselves, seemed to be intent upon making the position of the players as difficult as possible; that the attempts to impose upon players such conditions of employment are tantamount to slavery; that should players have the misfortune to be stricken with illness or crippled physically they also wish to cripple them financially.

The meeting then carried the following resolution:

That this meeting of delegates of the AFPTU strongly condemns the proposed addition to players' agreements; this proposed addition is a serious matter to all players (and the game) and we demand that it be withdrawn. If it is accepted by the clubs, the union will take drastic action and fight the matter to the end…

UNION AGM REPORT by Thomas Hinchcliffe

Syd Reid
The Union Case: v Luton Town FC
This is a compensation claim in which one of your members Sydney Reid received injury on the 21st day of January, 1928, while playing for his Club, consisting of a loose cartilage of the knee joint. The matter was placed in my hands by your Union for attention. The usual proceedings were commenced, and eventually liability was admitted, and full weekly compensation of 30/- per week up to date of settlement. After numerous interviews and correspondence with the Insurance Federation's Solicitors and Reid, a settlement was arrived at, the sum of £250 being paid by way of damages, which, with £31 10s. 0d. received in addition by way of weekly compensation, makes a total of £281 10s. 0d. Our costs have also been paid, and we have no charges against you in the matter. This settlement was very satisfactory to Reid, and he was thankful for, and appreciated the assistance afforded him by your Union.

His career:
Although only 5ft 6in tall, Syd Reid was a prolific goalscorer for Luton in the 1920s, netting 70 League goals in 134 starts in Division Three South. Born in Cannock Chase but moving to Aberdare as a youngster, Syd was spotted playing for Troedyrhiw Star and moved to Luton in 1922 as a 19-year-old to replace another natural goalscorer, England international Ernie Simms. Syd was badly injured during a 3–3 home draw with Bournemouth on 21 January 1928 [the case above] and in the Luton Club minutes it is stated that the Luton trainer thought that Syd would be fit to play after a few days. The decision to try to make him kick a ball was no doubt the cause of his claim for compensation as he was not able to play again. It is also minuted that Luton prevaricated over paying the compensation and it took a letter from Hinchcliffe and Co., solicitors of Manchester, and threats from Fred Charnley, secretary of the Football League, before the money was paid out!

The proposal was withdrawn, a significant coup for the union. However, relations between the League and union would remain poor, made poorer still by signs that the employer's body was standing in the way of progress. In August 1934, in the midst of the bickering over injury insurance, a solicitor from Liverpool had come up with a startling suggestion that could have lifted professional footballers and the game on to a different financial plane of existence entirely.

UNION AGM REPORT by Thomas Hinchcliffe

Tom Kelly

The Union Case: v Barnsley FC

You will no doubt remember the facts of this case. Kelly was injured while in the employ of the above named Club on the 15th January, 1925, at Oakwell, while playing against the Millwall Football Club, and the nature of his injury was 'twisted right knee'. Kelly consulted your Union and in due course you instructed me, on his behalf, to take up the claim and protect his future interests. The Club paid his wage up to the end of the playing season, and subsequently they admitted liability, and full weekly compensation, at the rate of 30/-, was paid to Kelly, when negotiations took place for a settlement by payment of a lump sum, with, I am pleased to report, successful results. The Federation agreed to pay Kelly £150 clear of costs in full settlement in addition to the sum of £61 10s. also paid in weekly compensation, making a total of £211 10s., a settlement which the Court readily approved, and a cheque for £150 was paid over to Kelly, who expressed himself very grateful and pleased with the efforts made on his behalf. My costs have also been paid and I have no further charges against you in this matter.

His career:

Tom Kelly was a centre-forward, born in Manchester on 13 January 1902. He signed for Barnsley from Corpus Christi FC (presumably a church team) in April 1924. On 26 April that year he made his debut and scored one of the goals in a 5–2 home win against Crystal Palace. He played his last game for Barnsley on 28 February 1925 in a match against Leicester City which Barnsley lost 6–0. He went on to join Rhyl Athletic. His career record at Barnsley was 17 League and Cup games, scoring six goals.

Since the start of the 1930s, the football pools had grown rapidly to become a multi-million pound industry, earning almost everyone untold riches: the government received millions in taxes, punters regularly struck lucky and the pools companies themselves made healthy profits. Unfortunately, the game and the men upon whose labours it all rested received not a penny. In 1934 a certain Watson Hartley devised a scheme whereby the Football League would patent its fixture list and then charge the pools companies for its use.

He took it to the League but was rebuffed. The union argued that with the money the League might receive from granting companies use of its patent and the money the pools companies were more than willing to pay, the football industry's multiple problems such as providing players with proper insurance from injury would be solved. It was the stuff of which Jimmy Fay's dreams had long been made: a pension fund for men of five or more years service on retirement; centres for training young players in football skills; official hostels for injured and sick players paid for by private insurance; assistance for clubs in financial difficulties; and increased pay for players – all might be possible under this imaginative scheme.

The men who ran the League were unimpressed, however, declaring that they would have nothing to do with gambling. The union was aghast that such an opportunity had been squandered and angry at how helpless it had been to influence affairs that affected its members so closely. There was, however, a growing conviction that it was moving into a position where it could start to influence events rather than simply react to them.

The year 1937 saw the union bracing itself for a struggle. At that year's AGM it was announced that only 11 clubs in all four divisions were now non-union and that membership figures, now approaching 2,000, were the best since 1920. Along with increasing popularity and membership came confidence. There were also one or two small 'perks' accompanying membership – a discount scheme offered to union members on purchases from a large London warehouse company; and a subscription withdrawal scheme whereby retired members could claim three quarters of their subs paid during membership.

However, the advent of war in 1939 more or less halted the union's progress in its tracks. Its declaration came as no real surprise – daily life in Great Britain had been subtly shaped by the growing threat of hostilities for quite some time. The sudden ending of normal life saw people rushing in all directions: sending children away to the countryside, hurrying to call-up points, digging shelters and preparing for the worst.

Professional football ceased just a week into the new season 1939–40 and many footballers found themselves stranded or involved in dashes back to distant homes in search of jobs and somewhere to live. Within months of the declaration, some clubs had virtually no players at all to call upon, even had there been games for them to play in.

For the Players' Union, the first few months of the war brought a flood of enquiries: the sudden cancellation of agreements and the abrupt stoppage of wages meant there were many men without a penny, especially those who had just finished a summer on the retained list and had thus received no cash for some months. There were anxious requests concerning how much money clubs were obliged to pay regarding contracts already signed. The League eventually announced that those players who had been 'on call' to play on 8 September – the second Saturday of the season – were entitled to that week's pay. Inevitably, various clubs did not respond and the union had to do a great deal of chasing up. One such case would result in a certain Jimmy Guthrie joining the union on behalf of his playing colleagues at Portsmouth – and staying in.

The union's own running costs were cut to the bone. The office was removed to Jimmy Fay's home above the shop in Southport, thus saving on travel, wages and rent, while application was made to the chief registrar of Friendly Societies for a relaxation in the union's rules regarding helping players financially. The healthy state of the union's finances meant that it was in an ideal position to help men suffering hardship. Thus the union found itself paying out to men for travel, rail-fares and removal costs; there was also extra money paid to families who had recently lost breadwinners. Many men took advantage of a relaxation in the union's rules relating to rule seven (whereby a retiring member could claim back most of the subs he had paid in during the course of his membership – usually a sum of about £20) which proved extremely popular, helping many men out at a tricky moment.

Although battening down, the union would remain in situ. At the 1940 AGM a new trustee – Mr S. Sanderson, JP, and secretary to the Card and Blowing Room Operatives Association – was introduced to take the place of Charlie Roberts who had died some weeks previously. Sanderson was also provincial secretary of the National Association of Trades Union Approved Societies – thus he could speak for over one and a half million trade unionists. Even in 1940 he could see the germ of coming changes:

'The first step is to win the war. That in the midst of peace wise men prepare for war is without doubt a profundity. Equally so is the truism that in the turmoil of war wise men prepare for peace.'

Jimmy Fay echoed the sentiment, and made a prediction:

'The administration must go on, we must keep in touch with the members so that when this terrible struggle is ended we may be in a position to represent the members in an endeavour to make the livelihood of the professional footballer more secure and much more equitable than it has been in the past. When that time arrives, great leadership will be necessary and I feel sure that your management committee will not be lacking in efforts on your behalf.'

3. Paying to Play 1909-39

The union which emerged from the traumatic events of 1909 was no puppet organisation, but its very independence merely highlighted what little power it possessed and how easy it was for football's authorities either to bully or ignore it.

For the next three years it would struggle along, tilting at the familiar windmills with high hopes but little success. There would be some small reform of wages and the union would claim to have played a part in bringing them about, but in truth they were the handiwork of one man: Football League solicitor, C.E. Sutcliffe.

The 1909 'strike' had proved to be the last straw for the FA and in January 1910 an FA spokesman wrote: 'It is incompatible with the position of the FA as the governing body of a national sport that it should be concerned in the financial arrangements between clubs and players other than seeing that the engagements which they enter into are observed.'

The union must have felt that radical change was close at hand. In January 1910 the FA distributed voting papers to 74 clubs and 1,725 players to ascertain their opinion regarding the abolition of the maximum wage. Although only 31 clubs bothered to reply (12 for abolition and 19 against) 1,055 players did return their papers, 795 voting in favour of abolition. In February of that year the union Management Committee, after considering various wage schemes, declared that 'the only solution to the vexed question between clubs and players is the abolition of the wage limit'. After some wrangling, however, the resolution was extended to read: 'but the union would willingly accept any scheme that tends to improve the now existing conditions'.

Eventually a wages conference was held on 25 February 1910 at the Grand Hotel, Manchester, the union being represented by Evelyn Lintott, Jimmy Sharp, Herbert Broomfield and Syd Owen. The union scheme, drawn up by Owen, was given 'a courteous hearing', but it would be the League's proposals that would eventually be adopted in full.

The only straightforward changes, however, that players and club managements could easily understand and which looked automatic were the introduction of talent money schemes. Bonuses could be paid to players by clubs finishing in the top five of any division. The top club could disperse £275 among its first team, the runners-up could disperse £220 and so on. These payments, however, were not compulsory.

The changes proposed to the basic weekly wage were designed to reward long-serving (or 'loyal') players. After two years a player on the maximum wage *might* be offered an extra 10s a week for two years. After four more years service another 10s rise *might* be awarded. Thus, it would take a player six years to move from the £4 maximum a week to £5. Since the great majority of players were not on £4 a week anyway, this 'concession' had little effect on the bulk of pro-players.

Where players' 'benefits' were concerned, the new proposals looked logical enough. After three years service a player could ask his club for a 'benefit' to be awarded for five years service. After that, he might ask for a 10-year benefit.

A 'benefit' generally consisted of the proceeds of a particular match granted to a particular player, usually a star, and usually when approaching the end of his career. It served as a pay-off lump sum with which he might set up a small business when his career ended.

After World War One a specific sum was guaranteed rather than the proceeds of a particular match and the payment evolved into a contractual right rather than a 'gift', with specific sums added to the player's weekly wage. The downside where this arrangement was concerned was that, for many years, this 'gift' was taxed.

The benefit was, however, discretionary. What was more, if a player was transferred before the five year period was up he might be granted an 'accrued share' of what he would have earned – *if* the club wanted to pay it and *if* the player had been wise enough to have such an agreement included in his contract.

As Charlie Roberts wrote, life was never as simple as that:

> I know that a player can make an agreement after three years service for a benefit, but how many clubs will allow him to make it? At the end of his third season, take it that a player asks for such an agreement, and the club refuses. What then? If the player refuses to sign on, what happens? The longer he delays signing, the more wages he continues to lose. He has no power to force the hands of the directors and he cannot go elsewhere owing to the stringent transfer rule.

The sums players might earn depended on each man's worth in terms of the affection fans felt for him and the relative power of the club. Clearly a top club could pay a top benefit. Before 1914 the typical amount paid out by the two Sheffield clubs could be anything between £150 and £250. At Aston Villa it was between £300–£450, rising to £500 for a player like Joe Bache. Billy Meredith, however, at Manchester United, reaped over £1,000 in 1912.

Colin Veitch had always taken an optimistic line: caution and patient plodding would eventually reap rewards. Thus, he set about planning the union's proposals for 1911, imagining that a process had begun that would simply accelerate. In April 1911, along with Charlie Roberts and Arthur Bridgett, he took his ideas along to the League for consideration.

Veitch's proposals were that players not offered a 'reasonable' wage should be given a free transfer; that players in service for five years should become exempt from the maximum wage (should attain freedom of contract); that players having, on 30th April of any year, completed four years' service be granted a rise of £52 a year; those completing two years, £26 a year; plus a new set scale of talent money: £2 for a win, £1 for a draw with £3 for a first-round Cup win rising to £15 a man for the Final. Added to all this it was proposed that a transferred player should receive a percentage of the fee.

According to the official League history, 'A long discussion took place in a very friendly spirit.' C.E. Sutcliffe for the League, however, was in no doubt that the proposals were unreasonable.

> 'It is no use mincing words, the clubs cannot stand the ever-increasing drain…The club manager is often at his wits' end to pay his way. He is signing bank guarantees and finding money out of his private means to meet players' demands. Why should he be compelled to go further?'

He even went as far as to say: 'I boldly assert that very few clubs had value for money spent in the season 1910–11 and I should say the majority of directors and managers are glad that the worry is at an end for another season.'

It was useless for Syd Owen to write a week later wondering where exactly the money went when individual clubs were drawing 20,000–30,000 spectators every fortnight and still declaring losses. Useless also to point out that the union's proposals for Cup bonuses would result, if implemented, in a total of £3,431 being paid to players while the competition as a whole would earn £70,000. Veitch's proposals were rejected. The consultations concerning wages were over.

★★★★★★★★★★★★★★★★

World War One saw any serious payment to players cease. When football commenced in 1919 players were allowed to earn just £2 a match but with clubs soon earning massive amounts as the crowds flocked back, the League could hardly continue paying men such a niggardly amount. Wages, however, were still pegged back during the 1919–20 season, and, despite union demands for increases reflecting the inflation that had occurred since 1915 (anything up to 75 per cent on pre-war prices), the League eventually awarded them a 50 per cent increase on the pre-war maximum (and this to be paid only during the playing season).

Thus, the year-round weekly pay of professional players went up to £4.50 a week, not much of a reward for men who had made so many financial sacrifices for so many years – and nowhere near the extravagant promises made by League Management Committee men when they had cut wages in 1914.

By 1920, however, even C.E. Sutcliffe had to concede that clubs could afford more. In March he wrote:

> 'The arguments for better wages are unanswerable. In view of the decreased value of the pound, players must have more and in view of the increased popularity of the game and increased gates, the bulk of the clubs can pay more.'

Just a month earlier, in February, the third round of the FA Cup had drawn over half a million spectators paying over £33,000 in gross receipts. Grounds were groaning – spectators literally so. At Chelsea there were scores of injuries when a roof upon which people were standing collapsed onto spectators below. Even teams with nothing tangible to play for were reporting record takings: Bradford City finished the season in mid-table and were knocked out of the Cup in the second round, yet they registered gross takings of over £35,000, and profits after all expenses and taxes of £22,000.

C.E. Sutcliffe's team, Burnley, were another small club reaping a financial harvest, though in their case it was as much due to success on the field as general euphoria off it. Burnley were League runners-up in 1920, champions in 1921 and third in 1922 – and during their championship season they made a clear profit of £13,000. No wonder Sutcliffe could afford to sound magnanimous and encourage other clubs, despite 'certain difficulties', to 'act favourably towards the players…it is evident that further concessions must be cheerfully made to them…'

He had by the time he made those statements already announced that for the season 1920–21 wages would double – the maximum rising from £4.50 to £9.00 a week – to be paid all the year round. In addition to this there would also be the possibility of 'talent money' consisting of £2 a win and £1 a draw, as well as various FA Cup bonuses.

The Players' Union could claim credit for the pay rises, as Sutcliffe would comment:

> 'The arguments of the deputation from the union were lucidly placed before the League committee with a reasonableness yet earnestness and sincerity we all admired.'

Players' representatives, however, were still in the position of being supplicants rather than equal negotiators. At the grass roots there were increasing grumbles. In the early 1920s a 'sliding pay scale' was introduced by many clubs. New players might be started on £5 a week and earn annual rises of £1 a week over four years. Thus, a new maximum wage of £468 a year had been created. What was more, the sliding scale gave club managements flexibility in dealing with players, and many used it as a device to intensify competition between men in the same club.

The union soon brought to the attention of the League its members 'extreme discontent' with the way the system was working. In 1921 they demanded its abolition and called for the institution of a maximum wage of £10 per week with freedom of contract up to that amount. They also drew the League Management Committee's attention to the fact that 'there is a more serious state of unrest than is generally realised' among the players, particularly concerning the way the League committee had been cutting the shares of transfers awarded to certain players by their clubs.

The League nevertheless turned its back on all but the most minor of adjustments. The sliding pay scale would remain: making maximum pay awards compulsory, it was said, would be 'unjust' to the clubs. To the suggestion that the cost of living was rising the League retorted that it was rising for clubs, too. What was more, the public was now demanding all sorts of improvements in facilities which would cost money to provide.

The players were being told to get to the back of the queue. As it was put at the League's ANNUAL GENERAL MEETING in July 1921, beneath the chandeliers of the commodious Connaught Rooms: 'We have gone quite far enough where wages are concerned!'

Unfortunately, the principal of 'dog eat dog' engendered by the new pay system hardly made for good fellow feelings among teammates. This was especially true where the vexed question of benefits were concerned.

Soon after World War One one of the top benefits received was that by George Utley who walked away from Sheffield United with £1,100. Utley had been a prominent player for Sheffield United since 1913 when the club had bought him for a record £2,000 from Barnsley. His bargaining skills secured him a five-year contract, the team captaincy, the tenancy of a sports-goods shop in Bramall Lane that supplied the club itself, plus the promise of that lucrative benefit.

In 1913 Utley had been offered £800 or a match; he had chosen the match. Although the League subsequently decided that benefits should be limited to a maximum of £650, Utley's agreement predated this, but his teammates were unhappy and in 1922 certain senior men wrote a letter to the club's directors concluding:

> …why should Utley have preferential treatment seeing that in regard to service he is less entitled to a benefit than some of the undersigned?
> We remain Sire, your obedient servants,
> (signed) W. Gillespie, W. Cook, J.E. Kitchen, H.H. Pantling, W.H. Breisford, I. Simmons, H. Gough, A. Sturgess, S. Fazakerly.

Some of the eight appeared before the board and were mollified by offers of benefits to those players who had requested them. Each of the benefits was £500. The varying fortunes of some of Utley's teammates following this controversy might have impressed upon some the necessity for change that only a union might bring.

Fazakerly, having been refused a benefit, eventually forced the club to sell him after dodging training and intentionally playing badly, angering fellow players and supporters alike. When the veteran international, Gough, took a pub to provide for his imminent retirement, the Sheffield United directors summoned him to a meeting and informed him that he had broken his contract (Sheffield players were expressly forbidden to become publicans while under contract). Gough replied that he was prepared to take the consequences and the directors resolved that 'the player was to be informed he would be held liable to make good any damage or loss which the club might sustain in consequence of his breach of the agreement'. He was eventually forced to pay back wages he had received under the 'broken' agreement and was

Player	Playing Season Wage £	Close Season Wage £	Bonus for for 1st XI Appearances £	Bonus for for 2nd XI Appearances £
Barclay	8	6	–	–
Barker	5	3	3	–
Boyd	8	6	–	–
Hall	5	3	3	–
Hobson	3	2	1	–
Holmes	8	6	–	–
Jackson	5	3	3	–
Killourhy	6	4/10/-	2	–
Pickering	8	6	–	–
Williams	6	6	2	–
Anderson	5	3	3	–
Coward	2/10/-	–	2	1
Earnshaw	2/10/-	–	2	1
Goodison	2/10/-	–	2	1
Gooney	6	6	2	–
Hooper	5	5	3	–
Johnson	5	3	3	–
Smith	5	5	3	–
Stacey	6	6	2	–
Wildsmith	1	–	2	1
Wilkinson	5	5	3	–

Players' Weekly Wages 1934-5, Sheffield United FC

Players' weekly wages 1934–35, Sheffield United FC. With acknowledgements to Nick Fishwick.

reported to the FA who suspended him. The club thereafter refused to release him unless another club paid a prohibitively large transfer fee of £2,000 – for a man of Gough's age and lengthy career, such a fee meant that his football career was finished. The Players' Union decided that it could not help him.

The Utley case illustrates how individual players had to rely on their own wits to negotiate with clubs, with the union being a largely peripheral player. There would be no more trouble where benefits were concerned, however. The ceiling established at £650 in 1924, would, just like the £1 talent money, remain almost the same for the next thirty years!

As the inter-war years progressed the downward pressure on players' wages would intensify. With each succeeding slump in general trade there were calls from various clubs to reduce wages across the board. Although no such reductions were made, the freedom clubs possessed to squeeze down the wage bills was exercised with ever more ingenuity.

During the 1930s Grimsby and Sheffield Wednesday pioneered an 'incentive' scheme in which the best players were guaranteed a weekly wage of £6 with £2 extra if they kept their first team place. Thus, you could only earn the maximum if you were playing in the first team. Being dropped meant a significant loss of wages.

The version of the 'sliding scale' was the principal method employed. Briefly, it might work as follows: a player in the first team received the maximum £8 a week; if the second team, £6 a week; if unable to secure a place even in the 'stiffs', his pay might drop to £4 a week. Once out of the first and second teams, the extra bonuses for wins and draws went as well.

In an industry where form was often a matter of tactics, individual judgement or perhaps of just plain fate, such a system of payment engendered insecurity, anxiety and often deep discontent among playing colleagues. Indeed, suspicion, resentment and a sense of injustice were almost natural products of the system – one that players had no say in either formulating or applying.

Although the average football fan considered all players well-paid there were, in fact, wide variations, not only between clubs and divisions, but within clubs a definite hierarchy existed. At the bottom were the majority of lower-paid players; above them, players earning more or less the maximum; and above them an elite of 'stars' who could expect to supplement the maximum wage by other earnings directly or indirectly derived from their status.

By 1939, according to the Players' Union, fewer than 10 per cent of players were in the top bracket, a figure not dissimilar to that achieved in 1910, although the actual number may have been higher as more men received it than were guaranteed it by contract. Second and Third Division players never saw the

The car ban comes on at the start of the season for Huddersfield Town players. It will hit Billy Hayes, Irish international back, particularly hard. Billy has a business dealing with used cars. *The Weekly News,* Saturday 29 July 1939.

maximum, and there were many examples of even the best men earning no more than £7 in season and £4 in summer.

In 1937 there had been a small increase in bonuses offered by the League for wins, etc. but this only threw into starker relief the fact that there had been wage stagnation since the early 1920s. With 'gates' now recovering after the Depression and clubs earning regular profits, the union declared it was 'time for a deputation to be met by the League in 'order that "better terms and more equity be obtained" for players'.

The request, sent following the August AGM, took the usual season to come to fruition. In March 1938 the League finally consented to a meeting – the first for a decade! Sutcliffe declared that the League Management Committee was 'prepared to listen to all they (the Union) had to say and that Fay and his committee should 'not be afraid of voicing their opinions on the requests and grievances which had been put forward'.

After two hours, during which the union pressed for a maximum wage increase of £1, insisted on a fixed retaining fee of £260 per annum (or else a free transfer) and emphasised the unreasonableness of the amount players received as a percentage of any transfer fee, Sutcliffe closed the meeting with yet more platitudes concerning frankness, candour, calm and courtesy.

Of course, nothing was subsequently granted and nothing conceded. Thus, at the 1938 AGM held in August, delegates were angry and bitter. There were now demands for another meeting, with 'drastic action' being threatened unless something concrete emerged. Early in 1939 Fay organised two special 'extra-ordinary delegate meetings' – one in London and one in Manchester – in order to gain maximum backing for action should the League once again turn a deaf ear. These meetings, both in their size and in the determination expressed by the delegates to stand for no more prevarication from the League, demonstrated the serious nature of the rift between employers and employees.

At the London delegates meeting attended by 59 club delegates representing over 300 members, the 'outdated, one-sided' regulations were attacked and demands voiced for representation on the governing bodies of football; for 'modern' employer/employee relationships; and for the truth to be told about exactly how much pro-players received by way of pay.

At the Manchester meeting the press were called in to hear the comprehensive demands of both meetings:

- an immediate pay rise;
- a minimum wage of £4 a week;
- two weeks pre-season training to be paid at playing season rates;
- contracts to run from the beginning of August to the end of July to prevent clubs saving money by keeping men out-of-contract during the summer;
- larger shares of transfer fees;
- 100 per cent increase in bonus payments;
- compensation/injury payments to be fixed and compulsory;
- representation on the Jubilee Fund.

Compulsory Service For Footballers

Players Who Don't Know What Work IS

By THE MAJOR

EXERCISING the minds of the Football League Management Committee is a proposed scheme of compulsory service for professional footballers. Or something very much like that. If the scheme becomes a fact it will run in conjunction with the League's Jubilee Fund.

Briefly, the scheme is that young fellows signing for Football League clubs shall undertake to undergo vocational training. There may even be a clause inserted in the contracts which the players sign making this vocational training compulsory.

THEY'VE NEVER WORKED

There is a lot to be said for this idea. Its sponsors have their fingers on the football pulse.

One thing they have recognised is the remarkable fact that a host of young men coming into the game have never had a job of any kind.

Problem facing football: What is going to happen to these players when they finish with football?

Even more urgent is the problem of what will happen to them should their football careers end abruptly through accident.

What could they do? In nearly every case the answer would be—nothing. Except apply for relief from the Jubilee Fund.

And the chances would be that money from that source would just be frittered away. The paying for this vocational training, in fact, might be a sounder way of spending Jubilee Fund money than doling it out to players unable and unfitted to find a place in the labour market.

VOCATIONAL TRAINING

It is to enable players to find a place in this market that the scheme of vocational training is now under close consideration.

Players trained to a job would stand a much better chance of finding a position. As things are, many players have no idea what work actually means.

Something on similar lines has already been adopted by clubs, Blackpool, for one.

The aim of the Football League scheme is to establish the training on a comprehensive basis and in a thorough manner.

The Weekly News, Saturday 14 January 1939.

The Weekly News, Saturday 16 September 1939. On guard – but not in Stoke City's goal. Norman Wilkinson keeps as sharp lookout now as he did when between the sticks for the Potters.

Delegates gave the management committee their full backing, pledging to 'stand by the union whatever action it may be deemed necessary to take in the future'. Acting League president Will Cuff (Sutcliffe having died in January 1939) thus came face to face with probably the most determined union Management Committee of the inter-war years – certainly the most confident and, in terms of cash and membership backing, the strongest. Moreover, some kind of confrontation seemed inevitable from the moment Cuff demanded to know the exact membership figures of the union before discussions had even started – only to be told by Fay that membership stood at approximately 1,850, 'and eighty or so non-League members, many of these having been forced out of League football to try to earn a living owing to excessive transfer fees placed upon them...'

Cuff was no conciliator. One senses that a fight with the union would have suited him perfectly in order to demonstrate his fitness for the job of president. Thus it came as no surprise when all the union's demands were turned down at the Football League AGM a few months later. The union's response was to prepare for 'drastic action' at the commencement of the 1939–40 season. However, within days of the resolution, football was suspended as war was declared: the antagonists were thus to remain frozen in mutually threatening poses until 1945.

PART THREE
EMERGING FROM THE SHADOWS 1939–63

1. First Victories! 1939-56

With the commencement of the war in 1939 the League programme was immediately halted. Just as during World War One professional footballers ceased to exist as legal entities: their contracts were cancelled and they were no longer covered for injury under the Workman's Compensation Act. The clubs themselves continued to operate though, and retained their hold on players whose contracts they were no longer obliged to honour. Many ex-professionals were given special tasks related to fitness training within the armed forces, while the men at the very top of the profession enjoyed various privileges, such as the freedom to leave their units in order to play in internationals and representative matches. By 1943 enemy bombing raids were much reduced and crowds began to flock back to watch a reorganised Football League. The professional game started to generate vast sums of money for a variety of wartime charities, while many clubs also began to make healthy profits once again. Those players not in the forces, working in factories, munitions or reserved occupations, continued to turn out each weekend but it was a part-time career and, as a letter to Jimmy Fay from Jimmy Guthrie, Portsmouth captain and future chairman of the union, written in early 1943, demonstrates, there was a certain amount of resentment building up:

> The football player has been hard hit and I am sure no one will deny that 30/- is a very meagre sum. Many players are having a very hard time making ends meet. Why not make a limit of £3 and a minimum of 30/- and allow clubs to pay for time lost? Take my own case, for instance. We play every Saturday for 30/- but by doing so we deprive ourselves of earning more money over the weekend, but what can we do? Football is our life and we must play to keep in the game…play or else get out of the game…All we ask for is a square deal. I don't think we are getting one.

The consolation for men such as Guthrie was that with the end of the war in sight the future for working people looked brighter than ever before. The expectation was that society would be more rationally organised and planned: a National Health Service, slum clearance and municipal housing, new towns and an educational overhaul. In short, a planned society that would sweep away all the old worn out relics of the past and replace them with new, vibrant, dynamic structures.

Sammy Crooks Chairman 1937–46

Originally a miner, despite his frail appearance Sammy was a fast and tricky winger with a direct style, specialising in centres of pinpoint accuracy. He played for Derby County for the whole of his professional career. Too slight to play inside-forward, he was occasionally switched inside during a game when a vital score was needed. He certainly had an eye for a goal: in all he netted 111 in 445 League and FA Cup games! He was also one of England's fastest and most effective wingers. Selected 26 times before the war, he was good enough to keep Stanley Matthews out of the international side. After spells in management, Sammy concentrated on running a sports outfitters in Derby in partnership with former Derby wicketkeeper Harry Elliot. He became Derby County's chief scout and in 1950 was Shrewsbury Town's secretary-manager.

As Jimmy Fay wrote to Ernie Thompson (ex-management committee-man but now a company sergeant major in the Glider Pilot Regiment):

> I can visualise a great opportunity for the player to demand a thorough overhauling of the out-of-date rules, particularly those affecting agreements, wages, benefits, transfer fees, retaining fees, compensation, insurance, etc. There is something to work upon, such as the Beveridge Report and the Atlantic Charter.

But, he added ominously: 'These appear to cover everybody except the professional footballer…'

****

In 1944 the post-war planning committee of the Football League reported its recommendations. There would be, prior to League football's recommencement proper, a 'transition period' during which all players would remain part-time (thus remain in their jobs wherever possible) and be paid a maximum of £4 a week, with no bonuses.

The Players' Union was quick to react: 'It is an insult to offer such terms and will meet with great opposition from the players,' it declared at its first post-war AGM. There had already been complaints concerning the niggardly amounts of money the League's Insurance Federation had been paying out to men injured during wartime games. While there were no reliable gate-figures available it seemed that crowds at football matches had never been higher.

A demand was made immediately for the £2 match fee to be doubled as 'it was generally agreed that the majority of clubs last season made fairly large profits and are sounder financially than they have ever been in the past'. This was ignored by the League and by mid-1945, with the war rapidly approaching its end, the union was pressing for immediate action.

With the 'transitional' season of 1945–46 about to start, the union demanded an immediate £8 match fee maximum. It would, it declared, 'be an opportunity for clubs to show their appreciation of and recognition to the experienced players for their splendid services during the war. The majority of clubs can well afford an increase and would willingly approve.'

Union delegates met in Manchester for their 35th AGM and Jimmy Fay announced:

> 'We have suggested schemes to the League to provide for players in the future at the end of their playing days. Schemes by two of the League clubs to end all financial troubles were circulated to the whole of the League members and wonderful schemes they were. They appeared to be received with jubilation by many of the clubs, but not a word was raised about them at the AGM of the League. No doubt you will be wondering why this unprogressive spirit, why no effort to bring the game up to date with the changed times…The answer is that there is sufficient money in the game to provide security for all. It is big business and should be in the hands of big businessmen…'

Fay's indignation at the League was surpassed by the anger of many of the delegates. Calling the meeting to order with a great deal of difficulty, chairman Sammy Crooks summed up. There were two possible courses to take. The first was simply to refuse to restart the football competitions. As no one was reliant for a living on football at that point, players being either part-timers or still in the forces, this course of action would be relatively painless to members. It would, however, threaten the football pools. As Guthrie had written to Fay some weeks earlier: 'Think, no Pools! What will the man in the street think?'

The second course would be to demand an immediate meeting with League officials while commencing the season 'under protest'. The second course of action was chosen. Having notified the League that another meeting was essential, the management committee proceeded to draw up new demands.

At 2pm on 29 August 1945 at the Midland Hotel, Manchester, Players' Union officials Sammy Crooks, Joe Mercer, Allan Brown, Jimmy Guthrie and Norman Low met a sub-committee of the League Management Committee led by Will Cuff. The case was straightforward: a £12 a week maximum wage and a £5 minimum, plus a list of demands relating to agreements and accident insurance. The meeting concluded with the usual caveat that everything would have to be decided by the clubs

Johnny Shepherd figures out £4 wage cut

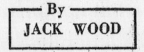

By JACK WOOD

MILLWALL'S Johnny Shepherd talked last night of the fear which haunts hundreds of footballers in England, the fear of going on the breadline.

No squealer, this Cockney boy with the shoulders of a heavyweight, just a sensible youngster with the welfare of his family at heart.

Shepherd, twice the club's leading scorer in five years, demanded a transfer over the week-end, because he could not live on the £12 a week paid by Millwall to their players when out of the first team.

Withdrawn

After a talk with manager Ron Gray yesterday he agreed to withdraw the request . . . for the time being. But take it as certain that Shepherd will never be content to draw only £12 a week as his footballer's pay.

In two modestly furnished, self-decorated rooms in Notting Hill Gate, Shepherd and his attractive Spanish-born wife gave me details of the weekly budget which regularly takes most of his first team pay of £16, less tax and National Insurance.

"This place costs us 25s. a week," said Johnny. "But we don't want to live always in two rooms. We try to put something away each week for the house we hope to buy one day.

£1 on clothes

"Our insurances are nearly £1. Repayments on furniture, television, and other things amount to £4. My fares to the ground are £1 weekly, and coal, light and gas take another 15s."

"I can't go to the ground in any old clothes. So I have to reckon on having three reasonable suits. With things for the wife and our baby Julie, who is six months, you can say another £1 a week on clothes."

Johnny, Esther, and I did some quick arithmetic. So far, the outgoings came to £9 a week, which would leave the Shepherd family £3 for food, holidays, and savings.

"I'm a big fellow, and I eat a lot to keep fit," said Johnny. "In the summer my wages dip to £11 a week. So we have, in the past, aimed to save through the season, so that things won't be so tough in the summer."

On £16 a week, Shepherd and his young family just manage. There is not much left for life's luxuries.

On £12, to which his wages dip as a reserve-team player, the Shepherd family would find it impossible to carry on.

"I have to keep up appearances, look smart at the ground and when we go away," said Johnny.

"I could probably walk out in the morning and get a job as a labourer for more than I would get in the reserves. But I love football."

Benefit hold-up

I mentioned benefits—the nest egg, payable every five years, to which men like Shepherd look forward.

This is a sore point with Shepherd, and a string of Millwall players.

Shepherd was due a full one in October. So far, the subject hasn't been mentioned at the Den.

"I don't really hold much hope for a while," said Johnny. "Stan Anslow has been waiting two years for his, Ray Brand 18 months, Roy Summersby a year. I'm way down the list, it seems."

When next you accuse men like Shepherd of moaning, think of the budget I've presented. And ask yourself how you and the wife and family would cope if the pay packet suddenly dipped by £4 a week.

Johnny and Esther put baby Julie to bed.

Daily Herald, 1959.

themselves 'at the earliest opportunity'. In fact, it would be another two months before the Football League clubs finally met to reject everything the union had put forward and to pass a motion that players' wages should return to pre-war levels!

The union lost no time in balloting the membership on strike action. On 5 November the result was announced: 62 clubs had voted for a strike, only two were against, with the rest having failed to reply. The stoppage was set for the 19 November, a fortnight hence. It was now up to the Football League.

The press was generally well-disposed towards the union. Clifford Webb in the *Daily Herald* wrote:

> The players are not asking for the moon. They are not suggesting for a moment that every player should be paid £12 a week or, while still in the forces or an essential work, £8 a match. These figures are suggested maximums. The players are equally concerned with fixing a minimum figure which they suggest should be £5 a week. Could anybody regard that as an outrageous proposal?

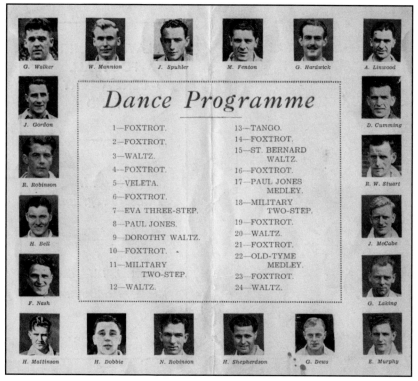

Players' Union Football Benevolent Fund souvenir dance programme, held at the Town Hall, Middlesbrough, Monday 31 March 1947.

Here are Stalwarts of Union's Battle

WHEN the Football Players' Union Management Committee met, in Manchester last month, R. W. Stuart (formerly with Middlesbrough and recently transferred to Plymouth Argyle) wanted to resign. He felt his journeys to meetings would be too long.

J. Guthrie (re-elected chairman for the next two years) praised Stuart's work during the long-drawn-out wage

negotiations. It was decided not to accept Stuart's resignation and to ask him to reconsider his decision.

Pictured above are the stalwarts who have led the Union's fight and achieved so much during the past couple of years (left to right): Stuart, N. Low (Norwich City), F. Broome (Derby County), J. Guthrie (chairman) and J. Fay (Secretary).

TRIBUNAL AWARDS FLOUTED

F.A. LAWS USED TO SLICE WAGES

ALTHOUGH it was clearly laid down more than a year ago by a National Tribunal that professional players should receive minimum wages of £7 (winter) and £5 (summer) and maximum £12 (winter) and £10 (summer). several clubs are paying far less than the legal rates. In some cases, players are paid on a matchly basis (no-play-no-pay). This has been defended by the Football League on the grounds that it is in accordance with Football Association rules.

A list of Union members receiving only so much per match was forwarded to the Football League with the warning that if these men were still dissatisfied by January 1 their cases would be placed in the hands of the Union's solicitors with instructions to take further action.

In a letter to the Union, the Football League state: ". . . so long as the Football Association permit players to be engaged on a matchly basis there is nothing the League can do to stop League clubs engaging players that way.

"A League club is just as much entitled to engage players on a matchly basis as any other club. What we can do is to see that the matchly terms are reasonable.

"We have had no complaint with any of the players on your list that the terms are not reasonable."

OUT-OF-DATE

F.A. Rule 34 states: ". . . Agreements may provide that a player shall only be paid when played in matches, but if any such player is not played for a period of four weeks he may apply to the club to cancel his agreement and registra-

tion, and, if refused, he shall be at liberty to apply to this Association for the cancellation of the agreement upon such terms as may be deemed reasonable."

This rule, of course, has been made out-of-date by the National Tribunal Award, yet some League clubs. apparently backed by the Football League, use it to elude the conditions of the Tribunal award.

This "passing the buck" between League and Football Association

over the question of wages cannot be allowed to continue, and was one of the chief topics for discussion at the last meeting in Manchester of the Players' Union Management Committee, where it was urged that the authorities should give immediate attention to the rules, some of which should be abolished and others amended.

F.A. Rule 31, for example, despite the Tribunal ruling, still declares ". . . Clubs shall be entitled to retain players who they are prepared to pay at the rate of £208 a year."

The Union suggests that full-time players should get a minimum £340

(Continued on page 15.)

"SOCCER's" Friends

"SOCCER" has quickly found friends among the big newspapers. We thank the following for giving permission to use copyright photographs or allowing "star" writers and artists to contribute articles and drawings:

"The Star" (London): Specially-drawn cartoon by Roy Ullyett.

Northcliffe Newspapers Group Ltd.: Photographs of Roy Bentley, *George Swindin and George Farrow.*

"Daily Mail": Photograph of Union Management Committee.

"Sporting Record": Club Curiosities Series.

"Derby Evening Telegraph": Photograph of Peter Doherty.

Soccer Magazine, January 1948.

At 10am on 12 November, once again at the Midland Hotel, the union management committee was presented with the League's proposals: proper full-time contracts were agreed along with injury compensation and regular union/Football League meetings. Where the wages demand was concerned this was dismissed as 'impossible'. Instead, players were offered a maximum of £9 a week –just £1 more than in 1939. There would also be a £5 match fee for men still in the services or engaged on essential work and bonuses would be introduced at the rate of £2 a win and £1 a draw. It was a take it or leave it offer. After one more attempt at compromise, the union delegates decided to accept the League offer.

Thus was sown the seed of great bitterness among the majority of players as they prepared to resume their full-time status – those, that is, who could obtain contracts. Many clubs immediately began to search for ways of exploiting the inevitable post-war confusion. With no minimum wage established some men were offered employment on a match-by-match basis; others were signed on as reserves to play in Combination leagues where the new rates of pay did not apply, thus enabling the clubs to secure men for just £3 and £4 a week. The ruses employed to cut and whittle down what professional footballers were to be paid were legion; the motive, it would appear, was simple greed.

The majority of players had no choice but to accept what was offered. There were the occasional 'rebels' however. Ephraim 'Jock' Dodds was a free-scoring forward with Blackpool who had made his name before the war with Sheffield United. Dodds was a good-looking, debonair character who had always been happy to flaunt his relative wealth. Dressed by Sheffield's top tailor, Barney Goodman, he was regularly seen driving an open-top Cadillac and wearing a fedora and silk scarf. His reputation was such that when singer Gracie Fields performed in the city she specifically requested a meeting. Dodds also had a taste for gambling and while at Bramall Lane raced his own greyhounds at the local Hyde Park track.

When in 1946 Blackpool offered him a new deal worth £7 a week, £2 less than the maximum wage, Dodds was understandably affronted. Manager Joe Smith blamed his board for the frugality of the offer but Dodds decided to step outside the Football League and negotiate a deal with Dublin's Shamrock Rovers. He received a £1,500 signing-on fee and £20 a week while Blackpool received no transfer fee because Dodds had moved beyond the League's jurisdiction. Dodds later commented:

> 'I was banned sine die, until further notice, for contravening their regulations. They'd brand you a troublemaker, but they were the troublemakers. They gave you a one-year contract, you'd carry out that duty, but then you couldn't leave when the year was out because they owned you.'

Unfortunately, like so many top players before him, he was not prepared to use the Players' Union and challenge the situation in court. He was clever and attractive enough as a player to make good and thus he was able to act independently. He would

Editor: JOHN BATSON.
Editorial Offices:
41, Kensington Place, London, W.8.

George Swindin's Column

FOOTBALL'S BROKEN MEN ASK FOR AID

FOOTBALL has more than its fair share of hardship cases. Some were considered at the recent meeting of the Football Players' Union Management Committee in Manchester. Members of our Union as well as the general public should know some of the pitiful details, although I have no intention, of course, of revealing anything which would identify a fellow footballer " down on his luck."

Editorial

THE Football Association have made a grave error of judgment and shown lack of knowledge of psychology in publishing a " Black List " of 87 professional footballers against whom cautions were recorded during the period August 23-December 13.

No good can come of it. On the other hand, a great deal of harm can be done.

There *are* certain players whose general behaviour is not above reproach. They are so few, however, they could be numbered almost on the fingers of one hand.

Yet the F.A. in one swoop attaches the stigma of unsporting conduct to 87 men, most of whom got into trouble, because their love for football made them over-keen.

There is no appeal against a F.A. judgment, although players and clubs are often convinced men are sometimes reported unjustly. This is no attack on the present standard of refereeing. Still, who has not seen free-kicks awarded for fouls to the wrong team?

Public "Black-listing " excellently illustrates " giving a dog a bad name, etc." Does the F.A. *really* believe it will make the real Bad Lad better? Of course, it won't. He will probably become defiant. Not sorry.

As for the player who believes he was innocent or committed a minor offence when worse offenders got off scot free, who can blame him if he becomes resentful?

Even if clubs and players do disapprove of the " Black List," they may be influenced when they come up against a man who figures on it. Referees, consciously or subconsciously, may also react against a player, not to mention spectators.

There are the makings of broken careers in every " Black List."

The F.A. would have displayed better judgement if they had "Black Listed " clubs not giving professionals a square deal with regard to pay and conditions.

One case concerned a loan a player wanted from the Union to aid him over a difficult period. Injury has not only finished his playing career, but also caused an internal complaint for which he must have an operation before even being able to take up light work.

His income amounts to £3 2s. 6d. a week. Out of that he pays £1 14s. weekly for rent, rates, coal, light, etc. (he is searching for a cheaper house in order to curtail his living costs). Obviously, out of what remains he cannot afford the extra nutrition necessary to maintain his health even in its present poor state.

BOMBED OUT

Another case the Union have asked me to investigate concerns a player asking for a small loan with which to start a little business.

There are eight in the family, which lives in a Nissen hut.

The man was not injured while playing football. He and his family were bombed out during the war, he himself suffering injuries which left him completely broken in health.

In this case, previous grants have been made by the Football Association, Football League, and the player's old club as well as the Union. The player's wife thinks that the little business they would like to buy would provide an income sufficient to keep the family going, and would give her husband the stimulus necessary to restore him to something like reasonable health.

My job is to visit the family, and the person from whom it is proposed to buy the business. The Union Management Committee will then consider my report, and consider what action is necessary.

JUBILEE FUND'S JOB

Union funds are extremely limited. This broken player did, after all, play in those matches whose " gate " money went to swell the Jubilee Fund. I

GEORGE SWINDIN, Arsenal goalkeeper and a new member of the Football Players' Union Management Committee, has been one of the big reasons for the League leaders' great run of success.

feel that all hardship cases should be helped by that Fund.

As a Union, we feel very keenly when we hear of old colleagues broken in health and penniless. Invariably, we do our best to help.

But the Union funds, strictly speaking, are not for charity. The Union has a job to do. The fight for better wages and conditions and raising players' status is costly.

I suggest that the Jubilee Fund should deal with all cases of hardship. A visiting committee (including, if necessary, members of the Union Management Committee) should be appointed to look into cases on the spot, and to recommend grants.

There is a huge sum of money available. Who has better claim than men whose playing efforts helped to raise it and who are now in dire need?

Soccer Magazine, January 1948.

Joe Mercer

Management Committee member, 1940s

Joe signed for Everton in 1931 and made his debut at wing-half in April 1933. An outstanding player with a biting tackle, deceptive speed and a never-say-die attitude, he won five international caps for England. After the war he returned to Everton until he was transferred to Arsenal for a fee of £8,000 in 1946. Appointed captain, he led the Gunners to the 1947–48 League Championship and the 1950 FA Cup victory over Liverpool. That year he was voted by the Football Writers' Association as Footballer of the Year. Joe served on the Players' Union management committee during the turbulent time when the union was first establishing itself as a force in football. Joe won his third championship medal with Arsenal in 1952–53 before retiring to run a grocery shop in the Wirral. In August 1955 he became manager of Sheffield United. Soon after he moved to Aston Villa and in 1960 helped them win the Second Division title before joining Manchester City in 1966. Over the next few years he had great success winning the Second Division (1967), First Division (1968), the FA Cup (1969), League Cup (1970) and European Cup-Winners' Cup (1971). In 1974 Mercer was the temporary manager of the England national side. Joe died in August 1990.

trouble football's authorities some years later when acting as a go-between for various top English internationals who also broke free of their contracts to take up lucrative offers in Colombia. That, too, was a piratical affair and doomed to failure. Jimmy Guthrie understood that real change could only be achieved through collective action.

****

Guthrie was convinced that the clubs had been let off lightly in 1946 and that the next time the union should stand firm. He immediately began making plans for the next wage round in April 1946, meeting with journalists and MPs.

Once again the union's demands for a £12 maximum and £5 minimum were rejected. Instead the League offered a non-negotiable £10 maximum (dropping to £7 10s in the summer). The union Management Committee accepted it, but at the subsequent ANNUAL GENERAL MEETING in November great dissatisfaction was expressed by rank and file members at the fact that the committee had not called for strike action.

Soundings suggested that there was not a club in the League whose players would not support direct action and when the League Management Committee refused a further meeting, the press were informed that a complete stoppage of football was now the union's only alternative.

Just how aware the union Management Committee was of the wider political implications of such a decision is unclear. Nevertheless, they seemed genuinely taken aback when, a few days later, they were contacted by the officials at the industrial relations office of the Ministry of Labour who had apparently read about the proposed action in the newspapers. Under the War Emergency Act – then still in force – a strike was technically illegal. The new Labour Government, desperate to keep production up at a critical period of reconstruction, was doing all it could, with TUC cooperation, to prevent industrial stoppages. Whether they liked it or not, both the Players' Union and the Football League were now to become deeply entangled in the intricate web of industrial relations. Their claustrophobic little world was about to be invaded by strangers. What was more, the conflict and possible strike action caught the imagination of an entertainment-starved nation. For instance, a *Pathe News* special appeared in cinemas up and down the land featuring a short interview with chairman Sammy Crooks, the first-ever such appearance of a football 'politician'.

Urged by the Ministry to get back together again, a meeting took place on 19 September 1946 at the Midland Hotel in Manchester. The League Management Committee and Will Cuff in particular were indignant that the Ministry of Labour had been involved at all. They simply refused to negotiate at all. After Guthrie suggested voluntary arbitration, which was again refused, the union committee announced they would be seeking compulsory arbitration and the meeting ended abruptly.

A month later, on 17 October, at the Ministry of Labour offices in London, Jimmy Guthrie, Frank Broome, Bob Stuart and Jimmy Fay sat down opposite the Football League management committee with the Labour Ministry's relations officer, a Mr Stillman, in attendance. Times were certainly starting to change within the football 'industry'.

After three hours of acrimonious argument Stillman called a halt and asked to talk in private with the union men. He complained that the discussions could go on for hours; new questions were being raised all the time and it had become far too complicated for him. In fact, he would be able to make no recommendations at all to the Minister.

Guthrie was angry and impatient; time was being wasted and the League was clearly not negotiating in any recognised fashion. However, Stillman managed to persuade both sides to form yet another joint sub-committee to meet as soon as possible to thrash out a basis for a possible settlement.

Two weeks later, at the Football League's offices in Preston, the two sides faced one another again. Cuff set the tone of the meeting by announcing that, in his opinion, the whole process was unnecessary especially as the Wartime Emergency Powers Act only applied to industry, not football, and that any arbitration award would be challenged by the League in the courts.

That small pleasantry over with, the two sides proceeded to work out a possible agreement covering all aspects of pay, injury compensation, benefits, minimum wages and shares of transfer fees. Cuff emphasised that the agreement had to be acceptable

Soccer Magazine, March 1948.

both to the League Management Committee and the clubs and that a decision would have to wait until at least the end of February. Three months later, on 24 February, the League clubs met in closed session and, without offering any explanation, threw the whole agreement out. It seemed they simply could not deal with the new world forming around them.

On 25 February Jimmy Fay wrote to the Ministry of Labour to request that the issue go to compulsory arbitration and on 10 March, at an extraordinary meeting of union delegates in Manchester, the union committee was roundly criticised for allowing the League to constantly play for time, so much so that almost a whole year had now passed since the dispute had begun.

Strike action was once again set for 21 March but mercifully for all concerned the Ministry of Labour at last decided to refer the whole dispute to the National Arbitration Tribunal under the chairmanship of Lord Terrington, a solicitor, civil servant and experienced industrial negotiator. It took the tribunal just two weeks to come to its historic decision, with the union being granted almost everything it had asked for!

The claim for a £12 maximum during the playing season (£10 in summer) was granted; a minimum wage of £7 during the playing season and £5 during the summer was secured for all full-time players over the age of 20, with agreements to run from August to August. On the question of the transfer system the tribunal made no recommendations but felt that there was a need for an authoritative joint negotiating committee for football along the lines of the Whitley Councils operating in other industries: this, it was felt, could deal with transfers and benefits, as well as 'stabilise amicable relations between clubs and players'.

It was a significant landmark in the history of professional football in England. It was also the beginning of the rise of players' union's into a position of prominence in the English game.

The joint negotiating committee consisting of representatives of the Players' Union, the Football League and the Football Association would eventually be established with a definite set of rules of engagement but it was clear from the outset that the Football League regarded it as a necessary nuisance, certainly not a true negotiating body. As Guthrie ruefully remarked when assuming its chairmanship in July 1951: 'The past two years have been spent in exploration and while we have not made the progress expected it has been the means of getting to know each other better.'

Ideas would be exchanged, some argument would take place, but the real decisions would be taken, as ever, at the League's AGM and then presented on a take it or leave it basis. Thus, at regular intervals in the early 1950s the union would find it necessary to turn again to the Ministry of Labour to register a dispute and embark on a long and expensive legal process. Recommendations would be produced, published and then it would be back to the joint committee once more for yet more acrimonious and frustrating 'discussions'.

This process would eventually lead to a major setback for the union and its chairman Jimmy Guthrie. In April 1951 the union presented the joint committee with a proposed new agreement based on a players' charter drawn up by Guthrie. This ambitious document suggested far-reaching reforms such as the abolition of the maximum wage, the dismantling of the transfer system, legal and union representation at FA and League disciplinary hearings, increases in international fees, compulsory bonuses, etc.

At a subsequent special meeting of Football League clubs, not only did they throw out the charter completely, they actually altered the existing contract, reverting to July to July signing-on dates rather than August to August, thus enabling clubs to save money when men refused to sign on or when they were placed on the transfer list! The union decided to approach the Ministry of Labour once again and were rewarded when a far-reaching enquiry, led by John Forster, was established to look into players' conditions and their demands for radical reform.

However, the union's high hopes would be dashed. After lengthy consultations the report endorsed almost every Football League argument, from the need for the maximum wage to the essential nature of the retain-and-transfer system! It merely recommended that certain obvious anomalies be changed, such as the non-payment of men on the retain-and-transfer list; legal representation for men appearing before League/FA commissions or enquiries; match bonuses and talent money to be obligatory rather than at the discretion of the club; and increases to be made in international fees – significant gains but peripheral to the main thrust of the players' charter. It had also been a costly business for the union with lengthy legal submissions incurring hefty lawyers fees at a time when subscriptions were starting to fall away.

Within a few years, however, Guthrie would secure a victory that would have far-reaching financial consequences for the union, greater than could have ever imagined. In February 1956 relations between the Football League and the union reached breaking point when the League announced that it would take no further part in joint committee meetings after an argument over extra payments for players taking part in floodlit and televised matches. On 5 March a circular was sent out announcing a ban on union members participation in such games until the League returned to sensible negotiations.

The main victim of the dispute would be Wolverhampton Wanderers, then one of the most powerful and successful clubs in the League and led by England captain Billy Wright. During the 1950s, prior to the development of proper European competition and following the introduction of floodlights at Molyneux in 1953, Wolves staged a series of famous evening friendlies against some of the great Continental teams of the time, such as Moscow Spartak, Moscow Dynamo, Honved and Real Madrid. The matches gained the club world renown and earned it a great deal of money.

ASSOCIATION FOOTBALL PLAYERS' & TRAINERS' UNION

BULLETIN

Registered Office:
504-6-8 Corn Exchange Buildings,
Manchester 4, Lancs.
Telephone : Blackfriars 7554

Chairman's Address:
12 Westbourne Road,
Croydon, Surrey
Telephone : Addiscombe 3514

Management Committee:
J. GUTHRIE (Chairman)

| C. LLOYD (Secretary) | O. HOLD | G. WARDLE | F. WALTON |
| A. BANNER | G. FOX | J. HILL | J. CAMPBELL |

| No. 1 | VOLUME 2 | September, 1956 |

Union Charter

1. **A Standing Joint Committee for all employed in Association Football.**

2. **A Provident Fund for all employed in Association Football.**

3. **A New Form of Agreement for all employed in Association Football.**

4. **A Coaching, Physical Training and Educational Scheme for the purpose of employing ex-members full time.**

5. **A training Scheme for Referees for the purpose of employing ex-members full time.**

6. **Allocation of Cup Final Tickets.**

7. **Link up or closer contact with Football Supporters' Clubs.**

8. **World Federation of Association Football Players.**

9. **Accident Insurance Scheme for all employed in Association Football.**

10. **Television Match Fees for all employed in Association Football.**

11. **Fees for all Matches other than the normal cup programme for all employed in Association Football.**

1

Jimmy Guthrie's template for the future!

It so happened that a prestigious match had been arranged against Spanish champions Athletic Bilbao for 14 March. The tickets had been printed, the world's number one referee had been hired to take charge and the Bilbao team were booked to fly in on 12 March – a day before the threatened players' strike was to take place.

On 7 March, with the Wolves' players having voted to support the strike, the club announced that the game had been cancelled. It had not been quite as straightforward as later reports suggested, however. Some years later Guthrie revealed that some of the Wolves players had resented the union banning such games without first consulting the players: 'I had to go to Wolverhampton and straighten their thinking. They came round and dropped 35 "we strike" votes into my hat after the meeting.'

In fact, the voting was a lot closer than Guthrie suggests. Manager Stan Cullis, a biased witness it is true, claimed that the vote was just 13-12 in favour of the ban. Tellingly, a few days afterwards the Wolves players wrote to the union indicating that they had no confidence in the management committee and that they would prefer more playing members on it. Billy Wright, when questioned about his union allegiance, declared that he would be happy to serve. In fact, Wolves players, including Wright, would cease paying their 'subs' until Jimmy Guthrie was eventually removed from office.

Nevertheless, as Guthrie claimed, 'This was the union's greatest victory…But if we had lost, the union would have been slapped down…probably for good.' He was quick to point out, however, that without declarations of support from the wider union movement, the result might have been different.

With the abandonment of the Bilbao game, the League wasted no time in climbing down. On 12 March both management committees were in London at separate hotels. League secretary Fred Howarth proposed a deal. He called for an immediate withdrawal of the TV ban plus a statement by the union that it accepted the principles of the retain-and-transfer system plus the maximum wage. In return the League would talk about money.

Union secretary Cliff Lloyd replied that they wanted a proper negotiating machinery set up, as well as serious discussions concerning conditions of service. After a short stand-off the League offered to meet the union representatives in person. The union agreed; negotiations resumed and the ban was called off.

After a further five meetings during the second half of 1956 the results were anything but earth-shattering. Match fees for 'additional matches' were set at a maximum of £3 and £2 minimum; match bonuses in general were increased to £3 for a win; the Players provident fund payout was increased from 7.5 to 8 per cent; while on the question of TV fees negotiations were to continue. They would eventually result in the union being granted a percentage of all TV revenue. It would be the key to the union's eventual transformation as television assumed ever more prominence in the decades to come. It would, however, prove to be the swansong for chairman Jimmy Guthrie.

Jimmy Guthrie Chairman 1946–57

Jimmy Guthrie would always be a controversial figure, even as a young player. Born in 1913 in the country village of Luncarty, near Perth, he was signed by Dundee when aged just 17, the club chairmen handing him an envelope containing £100 for his mother. In 1936, aged 23, he was sold on to Portsmouth after demanding an unrealistic pay rise from Dundee. A season earlier he had led the Dundee players in a successful struggle to obtain summer wages when the club chairman had tried to cut players' wages across the board. A tough, uncompromising half-back, he was a good leader, captaining the Portsmouth side to a surprise FA Cup win over Major Frank Buckley's young Wolves side in 1939, the last Cup Final before the war. Two years later his Portsmouth side reached the Wembley (Southern) Cup Final but were beaten by Brentford. During the match Guthrie missed a penalty and conceded an own-goal, but his concentration may well have been affected by the fact that he had led the Portsmouth players in a last minute dressing room confrontation with the club's directors to demand various outstanding payments.

After the war Jimmy coached at Crystal Palace for a short time before devoting himself full-time to the union. He joined the management committee in 1943, having been pressing for tough action on behalf of the players for some time. Immediately after being elected in 1947 he embarked on a determined and often controversial campaign of confrontation with the then all-powerful Football League. He worked tirelessly, travelling the length and breadth of the country, meeting MPs and lawyers, briefing the press and talking directly to players and directors. Guthrie caught the headlines, principally because he based himself in London and developed close links with the press – the first union chairman to do such a thing.

In 1955 the Players' Union joined the TUC, the first time it had been a part of the wider union movement since 1909. At the TUC's National Conference at Blackpool that year Guthrie made a famous speech in which he spoke of professional players as being little better than slaves: 'I stand here as a representative of the last bonded men in Britain. We have had enough of human bondage – we seek your assistance to unfetter the chains and set us free!' This drew a mixed response from professionals up and down the land, many of whom disagreed with Guthrie's left-wing politics.

Jimmy left the PFA in 1957 following an AGM vote to disbar non-playing members from holding office. He later wrote regularly for the Sunday People. Jimmy died in September 1981.

2. The 'Ball Game Bulganin' 1944-56

There could have been no other candidate for chairman after Sammy Crooks's retirement than Jimmy Guthrie. Ever since he had first made contact with Jimmy Fay back in 1939, asking advice as to how to claim a week's back pay for himself and his Portsmouth colleagues, Guthrie had demonstrated a determination and commitment to the cause of the pro-player unsurpassed by anyone else in the union's chequered history.

His impatience to get to grips with the game's problems (not to mention its rulers) would be both gratifying and problematic for secretary Jimmy Fay: gratifying because Guthrie undoubtedly took on a great deal of physically demanding work – meeting MPs and lawyers, briefing the press, travelling to clubs to talk to players and directors; problematic because he also generated a great deal of controversy which often made matters difficult, and Fay would often be left to pick up the pieces.

They made an unlikely duo: Fay the white-haired, immensely experienced, cautious Lancastrian; Guthrie the restless, sometimes bombastic, radical Scot. From the moment Guthrie assumed the chairmanship the latent possibilities of the position were unleashed. Until then the chairman had been a man of responsibility without a great deal of influence. Fay, with his decades of experience, his knowledge and above all his permanency, had actually run the union. Sammy Crooks had been his willing partner but, like Dave Robbie before him, had been essentially an ambassador.

Guthrie saw the chairman's role as more important and crucial than that. He had been elected by the membership and was thus 'head' of the union. This is not to say that he attempted to downgrade Fay – that would have been impossible, not to say inadvisable. However, from the very start Guthrie went his own way, a tendency made much easier because he based himself in London and made no secret of the fact that he thought that was where the union's permanent offices ought to be.

Guthrie also placed a great deal of store by 'influential people': he cultivated friendships with MPs such as J.P. Mallalieu and Ellis Smith and lawyers like Terence Donovan and Walter Moncton, who would prove to be good friends to the union.

On one level such lobbying was practical: as Guthrie put it, 'For the price of a round of drinks I got the best legal advice and my friendships meant that when work was required for the Courts we were represented at the lowest possible fees.'

Such increased contact with lawyers, MPs and trades union officials had a more serious purpose. Professional footballers had to break out of the closed football world in which they were at the mercy of their employers, the Football League and their rulers, the Football Association. That was the main struggle: whereas the latter organisations strove mightily to keep government, trades unions, the pools, the public and even the press at bay, the union should, according to Guthrie, be determined to win their cooperation.

In short, Guthrie wanted the Players' Union to become more politically-orientated. He agreed with Barnsley's Joe Wilson who had criticised the union set-up just after the war as 'weak-kneed' and inadequate, and in the immediate post-war years he challenged the traditional Players' Union rule that only the secretary should be paid and thus be full-time. The management committee and Guthrie became its first full-time paid employees. They insisted, however, that he give up his role as player-coach at Crystal Palace, a decision that would prove to be his Achilles heel.

From late 1946 onwards the union's agenda would be set by Jimmy Guthrie. Never in the history of the union would so much be attempted in so short a time: wage increases, the establishment of a Provident Fund, a magazine, new contracts, not to mention a complete overhaul of the structure of the union itself. With his players' charter, drawn up in 1947, Guthrie had truly caught the spirit of the time; with a Labour Government pushing through a massive programme of economic and social reform, he had a perfect example to guide him.

The danger was that he would move too fast for his management committee colleagues, perhaps even the membership at large; that he would lose contact with the realities of the game and thus cut himself adrift. For now, however, everyone seemed prepared to go along for the ride.

During the immediate post-war years the union could draw upon a fund of goodwill, not simply because the game itself was so immensely popular but because the Football League clubs seemed intent on behaving with a blatant disregard for public opinion. At times their flouting of agreements – even political directives – bordered on the breathtaking. Their meanness regarding the payment of players and their ingenuity in breaching both the letter and spirit of agreements was thrown into stark contrast by their continued, often rude, refusal to accept offers of financial help from the football pools firms. This, combined with clubs' apparently bottomless purses where transfer fees were concerned, caused widespread bafflement. To many observers it seemed incredible that clubs could plead collective poverty and cry out for government assistance while at the same time spending tens of thousands on star players.

Not surprisingly the popular press during this period was keen to support and publicise the players' arguments and here Jimmy Guthrie's assiduous lobbying and lunchtime Fleet Street briefings paid off handsomely. Journalist Alan Holby ('The Man Who Knows') of the *People* newspaper could almost have been Guthrie's mouthpiece at times, his outspoken column providing evidence to back up union claims and campaigns, his criticism of the League scathing, if perhaps a little melodramatic ('I Accuse Football's Fuhrers'.)

Holby's articles often concentrated on the harsher aspects of the lives of professional footballers and helped underline both Guthrie's and Fay's insistence that their battle was on behalf of the majority of hard-pressed working professionals rather than the men at the very top of the profession:

NEWS CHRONICLE, Wednesday, September 26, 1952

CHARLES BUCHAN'S DEBATE: No. 4

Are the players really free?

★ Is the transfer system a blot on the game? That is the fourth question asked by Charles Buchan in the News Chronicle's Great Debate on Football.

★ Players' Union chairman JIMMY GUTHRIE is of the opinion that it is; TOM WHITTAKER, the Arsenal manager, differs. And here they give their reasons.

Look at those balance sheets

By JIMMY GUTHRIE

DURING the past few months I have spent some time on a survey of the balance sheets issued by Football League clubs. Part of that survey has been to break them down into component parts to discover exactly what happens to the money, which the customers pass over the turnstiles every Saturday.

It may surprise you when I say that more than 50 of the 92 clubs last year lost money on their transfer transactions. And, further, most of those who showed a profit are members of the First Division.

That, to my mind, destroys completely the last argument of the legislators who wish to retain this feudal system as part of our greatest national sport.

You see, the only real point that can be made by the supporters of these fantastic transfer fees is that they circulate the available football wealth, taking some of it to the poorer clubs who need it most.

Almost without exception my investigations indicate that it was the Third Division clubs who lost money in transfer market deals.

The retaining clause

THE transfer system has arisen out of the retaining clause, a fact of which I am sure the majority of the Soccer public have no knowledge. In no other industry is it possible for an employer to retain a man's services after his contract has expired.

The ridiculous heights—or depths—to which the transfers have been carried only provided my argument with an added force. I am a great lover of football. I do not like to see the game cheapened.

Any sport begins to lose caste when it is surrounded with talk of illegal payments and other such inducements to make a man change his loyalty.

As a player myself I know of the strain entailed in trying to live up to a paper value running into five figures. And as one well acquainted with club management, I would venture to suggest that the present system is not in the best interests of the managers and directors.

It would be revealing to compile a list of men who have been transferred for five-figure fees in recent years. A high proportion of them are not now to be found in the League teams of their new clubs. It just is not possible to consider a footballer as a robot.

Our plan

BUT simply destructive criticism takes us nowhere. The most powerful backing which I can give is to put forward a plan which would wipe out the present system and, at the same time, further the interests of British football.

We of the Players' Union feel we have come very close to that objective in the proposals which we shall present to a Ministry of Labour inquiry in London next month.

We shall suggest that the present maximum wage clause be banished from the Football League regulations. Hand in hand with that, we will argue for the establishment of long-term contracts between the club and individual player.

Briefly, I envisage the day when a lad of 17, his heart set on becoming a professional footballer, sets out on a five-year apprenticeship. That, after all, is the usual way to become a competent tradesman.

During those years the youngster will receive a wage common to all the League clubs. The club shall have the option to dispense with the lad's services at the end of any particular season in that period.

But they must give him, in effect, what is now called "a free transfer" enabling him to sign up for another club without fee.

Contract system

AFTER that apprenticeship we would introduce a contractual system of from one to ten or fifteen years. The removal of the maximum wage is essential in order that these contracts should be negotiated without any "under-counter" offers from another club.

I believe that our system would have tremendous benefit, not only for the player but for the club as well.

If a manager has sufficient faith in his judgment he will be able to embark on a long-term policy of team-building. For recently there have been several cases of highly expensive men, purchased to fill a certain team weakness, demanding a move after a matter of months.

Similarly, our system would make for happier players. With a contract for a period of years in his pocket, Bill Smith can find himself a house, settle his wife and regard the area as his home. That is an important security which he does not at present enjoy. I think it would make for increased club loyalty.

All this sounds rather revolutionary. Really, it isn't. It merely establishes football, which nobody can deny is now a business, on the same basis as any other trade or profession.

Even were it revolutionary, the number of managers and directors who have said to me recently, "The game is crazy. We won't touch the transfer market," leads me to the conclusion that perhaps a revolution wouldn't do any harm at that!

News Chronicle, Wednesday 26 September 1952.

THIS IS WHY SOCCER NEEDS CLEANING UP

He is ruined by the game he loved

THAT great player Stan Mortensen once said to me: "You've got to have luck to be famous." Last week, while they were discussing football conditions in the House of Commons, I met one of those who wasn't so lucky.

His name is Dillimore—Jim Dillimore—and I don't suppose you've ever heard of him. He also was an inside-forward. He was so good that he once played in an English International Trial alongside such stars as Arthur Grimsdell, Colin Watson and Tommy Clay. Captaining the opposing side was Billy Walker.

On that happy afternoon Jim Dillimore touched greatness. Not only did he score the winning goal. He was virtually assured of his "cap."

But Dillimore, as I have said, lacked luck. The following week at Millwall—where he was an idol—he broke a leg. The following season—after five years with the club—he was given a free transfer. *But no benefit.*

Later, Dillimore went to Weymouth and then Chatham. His personal jinx went with him, for during his football career he broke *both* legs. He almost broke his heart, too, and tried to earn a few coppers—playing a mouth-organ outside the Millwall ground! A few coppers from the crowds who no longer recognised him....

Today he hasn't worked for three years, draws 37s. 6d. a week and holds a Disabled Person's Card—*disabled from football....*

"And to think," says this man whose last match was the unemployed men's final at Wembley—"that I gave up a safe £6 a week job to earn £5 a week from professional football!"

"Ah!" but I can hear you saying, "it couldn't happen now. Those were the bad old days. Millwall are one of the clubs which pay full benefits." Well, I agree that Millwall have changed their ways. *Yet it is happening now.*

Before the war, Dillimore applied to the Football League for help—he was then drawing 29s. dole. Here is the "warm-hearted" answer he received:

"The Trustees of the Football League have decided that only those players and officials who were in the active service of the League and its clubs on May 30, 1938, are eligible to participate in the benefits of the Fund."—Your faithfully, Fred Howarth.

No wonder the players call it the "Lost Fund"! Frankly, the Football League sits smugly on that £70,000 like a fat, over-fed turtle!

The same thing happened with the F.A. Benevolent Fund. They turned him down flat. Ironically enough, Dillimore played in about half-a-dozen charity games for the F.A. and still wears on his watch - chain a medal given to him by the F.A. after helping to raise money for the very Fund which turned him down!

But the old warrior is still fighting. "I was disabled as a result of playing professional football," he says, "and I reckon I am entitled to something from the game I still love and gave so much to...."

So do I.

★

By **ALAN HOLBY**

Alan Holby's *Daily Herald* articles revealed the harsh reality of the professional game, 21 November 1948.

Behind the clamour and glamour of the world's greatest game is often a bed-rock of loneliness and fear. Behind the current cascades of cash into the League clubs bursting tills and Pools promoters bulging pockets is a seamier side to an entertainment industry which still ranks amongst the poorest paid on the earth…

In November 1946, just after the first confrontation between the Players' Union and the Football League, Holby dealt with a problem then widespread in Britain: homelessness. He interviewed Queen's Park Rangers manager Dave Mangnall who revealed the plight of a number of his players:

'Seven of my boys are either separated from their wives and families or have no homes at all…' And he cited the case of Ivor Powell, a Welsh international who was on the maximum wage of £10 a week: 'He cannot find a home in London. His wife lives in Blackpool with her parents while Ivor lodges in a restaurant in Shepherds Bush. On his salary he has to send about £6 10s home, feed and clothe himself as well as pay tax with the rest and also spend nearly £3 every weekend on the rail-fare to Blackpool…' There were others such as Danny Boxshall ('six years in the army and proud owner of a military medal') who lived in one room with his wife and family in Harrow; John Barr, ex-PoW, Scottish centre-half reserve with a wife and baby up in Lanark who could not afford even a pre-fabricated house.

However, public anger and a sympathetic press, welcome though they were, could not alone produce results. The clubs proved immune to public criticism, convinced that no one outside soccer could possibly comprehend the complexities and problems of the game – certainly not the paying public and particularly not the press.

To fight such an implacable foe Guthrie felt that the union itself needed to overhaul its structure. Unless his proposed changes were introduced, he argued, the union would never be able to push through real, substantial change and would always be dictated to by the League and the FA. The tortured conception and gestation of the Players' Provident Fund only served to increase his determination.

The Provident Fund was a scheme to guarantee every professional player a lump sum on retirement. Jimmy Fay had long set his heart on such a plan, hoping that it would replace the 'benefit' system where a player received the proceeds of a special match or sometimes a regular League match. Benefits were unfair to the majority of lesser players whereas a provident fund would give many of the poorest paid men something to build on when their short playing careers were over.

In 1947 the Players' Union and the Football League had been brought together by the Ministry of Labour to thrash out a mutually acceptable proposal but the two sides would fail to agree on figures. The Player's Union scheme suggested a payout equivalent to 25 per cent of a player's gross career earnings. Backdated to season

1945–46, it would cost some £350,000 produced by a levy on football gate money. Attendances were then reaching record levels and clubs were reaping healthy profits. In 1948 alone Everton made a profit of £25,000, Tottenham £20,000, Burnley £19,000 and Manchester City £16,000.

The Football League saw things differently. Its scheme would cost close to £130,000, representing a four per cent levy on League gates. It would guarantee every player a sum equivalent to 10 per cent of his total career earnings, something like £130 per player. What was more, their scheme would be backdated only to 1948, would exclude all non-League professionals and would only pay out when a man reached 35 years of age.

Jimmy Guthrie was particularly angry about the exclusion of non-League men, pointing out that many such players had been forced out of League football by the retain-and-transfer system, while Jimmy Fay was saddened at the exclusion of so many veteran players who had been in the game just after the war and who had missed out on years of pay.

Deadlock was inevitable. In February 1949 joint meetings on the subject were terminated, so acrimonious had they become. A strike threat brought the Ministry of Labour on to the scene again and, on 14 March 1949 at the Ministry of Labour offices under the chairmanship of George Isaacs MP, the three sides – FA, League and union – gathered to attempt a solution.

In the end it was the union that gave way, its own broker suggesting that, although imperfect, the League scheme was a beginning and better than nothing. Thus the Provident Fund was born. Initially hailed as a breakthrough for the union at regular intervals over the next decade, the Football League would arbitrarily cut the levy and tamper with the pay-outs, gradually whittling them down. The union proved powerless to intervene. Guthrie was convinced that only a radically different kind of union could prevent the League acting in such a fashion.

He began his drive for internal reform in early 1948 but soon ran into stiff resistance. Briefly, he suggested that there should be three paid union officials who would not be players, as well as five playing members of the management committee. The FA and the League were composed of men who could devote their energies

---

Do you know of a Non- Unionist employed in the Football League ?

– IF SO, SEEK HIM OUT –

He should be inside the Association Football Players' & Trainers' Union

Advert published by the Association Football Players' and Trainers' Union.

full-time to their organisations, while the union, established on a part-time basis, was considerably handicapped. The paid men would be empowered to make decisions. He also felt that the union office should be moved to London, something Jimmy Fay was dead set against. Fay immediately made it known that if the office moved from above his shop in Southport it must return to its roots in Manchester.

Nevertheless, in May 1948 Guthrie was granted a regular weekly remuneration of £12 so that he could continue his work in London where he was responsible for looking after the union's block accident scheme, in addition to keeping up contacts with MPs and lawyers during what was considered to be a crucial period. Guthrie justified his remuneration thus:

> 'So long as we have playing members taking a leading part on the management committee we will have the danger of victimisation…your union spokesmen should be able to sit around the conference table and "say their piece" without fear of their livelihood being endangered…'

However, grave suspicion of Guthrie's ideas among union Management Committee members persisted. George Swindin, Arsenal 'keeper, had to be persuaded not to resign on account of his opposition to the idea and it would be 1950 before Guthrie would be allowed money to rent an office in London. Even then there were doubts about the legality of the meeting that approved it. In response, George Swindin and Billy Elliott, ex-committee members, persuaded their colleagues at Arsenal and West Bromwich Albion respectively to withhold their union 'subs', a move followed by a number of other clubs including Everton. At a special union meeting with Swindin present, however, Guthrie prevailed.

Equipped with an official London base he was increasingly able to ignore his management committee colleagues if he felt the need. With the law courts, Fleet Street and Westminster just a taxi-ride away, he could spend his days and nights rubbing shoulders with men and women more to his liking, people who had power, 'top' people. His attitude to the rest of the union was summed up in his book *Soccer Rebel:*

> Most of the action in those vital days was centred on London where I was in constant contact with MPs, solicitors, barristers and insurance brokers, whilst Fay and his two girl typists looked after the day-to-day administration. Most of their time was spent in receiving and acknowledging subscriptions because players had begun to contact me directly instead of going through channels whenever they had a grievance to air…

When management committee members had a grievance to air, one senses in Guthrie's dismissive replies a certain disdain for such 'provincials', the little people meddling in affairs they could not possibly understand. This approach was to lead him into serious trouble in 1954 – trouble that stemmed directly from his own deliberate flouting of management committee wishes and his growing sense of being almost a union in himself.

Guthrie's energy and reforming zeal had certainly won the union significant gains in the years since the war, but his regular outspoken attacks on both the League Management Committee and the FA, both in print and in committee, were disliked by those members who saw no mileage in what they considered merely bombast and insult. In March 1949, for instance, Guthrie wrote in the union's magazine:

> We cannot go on any longer under this football dictatorship. I personally believe that we would fare much better under state control, with a Minister for Sport, a role which would be well-filled by Sir Stanley Rous, Secretary of the FA, who has progressive ideas and whom we, the players, trust and respect. One – we are fed up to the back teeth with the League Dictatorship. We are tired of the humiliations and the planned procrastinations of this body. Professional football today is a stinking racket and the time has come for drastic action.

The political climate was changing, however. In 1951 the Labour Government fell. The outlook engendered by the Cold War rendered calls for state control, closed shops and strikes highly contentious. Guthrie's press nickname, the 'Ball Game Bulganin', derived from a prominent Communist politician of the time, though essentially frivolous, nevertheless had the effect of making him look a little out of step, even out of date. His protests in the union magazine that he was 'no Red' indicated his difficulty. The Players' Union had rarely, if ever, associated itself closely with party politics or ideology, and Guthrie's drive towards trades unionism proper during a period when the rest of the country was settling down for a period of cosy prosperity looked increasingly unattractive to members of a profession who liked to see themselves as 'upwardly mobile'. Guthrie soon found himself battling against a tide.

There was also the issue of money; the union was running out fast. The cost of the Forster Report had serious implications, not least for the union's ability to continue to provide crucial items such as accident insurance for its members.

More immediately, however, his general competence where day-to-day union business was concerned was increasingly being called into question. One of his chief responsibilities in London had been to handle the Block Accident Insurance Policy, something Jimmy Fay had been extremely proud of establishing immediately after the war. Men were guaranteed sums of up to £500 in the event of disability leading to retirement. The premium was high but for a number of years the policy continued without trouble. The problem was that the firm involved made little by way of profit: when there was a large increase in claims the premium paid by the union only covered some 25 per cent of that paid out.

By 1950 the amount guaranteed had been reduced to £300 and the premium was eating up over £6,000 per annum, a worrying trend that, added to the increasing costs of litigation and arbitration, was eating into the union's investments. During 1952–53, therefore, there was a move among members on the committee to find a better deal. Eventually, it was decided to place the insurance with another firm called Hammonds. In August 1953 Hammonds contacted Jimmy Fay claiming that Guthrie had informed them that their terms were not good enough and that he had placed the insurance business with someone else entirely! Confusion reigned for some days until Guthrie was finally tracked down and asked what he was doing. His answer was that he considered the terms that he had obtained (for which there was no evidence on paper) more advantageous to the union's membership and that the management committee should 'leave well alone'. He was instructed to do as the committee had originally told him and was unanimously criticised. Players' claims were being held up and even put at risk by the confusion.

It was at this point that pressure came from within the management committee for Guthrie's London office to be closed. With the imminent retirement of Jimmy Fay there was a need to find new premises for the main union offices as Fay was selling his Southport shop over which they were situated. The question was, where would the new offices be, Manchester or London?

Guthrie insisted on London, Fay on Manchester – and Jimmy Fay won. He moved quickly in early 1953 to secure two rooms in the Corn Exchange Building, Hanging Ditch, the very same building in which the union had had offices before the war, describing them to the rest of the committee as 'perfect'. 'It would' he declared, 'be impossible to find offices in London to compete with them.'

By early 1954 the London office had been closed at last, after much prevarication and ill-feeling, and Guthrie was having to work through Manchester. Gradually his position became less and less tenable. In August 1954, for instance, an emergency meeting of the management committee was called at the Charing Cross Hotel 'for the purpose of considering the chairman's action with regard to matters relating to insurance'. Guthrie had once again interfered with the placing of the Block Accident Policy and Cliff Lloyd, the new secretary, had had to sort out the mess.

Criticism of Jimmy Guthrie, however, ranged much wider to include his loss of office furniture when the London office closed; poorly worded, sometimes inaccurate circulars sent out to the membership; the trouble caused at joint negotiating committee meetings over his belligerent forays into print; his lack of accurate record-keeping and documentation, especially regarding his expenses; even his alleged inactivity regarding club visits. The list seemed endless. In the event, he was suspended for a fortnight.

Oddly, this deteriorating situation came at just the moment when Guthrie appeared to be have reached his personal apogee, delivering his famous 'Slaves' speech to the Annual General Conference of the TUC in 1955. The historic decision by the Players' Union to join the TUC in that year had been greeted relatively calmly – although both the FA and the League representatives at the joint negotiating committee expressed 'concern' at the union's action. Guthrie, however, was keen to exploit the new situation and his appearance at the TUC conference in September hit the newspaper headlines, made television news and was featured on a special Pathe newsreel. It was a defining moment in British football history.

The union put forward a motion that concluded: 'Congress calls upon the Football Association to arrange a conference of all interested parties to consider arrangements for a complete and comprehensive new deal for professional footballers.'

Guthrie's speech was a powerful one, citing various cases of injustice and attacking the 'heartlessness' of the retain-and-transfer system: 'A player and his family may starve while the clubs chatter about the fee to be paid for his transfer and what cuts the manager would receive when the transfer was completed.' He concluded with the ringing declaration: 'I stand here as a representative of the last bonded men in Britain…We have had enough of Human Bondage – we seek your assistance to unfetter the chains and set us free!'

Variety artist Wee Georgie Wood – the Little to Guthrie's Large – seconded the motion which was passed resoundingly.

The *Daily Herald* reported it thus:

> Television arc lights snapped as ex-soccer international Jimmy Guthrie ran up the rostrum steps at the TUC yesterday to make a scathing attack on the Football Association and to defend professional footballers – 'the bonded men of Britain'. Jimmy literally stole the limelight at the afternoon session – flashlights popped, movie cameras whirred under the great floodlights.

Guthrie could now claim that the players had the backing of the whole union movement. It was a publicity coup and ought to have seen him hailed by his profession as a prophet. However, his performance caused some confusion within the profession's ranks. While acknowledging the truth of what Guthrie had to say about the restrictions curtailing their freedoms, there was a definite undercurrent of resentment that footballers had been presented in such a sorry light. Guthrie was quick to spot the reaction: 'The press headlines all carried the word "slavery", a designation that was not appreciated by all of my colleagues.'

Stan Mortenson was one of them. The hat-trick hero of the Matthews final and an England international, he penned a newspaper piece entitled, 'We Soccer Stars Are Doing All Right, Thank You', just a week or so after Guthrie's TUC triumph. Although declaring himself a supporter of the union Mortenson felt that, 'we could take more care with our shooting. We are off target so often.' The current union proposal for five-year contracts and no maximum wage he considered 'dangerous talk' which could 'wreck the fabric of the game'. Complete contractual freedom at the end of each season would see soccer 'riddled with pay jealousies and the disruption of team plans.' What was needed was compulsory benefits, a rise in the minimum wage and 'an end to the non-payment of transfer-listed players at the end of their contracts'. Stars like himself, he felt, could ernment that nic crisis can merely on its nions need to elves whether ney.

nment that if, headed for a be shared and oulders of the

people that ne we are all re the respon the fight back

ks

sed a special Executives to omic policy. looked ahead ns could act. g the past few of the T U C ssible dangers

d these warn tive action to ved to exist?" onsibility of the e responsibility mployers could on their own

lan

ic crisis worsen General Council ference to work ithout waiting iled study pro-

will be about

General Coun to intervene to

Right on the ball

WEE GEORGIE WOOD and Jimmy Guthrie had something to smile about.

BRITAIN'S only supersonic jet fighter, the English Electric P.1, made its first public appearance here this afternoon before only a handful of people.

The P.1 was got ready too late for the crowds attending the first day of the Society of British Aircraft Constructors' great show.

It was a rush job. For this P.1 had to be modified before it could take the air.

The other P.1—there are only two prototypes — which it was intended to show off here had its canopy torn off during a trial.

Flashing by

The flying display ended just after five o'clock. Everyone had dispersed except aircraft technicians when with a roar the P.1 flashed by.

Flying it was Wing Commander Roland Beamont, the company's chief test pilot. He did a low fast run across the airfield for the benefit of the faithful few that had stayed on. But he was not flat out.

Then he showed the P.1's ability to manœuvre by doing several rolls.

Earlier, there were dazzling displays of aerobatics by Britain's premier test pilots.

U.S. claims new air record

LOS ANGELES. Monday.— The U.S. today claimed a new air speed record of 822.135 mph, more than 70 mph better than the officially-recognised figure.

North American Aviation Company said that Colonel Horace Hanes set this average speed in two runs eight miles up over the California desert in a Super Sabre jet fighter.

Wee Georgie Wood turns out against Soccer 'slavery'

HERALD REPORTERS

TELEVISION arc lights snapped on as ex-Soccer international Jimmy Guthrie ran up the rostrum steps at the T U C yesterday to make a scathing attack on the Football Association and to defend professional footballers—"the bonded men of Britain."

Jimmy Guthrie hits the front pages. *Daily Herald,* 6 September 1955.

look after themselves. As for being a 'slave': 'I've never felt like a slave, not for a single minute in 19 seasons.'

Mortenson's opinions were undoubtedly shared by many top players. The 'Crusader in a bow tie', as he was dubbed, was not every player's cup of tea. Nor were his attempts to transform the Players' Union into something more akin to one in the manufacturing industry.

His insistence that the union become a closed shop illustrated the divide. All the recent struggles, for the provident fund, the wage increases, the improvements in players' contracts, had been fought on behalf of the whole membership. Yet a substantial proportion paid no 'subs' and thus contributed nothing to the cause. As Guthrie commented, a little optimistically, 'This would not be tolerated in any other union, where a union card must be produced before the individual is allowed to start work.'

The problem with a closed shop was that it could only work efficiently with an employer's consent, which would clearly not be forthcoming in the football 'industry'. Suggestions that unionists should not play with or against non-unionists as a way of pressurising men to join posed obvious difficulties for a team competition.

The question divided the management committee. Jimmy Fay had always said how good it would be to have 100 per cent membership but had baulked at the idea of compulsion. In 1955, however, in the wake of Guthrie's Blackpool speech and the prospect of the TUC taking up the case of the players' charter, an additional rule was proposed by committee member Jimmy Hill as follows:

> No member of the union shall be allowed to play with or against professional players who are registered with the Football League who are not members of the union.

There was some heated debate among AGM delegates concerning this resolution, with the Norwich City delegate declaring that the 'Canaries' were against a closed shop in principle. An amendment was drafted and adopted, setting the 30 June 1956 as a date for the implementation of the rule.

The following April, with the union and the Football League locked in crucial negotiations regarding extra payments for floodlit matches and TV appearances, the League president, Arthur Oakley, announced that he had discovered via a Jimmy Guthrie interview in a Scottish newspaper that it was union policy not to play against non-unionists. 'If is was so,' he announced, 'there did not seem to be any point in continuing the discussion.'

The union representatives present, J. Campbell, Walton and Guthrie along with secretary Cliff Lloyd, appeared confused and unsure as to whether such a rule had actually been passed. The League representatives pressed home their advantage. No further talks could take place until the management committee had consulted its members and had the rule rescinded. The 'friendly atmosphere' in which the

Cliff Lloyd OBE Secretary 1953–82

The fourth of six sons, Cliff's childhood was happy, if predictably hard. His father had been a keen footballer, a useful full-back for Flint Town, with his footballing skills earning him employment at BICC Cables. Cliff was to follow in his footsteps. Signed as an amateur by Liverpool, and as a full professional in 1937, World War Two interrupted his career. He joined the Army Physical Training Corps and 'guested' for both Brentford and Fulham. He was selected for numerous representative matches, among them a Combined Services match at Wembley in front of 70,000 spectators, playing alongside Joe Mercer and Cliff Bastin. After the war he spent five happy years with Fulham, coached in Norway but by then his fitness was causing him problems. Having broken his right leg playing for Fulham in a Cup match, he had hurried back into action too soon and soon afterwards he hung up his boots for good.

By then he was on the Players' Union Management Committee, having taken on the job as delegate and collector for Fulham because no one else wanted to do it! His nomination for secretary in April 1953 came 'as a bolt out of the blue…no one was more shocked and surprised than me,' he admitted. Another Chelsea man, Danny Winter, simply said, 'In my view there's only one man for the job and that's Cliff…'

Cliff Lloyd was the quintessential player's man. He appreciated that unique blend of heartbreak and exhilaration the profession offered, and those who approached him with problems could feel confident, not only that he understood, but that he could do something to help.

He was very much a 'hands-on' administrator and was personally involved in everything. He travelled to hearings, to meetings, to clubs up and down the country in his small car in the days before motorways – yet returned every night to his home in Helsby. Being one of nature's 'worriers', he had no choice but to expend his nervous energy on each and every case, large or small. His finest moment came when he almost single-handedly saw the historic George Eastham case through to a successful conclusion – the perfect victory for one of the union's most dedicated and influential servants. He was awarded the OBE in 1976 for services to the game. Cliff died in 2000.

negotiations had hitherto continued could not be resumed until the matter had been settled. The union committee put up no fight; it simply did as it was told.

Clubs were circularised with a recommendation that the 'rule' be rescinded so that negotiations could continue. Twenty-six clubs replied: 20 were against the rule. This was duly reported to the League Management Committee in May and negotiations continued. In July, however, Cliff Lloyd discovered that there had, in fact, been no rule at all! There had only been Hill's proposal at the previous AGM which had not as yet been put to a vote. The swiftness with which the idea had been dropped by the membership at grass roots level suggested that the proposed link-up with the TUC was viewed with mixed feelings by professional players. No wonder Jimmy Guthrie could complain at the 1955 AGM that the union was no longer a militant one.

A parting of the ways looked increasingly imminent yet it was Guthrie who finally set the wheels in motion. Once again it would be insurance that would prove his undoing. Following yet more confusion over the policy's renewal and a suspicion that he was going to attempt some kind of personnel coup at the 1957 AGM, decisive action was taken.

The fact was that, due to the lack of enthusiasm among the membership as a whole, hardly any of the existing management committee were still actually playing. Most had continued serving when their playing days had ended because no one else had stepped forward to replace them. At the management committee meeting prior to the AGM proper the union accountant suddenly announced that 'there are several points regarding the legality of the position of several members of the committee of management and the chairman'. Only playing members of football clubs could be members of the union. The committee had to be elected from among them and the chairman had to be a member of the committee. Thus, several committee members were technically disqualified. 'In the case of the chairman,' the accountant continued, 'the situation is worse'.

Guthrie would later claim that he was thrown out of his job via a loophole in the system – that he had no union card. He did not have one because he had been told he could not work for anyone else and had given up his player-coach job with Crystal Palace. He was thus strictly a 'paid executive' and not a legal member of the union. As a non-member of the union he should not have been holding a position on the executive. As from that moment the chair was vacant. Guthrie later wrote:

> I was flabbergasted, breathless and the other committee-men –Jimmy Hill, Oscar Hold, Arthur Banner and Secretary Cliff Lloyd – sat like ventriloquists dolls saying not a word…

He insisted that he be allowed to open the AGM, which he did, explaining the extraordinary situation and suggesting that the delegates must decide whether or not to elect a new committee there and then. It was decided to let the committee continue – but without Guthrie. With that he left the hall and Jimmy Hill stepped into the chair.

Interviewed immediately afterward Guthrie appeared shocked and subdued. Asked by the press whether he thought his sacking was pre-arranged he replied, 'I don't think so. This is what the members wanted. That is all there is to it.' He held no grudges he insisted, though according to one journalist he cut a sorry figure, 'almost in tears as he stood alone in the meeting-room while the delegates hurried to catch trains.'

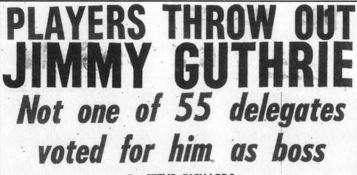

PLAYERS THROW OUT JIMMY GUTHRIE

Not one of 55 delegates voted for him as boss

By STEVE RICHARDS

JIMMY GUTHRIE, 16st. £1,000-a-year chairman of the Soccer Players' Union, who has fought for over ten years to unchain the footballers he called "slaves" was sacked yesterday—by the "slaves."

Not one of the 55 League club represen tatives at the Union's three-and-a-half-hour annual meeting in Manchester sto od up to nominate him as chairman for another year. He presided over the meeting until the unanimous vote was announced. Then he left the room for a beer—a dejected man.

Then, hard-hitting, bow-tied Guthrie, fam ed for his forthright declarations in defence of the English footballer, made his tamest- ever after-meeting speech.

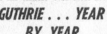

GUTHRIE . . . YEAR BY YEAR

AFTER seven seasons with Dundee, Guthrie joined Portsmouth as a wing-half.

● In 1939, he captained Pompey at Wembley and shocked Wolves in the Final.

● In 1948 he took over the chair of the Players' Union. The rebel, arbitrator, fighter, who never flinched. The Union grew to 3,000 membership.

● In 1955 came his greatest triumph. He addressed the T U C: "Professional footballers are the bonded men of Britain. . . . Human beings sold like cattle."

● In 1956 he called for a strike unless there was extra pay-ment for floodlit and televised matches. He was then dubbed the "Big Brother."

He said: "I did not expect this to happen after all this time. But it is one of those things—you can't have the luck of the draw all the time."

Asked it he thought the unanimous vote suggested his sacking was prearranged, Guthrie replied: "I don't think so. This is what members wanted. That's ; there is to it. The union has come a long way since I took over and is now a powerful body. I'm naturally sorry about all this—but I have no grudge against the union, don't think that."

No new chairman was appointed. The new committee was instructed to meet in the next fortnight to elect a chair-man, and to decide whether to appoint a "paid organiser"—a position for which Guthrie could apply if he desired.

The committee is:—
Harry Hough (Barnsley), Jeff Hall (Bir-mingham), Tony Ingham (Q P R), Ian Dargie (Brentford), Bill Reest (Bristol Rovers), Frank Walton (ex-Southend), and the two re-elected members, Jimmy Hill (Fulham) and Jack Campbell (Oldham).

Union secretary Cliff Lloyd said that the removal of Guthrie from office came "after reviewing negotiations and the outcome of several issues during the past two years."

Stood alone

Fighting Guthrie, Portsmouth's Cup-winning skipper in 1939, was almost in tears as he stood alone in the meeting room while dele-gates hurried to catch trains.

His only friends then and until he caught the midnight train to London were the Press—the people who had helped him in his battle for the players.

The Players' Union . . . with-out big, bold, blustering Jimmy Guthrie. Unbelievable. Here's how Soccer personalities reacted when we brought them the shock news last night:

JOHN DEAN (Fulham chair-man): "It is a shock. I am sorry. I don't think the Players' Union have ever had a better or more hard-working representative."

EDDIE LEVER (Portsmouth manager): "Good grief. What-ever have they done? Surely he was worth keeping on the com-mittee at least. In all my deal-ings with him I found him out-spoken but square-shooting."

EX-CHAIRMAN GUTHRIE . . . making his famed T U C speech.

AMERICA OFFERS JOE ERSKINE THE TOP PRIZE

By TOM PHILLIPS

LISTEN, ye millions of Welsh fight fans! Start sing-ing "Land of My Fathers" now! Get Joe Erskine into a sure-fire winning state of mind for Earl's Court, London, February 19.

For now Joe MUST beat Nino Valdes, of Cuba. Victory will give him the chance every young heavyweight covets—

TO FIGHT FOR THE WORLD TITLE

From New York last night I got the news: IF ERSKINE CONQUERS VALDES, FLOYD PATTERSON, THE WORLD CHAMPION, WILL DEFEND HIS CROWN AGAINST JOE IN NEW YORK IN JUNE.

Lew Burston, foreign agent for the International Boxing Club, of New York, told me: "The American public is tired of seeing the Bob Bakers and Tommy Jacksons. Either of them against Patter

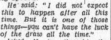

Daily Herald, 29 January 1957.

Jimmy Guthrie had wanted to run the union like an old-fashioned union boss. He would not or could not compromise and although the union would be heavily criticised for having 'ditched' him (Desmond Hackett of the *Daily Express* wrote 'It's a victory for the bosses') it was really only trying, albeit clumsily, to untangle a situation that had become intolerable. As Cliff Lloyd commented much later, 'Jimmy was a fool to himself and only had himself to blame.' Not everyone was happy. Both West Bromwich Albion and Birmingham City players protested at Guthrie's sacking and had to be mollified by new chairman Jimmy Hill before they continued as members. There was a suggestion in the wake of Guthrie's departure that the union would recruit a paid organiser and that Guthrie would be in the running for such a job. He quickly ruled that out saying:

'The job would have made me nothing more than a messenger-boy. I can imagine the procedure for Guthrie, paid organiser – "Oh, Jimmy, wait outside while we talk business with the League, will you?" I will never take such a job with the union.'

Guthrie remained on the football scene for many more years as a columnist with the *Sunday People* and he continued to lead the Saturday night choir of expatriate Scots at such celebrated Fleet Street watering holes as the Chedder Cheese and the Clachan. Few people ever had a bad word for Jimmy Guthrie; all admired his undoubted dedication to the players' cause and his personal kindness, particularly to the many young players arriving in London from Scotland in need of advice and a helping hand – just as he had once been.

His departure from the union shocked almost everyone, even those who had helped to engineer it. As the *Daily Herald* columnist Steve Richards wrote: 'The Player's Union…without big, bold blustering Jimmy Guthrie. Unbelievable!'

3. The Football Rumpus! 1961

Jimmy Hill, the man who ultimately replaced Jimmy Guthrie as Players' Union chairman, is often presented as the antithesis to the old-fashioned union 'boss' that Guthrie aspired to be. His image certainly presented a contrast. Much younger and sporting a 'bohemian' beard, he was a cartoonist's dream. Hill commented, 'Because of my beard they call me Rasputin, or the Rabbi or just Baa-a-a. But it's not a gimmick. Just vanity.' However, any thoughts that his arrival would mark a softening of attitudes and a less aggressive approach where players' demands were concerned were rapidly quashed. After welcoming him to his very first joint committee meeting with the Football League in April 1957 chairman Joe Richards expressed the hope that relations between the two sides would continue to be 'cordial and friendly'. Hill quickly disillusioned him. Earlier declarations by the Players' Union accepting the principles of the retain-and-transfer system and the maximum wage were a dead letter. Complete freedom was the goal. When asked by Richards if this was 'for the good of the game' Hill is said to have countered, 'We're not interested in the good of the game. We're only here to talk about our members.' Even Jimmy Guthrie could not have put it quite so bluntly.

What was more, Guthrie's courting of Fleet Street journalists would only appear a slightly more dated version of Hill's 'public relations' endeavours. Guthrie had, after all, revived the union magazine and had grasped the importance of the new medium of television. Hill simply took things to the next level. His business background made him aware of the burgeoning commercial possibilities then opening up for football, in particular the arrival of commercial TV with its massive advertising revenues, not to mention its subtle advertising techniques. His understanding of the importance of high quality publicity, of efficient, clear, simple presentation of ideas would also prove an important bonus to the union, especially when placed alongside the Football League's continued contempt for public relations.

Where Guthrie had liked to rub shoulders with the journalists and lawyers, Hill was not ashamed to be seen in the company of advertising executives (at one time he even shared an office with one). He was happy to participate in self-promotion and image-making, indeed, he had recently formed the International Club to help prominent players do just that. Advocating the 'upward social mobility' of footballers caused him no embarrassment at all. He was also blessed with just a little good luck. Within days of assuming control he was plunged into a football controversy that helped set the tone for his whirlwind chairmanship.

The investigations into the affairs of Sunderland football club in early April 1957 revealed little new about the murky world of football finance. Irregular and illegal payments had been made to players amounting to many thousands of pounds and stretching back many years. A joint FA/League commission of enquiry into the club's finances led to the suspension of various club directors for life and heavy fines for the club itself.

The Players' Union became directly involved when five Sunderland players were named as having accepted illegal signing-on fees and were summoned by the investigating commission. At this point the players approached the union for help and for the first time union representatives were allowed to be present as observers at such a hearing. The Football Association must have rued the day, however. On Players' Union solicitor George Davies's advice the union decided to take a bold course.

The men were instructed to say nothing at all that might incriminate them when asked any questions by the commission. British justice insisted that guilt, not innocence, be proved. In this way the union intended using the Sunderland enquiry as a means of challenging the supra-legal powers of both the League and the FA. They would argue that men faced with the possibility of losing their livelihood should be allowed – indeed, had the right – to a proper legal defence, a long-standing demand ever since the 1952 Arbitration Tribunal.

The immediate outcome of the commission on 25 April, however, came as a complete shock, even to George Davies. Faced with five silent men refusing to answer any questions, the commission simply suspended them all, sine die. The union was suddenly thrust into the driving seat. Its members had been suspended and were none too happy about the situation, even though the union had pledged financial support. What, then, was it going to do?

Hill's immediate response was to announce at a press briefing some three days later that the union was calling on the League and the FA to hold an enquiry into the whole question of illegal payments. The union, he said, would cooperate if three conditions were met: 'That no action would be taken against any player who gave evidence freely concerning illegal payments; That the five suspended players have their suspensions lifted immediately and reconsidered at a later date if necessary; The speedy implementation of any necessary changes agreed upon.'

The key element in the union's approach to the football authorities was its declared intention to collect as many signatures as possible (a thousand was the projected figure) of men who admitted to having received illegal payments. Such overwhelming weight of evidence, it was suggested, could not fail to force the FA and League to respond. The 'petition' idea, said to be the brainchild of a sports writer on Jimmy Guthrie's favourite Sunday paper, *The People*, was the factor that turned the Sunderland affair into something more than just another under-the-counter wages scandal.

Jimmy Hill – a cartoonist's dream.

Although not intended to be frivolous, it was in essence a stunt– and for that very reason perfect material for sports writers to seize upon and dramatise. For Jimmy Hill it rapidly became a personal nightmare. Having committed the union to securing a thousand signatures, he now had to produce them, not easy at the end of the football season with players disappearing on holiday. As Hill admitted in his 1961 autobiography, *Striking for Soccer*, 'We soon found we had taken on an impossible task.'

Driving up and down the country, he claimed remarkable success but would not reveal the figures to the press, leaving them free to speculate. As a consequence the campaign was dubbed a mess, a flop, a disaster: players were said to have refused to take the risk while others had simply laughed at the whole idea.

Jimmy Hill Chairman 1957–61

Jimmy began his playing career at Reading as an amateur under Ted Drake before turning pro with Brentford. In 1952 he moved to Fulham where he played alongside Bobby Robson, Johnny Haynes and George Cohen. Although a wing-half, he had a knack of scoring important goals. During Fulham's FA Cup run of 1958, which ended in semi-final defeat at the hands of Manchester United, he scored in every round. An enthusiastic, whole-hearted rather than skilful player, he holds the club record of scoring five goals in an away match. Jimmy was the first of the 'personality' chairmen, a player whose bristling beard brought him press notoriety as the 'bold buccaneer', the 'beatnik with a ball'. Hill never minded however. He understood that publicity was a good thing, particularly as television was beginning to have an influence on the game. After serving on the PFA Jimmy swiftly moved into management at Coventry, guiding the club from the old Third Division to Division One. The organisation he left behind had been modernised and galvanised. It had also been renamed. No longer the Players' Union, it was now the Professional Footballers' Association. In his latter years he played a key role in rescuing Fulham from extinction. TV executive and pundit, there is nothing Jimmy has not done in the game – he even ran the line in a League match at Arsenal when a linesman injured himself!

Len Shackleton incurred the wrath of his Sunderland teammates by insisting that the best way to change the wage and bonus structure was to go on strike. Signing confessions would not, he believed, help anyone: 'I am a union member but I still have the right to form my own opinion.' His opinion was a sound one, as events would demonstrate. As it was, the signature campaign made little impact on the League.

However, all was not lost where the union's overall strategy was concerned. Ever since the commission had suspended the Sunderland men the union Management Committee and its legal advisers had been sitting on the realisation that the League and FA had blundered badly. A member of Davies's law firm had discovered that, according to existing rules, the commission set up by the football authorities had no legal standing. Joint commissions of enquiry involving both the Football Association and the Football League had never been formed before. Thus, any decisions taken would be open to legal challenge because there were no powers granted to such commissions, least of all to suspend men for life.

How such a basic mistake had been made was a mystery. Perhaps the fact that the FA and League had never had to worry about legal niceties, that they had always considered themselves 'the law' where football was concerned, had dulled their legal wits. Whatever the explanation, Davies was convinced that an appeal would overturn the suspensions.

In the meantime, blissfully unaware of their mistake, the football authorities offered the Sunderland men a second chance to 'own up'. If they did it was promised that their suspensions would be lifted. This time, with the 'confessions' campaign having almost died a death and with the appeal against the original suspensions already underway, Davies advised the men to talk. They admitted to various illegal payments, were found 'guilty' and later punished by being stripped of part of their qualification for a benefit – an odd sentence as some of the men were not even eligible for one.

A significant spin-off from the Sunderland affair, however, was a heightened sense of dissatisfaction among players and fans with the ways things were in the football industry. The plight of the men involved in the Sunderland case only served to highlight the absurdities created by the maximum wage and of the hypocrisy of 'trying' five men for 'offences' that were being committed in every club in the land. In an increasingly affluent society professional footballers were beginning to look distinctly poorly paid. The media had played its part in highlighting the inequities of football finance. A *Pathe News* report, for instance, entitled 'The Football Rumpus' featured a selection of big-name players working at second jobs in order to supplement their incomes, while Jimmy Hill, interviewed at length, came across as well-spoken, earnest and reasonable.

Significantly, no impact at all appeared to have been made on football's governing bodies. Despite the fact that personnel changes had occurred in both organisations, attitudes remained depressingly familiar, particularly where the Football League was concerned. The new Football League Secretary, Alan Hardaker, while admitting to the need for changing the way professional football was run and organised, remained loyal to ancient League creeds and a significant exchange of letters with Cliff Lloyd in 1959 demonstrated this in eerie fashion.

Referring to the necessity of both the retain-and-transfer system and the maximum wage to the survival of the League Hardaker cited as conclusive evidence, 'the chaotic conditions that existed before the League was formed in 1888…'

Cliff Lloyd replied, 'This is surely a long time ago and I can hardly feel that those gentlemen who founded the League thought the maximum wage and transfer system would continue to be doggedly insisted upon without any real variation over 70 years afterwards…'

In April 1960, following the PFA's AGM, four principal demands were formulated: the abolition of the maximum wage; the right of players to a proportion of any transfer fee; a new 'retaining' system; and a new form of contract. In June the Ministry of Labour was informed that a dispute existed and the PFA demands were submitted to the League for its consideration.

Some five months later, on 8 November, an extraordinary meeting of League clubs offered the following: a rise in the minimum wage of £2; a wage of £10 a week to be paid to men on the transfer list; match bonuses to be paid to reserves; and the introduction of talent money. There being no mention of substantial changes to either the maximum wage or the transfer system, the offer was rejected out of hand by the union and after a series of rank and file meetings held in November, December and January the union felt confident enough to issue a strike notice to take effect on 2 January 1961.

The subsequent campaign for what the PFA would term 'The Two Freedoms' would be a heady time for English football. Arguments raged to and fro, and although the players would continue to pass motions in support of strike action, there were many men undecided about the wisdom of taking such action. Inevitably there was great pressure put upon players by management, especially at the smaller clubs.

At Luton Town club director P.G. Mitchell refused to accept the vote in favour of a strike and demanded that it be re-stated in front of him. Brendan McNally recalled: 'They had all the players into the boardroom, and he says, "I want a show of hands of the players who are not going to accept a maximum wage" – and all the hands went up except three. He was trying to put the squeeze on us, see who'd put their hands up and then they'd have their eyes on you. Ken Hawkes was one of the hands that went up in defiance of his chairman. He said, "I hope you know what you're doing, you're going to be out of a job." And Allan Brown, the union rep – Al was a pretty forthright guy – he says, "Are you trying to frighten me Mr Mitchell?" He says, "No, but it just won't happen. You're fighting a lost cause." And he did everything to convince us that it was silly.'

Crystal Palace players initially rejected action but were persuaded to join in. Hartlepool's men voted against action, as did Aldershot's, while in the Midlands Aston Villa players remained obdurately anti-strike action. At one point, when Villa

A lighter side to the dispute, *London Evening News.*

players boycotted a meeting of the Midlands clubs, they were attacked by Bobby Robson, then West Bromwich Albion skipper and England wing-half: 'I think it's absolutely disgusting that Villa players cannot even be bothered to attend a meeting which can decide their entire future. It is this sort of outlook which gives people the impression that footballers have their brains in their boots. The mentality of some professionals staggers me.' Villa players later apologised but insisted that they would retain the right to play whether or not the rest of the membership decided to strike.

Some of the mass meetings were poorly attended and PFA delegates had to do a great deal of explaining to reluctant members – but a Manchester meeting of delegates in January 1961 proved decisive. Roger Hunt and his fellow Liverpool players were promised transport to the venue by the Anfield hierarchy – with one proviso. Hunt recalled years later, 'Liverpool laid on two buses for us, provided we voted against scrapping the maximum wage. We all finished up voting for!'

It was at this meeting that the apocryphal story involving Stanley Matthews originates. Someone is said to have commented that his father worked down the pit and did not believe his son, a footballer, should be paid more. Tommy Banks, Bolton Wanderers and England full-back, stood up and countered: 'I have been down the pits, so I respect what your father says, but tell your dad to come out of the pit next Saturday and try to mark Stanley Matthews!' Bobby Charlton, a keen union delegate, considered that Tommy Banks's quip about Matthews changed the mood of the meeting. In a sense it underlined the fact that professional players were more than

Jimmy Hill talks to Arsenal players David Herd, far right, and Billy McCullough during the London meeting to decide the maximum wage crisis, 14 November 1960.

simply artisans. They possessed skills and abilities beyond the norm and deserved to be paid accordingly.

In many respects, this was to be Jimmy Hill's finest hour as a union man. He was at every meeting, cajoling, explaining and encouraging. He appeared on TV and radio and in countless newspaper interviews and was always a fund of bright, publicity perfect bon mots and ideas. In December he announced that he had started a strike fund with the fee he had recently received for advertising a television set. His aim was to provide strike pay for all players of £10 per week. There was talk of a 'pirate' league – with the teams using fictitious names – to raise money for the fund. It was also intended to run inter-city representative matches and seven-a-side and five-a-side tournaments. How this was to be achieved was not explained. The great Stanley Matthews appeared in a fund-raising match in December 1960 and was promptly reprimanded by the FA under a rule banning players 'under the jurisdiction of the FA playing with or against unaffiliated clubs'. Matthews gave a written undertaking not to do it again…

Nevertheless, the union appeared to have the country on its side. Ted Hill, TUC chairman, spoke out in support and warned other trades unionists not to attempt to break the strike in any way. Philip Goodhart MP went so far as to describe the Football League as 'inefficiently organised, semi-bankrupt and all too often a thoroughly bad employer'.

Although the Football League attempted to bluff its way along by suggesting it could stage the League programme without many of the strikers, it was in a hopeless position. By 9 January it had begun to shift its position and substantial gains for the players seemed possible. Five concessions were offered: longer playing contracts; the abolition of the maximum wage; the setting up of a joint negotiating committee; a minimum retaining wage per division; and testimonials for players every eight years.

With the retain-and-transfer system still largely untouched, the union felt obliged to consult its members again. The players held firm and at 2.30pm on Wednesday 18 January at the Ministry of Labour offices in London, Joe Richards, Joe Mears and Alan Hardaker for the Football League sat down opposite Cliff Lloyd, Jimmy Hill and George Davies for the PFA, with Ministry of Labour conciliation officer Tom Claro as referee to hammer out a deal.

After two and a half hours of talks the PFA men went to an adjoining room to consult with the rest of the management committee. At 6.45pm the Minister of Labour, Mr Hare, was summoned to make an announcement to a gathering of some 60 press and TV men. Agreement had been reached concerning the retain-and-transfer system. The battle, it seemed, had been won!

As telegrams were being sent to all League clubs informing them that matches would be played that Saturday as usual, Jimmy Hill announced: 'This is a historic moment for football in this country.' Mr Hare commented: 'One of the things that will please the public most is the fact that this agreement was reached with great goodwill on both sides – and so the future prospects of football look really good.'

The 'historic' settlement of 1961 was initially greeted by the press as a triumph for the players and while it was true that much had been achieved it was still a great deal less than was at first claimed. Even worse, it turned out to be a lot less than the union had initially believed had been agreed on.

With regards to the retain-and-transfer system, the League negotiators seemed to have conceded crucial ground. Once a player refused the terms offered to him (and he had until 31 May to do so) he would be placed on the transfer list and other clubs notified that he was for sale. If still on the list after 30 June he would automatically receive a minimum wage set according to his division. If not transferred by 31 July he would be retained on a monthly contract until 31 August when the League Management Committee would sort the matter out. Thus the 'retaining' element of the system appeared considerably weakened and it seemed that a player now had much more say in his future than had previously been the case. What was more, he now received a wage while waiting to move.

However, whereas the PFA Management Committee had the power to settle there and then and believed that it had done so, the League Management Committee now revealed that it had no such mandate. When, some weeks later, it took the deal back to a full meeting of all League clubs for ratification, it soon became clear that the clubs were unhappy. In fact, at an extraordinary meeting at the Café Royal, they rejected the deal completely, Joe Richards announcing: 'Come what may, the Football League will not alter the present retain-and-transfer system…it must remain an integral part of the League system…'

Predictable expressions of outrage greeted this volte-face. There were questions and statements made in the House of Commons and press headlines declaring that the League had 'died of shame'. Back the two parties went to the Ministry of Labour and by 16 May yet another agreement had been reached between the respective management committees. This time, however, the League representatives were careful to emphasise that they had no mandate. The clubs would have to ratify the deal, in particular clause four which stated that if a player did not accept terms offered to him he should be retained but placed on the transfer list. The League representatives, in fact, redrafted this clause to read: 'If he does not accept, the club will let it be known that he has refused terms and invites enquiries for his transfer at a stated fee.' The union negotiators did not object – it seemed merely a matter of wording. The whole package was then taken back to the League to be considered at its AGM on 3 June 1961.

By now, of course, the season had ended, the PFA's AGM had already been held and further strike action was impossible until the autumn. Perhaps because the pressure was off the Football League meeting turned out to be an unpleasant, acrimonious affair with the press being ejected from the room at the start to the accompaniment of derisory slow hand-clapping.

The discussion that followed saw all the familiar arguments wheeled out: that without the 'retaining' safeguard, players would 'hold the clubs to ransom'; that agents would take over; that the new agreement 'placed a premium on disloyalty'; and that no one else understood the system like they did.

When it came to a vote, with almost perfect historical symmetry, it was Burnley FC – C.E. Sutcliffe's old club – that proposed the whole deal be ignored. However, the clubs stopped short of such total folly. They simply deleted the troublesome clause four. Without it the 'retaining' element of the transfer system remained inviolate. A player could now refuse terms and still be held (although now on a weekly wage) for as long as the club wished it.

It had taken a year of meetings, arguments and brinkmanship, not to mention the expenditure of valuable nervous energy on behalf of Cliff Lloyd, George Davies, Jimmy Hill and the ageing Joe Richards to return, almost, to square one.

The PFA rejected the League's 'final' offer and declared the dispute still on; in June the Minister of Labour announced in the Commons: 'No final settlement has been reached because the AGM of the Football League decided not to implement the agreement in full'. Jimmy Hill, in a chapter of his autobiography entitled *The Great Betrayal*, would write: 'It has now become a battle for all Trades Unionists...' For Hill, however, such battles were over. In December 1961 he resigned from the management committee to take up the post of manager of Coventry City FC.

With his departure the 'new deal' and the fight for the two freedoms died in publicity terms, and although Tommy Cummings, the new PFA chairman, spoke immediately after his election about the battle being far from over, it was decided that the union would first wait to see if the spirit of the agreement would be carried over in practice before taking further action.

Soccer Strike off. Jimmy Hill, chairman of the PFA, shakes hands with Joe Richards, president of the Football League, watched by Labour Minister Mr John Hare (centre) and Football League Secretary Alan Hardaker (far left), 18 January 1961.

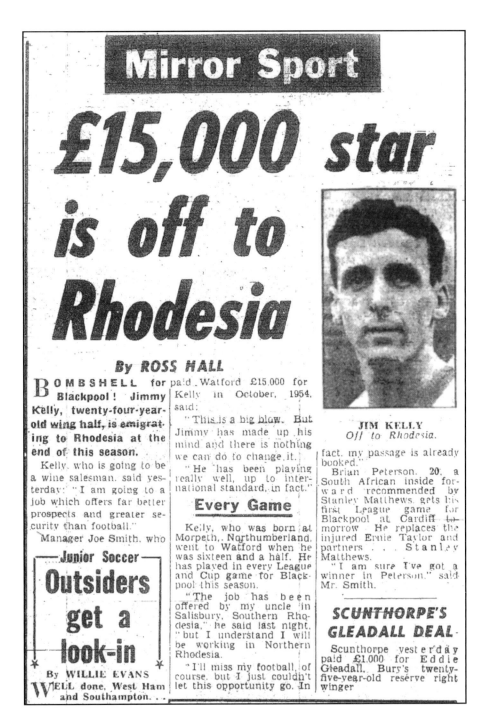

Mirror Sport

£15,000 star is off to Rhodesia

By ROSS HALL

BOMBSHELL for Blackpool! Jimmy Kelly, twenty-four-year-old wing half, is emigrating to Rhodesia at the end of this season.

Kelly, who is going to be a wine salesman, said yesterday: "I am going to a job which offers far better prospects and greater security than football."

Manager Joe Smith, who

Junior Soccer

Outsiders get a look-in

By WILLIE EVANS

WELL done, West Ham and Southampton. . .

paid Watford £15,000 for Kelly in October, 1954, said:

"This is a big blow. But Jimmy has made up his mind and there is nothing we can do to change it.

"He has been playing really well, up to international standard, in fact."

Every Game

Kelly, who was born at Morpeth, Northumberland, went to Watford when he was sixteen and a half. He has played in every League and Cup game for Blackpool this season.

"The job has been offered by my uncle in Salisbury, Southern Rhodesia," he said last night, "but I understand I will be working in Northern Rhodesia.

"I'll miss my football, of course, but I just couldn't let this opportunity go. In

JIM KELLY
Off to Rhodesia.

fact, my passage is already booked."

Brian Peterson, 20, a South African inside forward recommended by Stanley Matthews, gets his first League game for Blackpool at Cardiff tomorrow. He replaces the injured Ernie Taylor and partners . . . Stanley Matthews.

"I am sure I've got a winner in Peterson," said Mr. Smith.

SCUNTHORPE'S GLEADALL DEAL

Scunthorpe yesterday paid £1,000 for Eddie Gleadall, Bury's twenty-five-year-old reserve right winger

Even players at the very top found the game's financial rewards insufficient. *Daily Mirror*, March 1957.

Tommy Cummings Chairman 1961–63

Tommy joined Burnley in October 1947 from Hilton Colliery Juniors while at the same time continuing his apprenticeship as a mining engineer. Acknowledged as one of the fastest defenders in the English game, he nevertheless netted what has been described as Burnley's greatest goal in 1952 when he ran the length of a snow-covered pitch to score a late winner in a 2–1 victory over Newcastle United. He played for England B and also represented the Football League and probably would have gained further honours but for the brilliance of Billy Wright. Following an FA Cup Final appearance in 1962, Tommy hung up his boots nearly 24 years after his League debut. He later returned to Burnley where he ran a number of pubs. In retirement he was a familiar figure on the local bowling greens and snooker tables, playing with the same competitive spirit which he brought to Turf Moor.

In truth, the union was now in no position to launch another full-scale assault on the existing system. In the first place the earlier mood of militancy – so crucial to the success thus far and not entirely unanimous at the time – had almost evaporated. Unanimity, including the participation of top players such as Stanley Matthews and Billy Wright, had been essential in catching the public's imagination as well as ensuring that many lower-division players took the considerable risk involved in defying club managements. Top players, some of whom were already negotiating relatively lucrative new contracts, now had a great deal more to lose and little to gain in the immediate future.

The new agreement had seen the removal of the maximum wage which meant star players could now earn much higher salaries, up to £100 a week in certain celebrated cases. The majority of professional players at the time would doubtless have preferred a higher maximum wage – say £25–30 a week – plus unlimited bonuses for success. PFA committee members such as Jack Campbell, Ian Dargie and Tony Ingham were concerned that the removal of the maximum would threaten the livelihood of many lesser players, as it was being made clear by certain clubs that in order to pay the higher salaries there would have to be some trimming of playing staff. They had pressed for such a deal and in the early stages of the dispute League secretary Alan Hardaker and Cliff Lloyd had agreed on a higher maximum. This initiative had been rejected by the clubs – a disastrous move according to Hardaker.

In 1960 the maximum wage for a professional footballer over the age of 20 in England and Wales stood at £20 a week during the season and £17 a week during the summer. For a 17-year-old signing his first contract the maximum was £10 and £9; at 18 it rose to £12 10s and £11, while at 19 he could earn £15 and £13.

Across Europe at this time few other countries were able to offer as much as most were still only able to support part-time professionalism. There were wide variations in basic salaries. For instance, in Yugoslavia part-timers might earn up to £18 a month although the top players might get £60 a month. In Belgium, which had just started a full-time League in 1960, players might earn £12 and £7 a week; whereas in Holland a top international could expect only around £900 a year. In Sweden, where again most men were part-timers and did not even have club contracts, professionals could earn a maximum of £4 a game. In Portugal a married player might be offered £12 a week while a single man could expect £10. Meanwhile, in Denmark, there were some players on £1,400 a year.

As ever, the top stars earned the top money: in Spain, in 1961, Alfredo Di Stefano lived in a £20,000 house in Madrid suburb, was paid £300 a match and for a European Cup Final appearance he received £900 in bonuses. He also received a personal share of his transfer fee of £14,000. He was a peseta millionaire.

It would be a long time before players in England could expect such riches and most found that their clubs continued to operate private 'maximum' schemes. George Cohen, a player for Fulham and a future England World Cup winner, revealed, 'When they abolished the maximum wage in 1961 I was on about £45, which was three times what my father was earning as a gas-fitter. And when I made the England squad in the 1963–64 season, my wages went up to £80 a week which was far more than the basic wage Nobby (Stiles) was getting at Manchester United, for instance. Where we were worse off at Fulham was in terms of bonuses.'

As for Johnny Haynes, the original £100 a week man, he later recalled, 'Tommy Trinder, my chairman, opened his mouth and, not realising that the maximum wage was going to be abolished, said if it *was* abolished he would certainly pay me £100 a week. Of course, he then had to stick to it. To be fair to him, he did. I think he regretted it, but he had to live with it.'

There was a sting in the tail for Johnny however, 'Fulham did not increase my wages by a penny to the day I retired in 1970!'

4. Free At Last? 1963

Ever since he had become secretary, Cliff Lloyd had been coaxing the union back to living within its means. Administrative costs had been reduced from £1,363 in 1955 to £586 in 1958; and in 1959, with Jimmy Guthrie's expenses and London base gone, the union actually began making regular surpluses, although as the union auditor commented in 1959, 'it will be many more years before damage inflicted in the last decade has been repaired'.

In 1960, despite union subs being increased from 2s to 2s 6d (still a low figure when compared to other unions), membership began to show a gradual increase, although Aston Villa still stubbornly refused to join!

The management committee had been virtually transformed. Now serving were Harry Hough of Bradford (who had stood for the chairmanship against Hill); Jack Campbell of Blackburn Rovers; Ian Dargie of Brentford; Tony Ingham of Queen's Park Rangers Bill Roost of Bristol Rovers; Tommy Cummings of Burnley and Royston Wood of Leeds.

Men like Campbell, Hough, Ingham and Roost were of the same generation as Lloyd and shared the same point of view – that of the solid if unspectacular professional who spends much of his career with one club, the bread and butter player who is the essence of the professional game.

Campbell and Hough, in particular, would play active roles on the committee: outspoken and determined, they, along with Tony Ingham, would press the case of the ordinary player as against the 'stars' and in this respect they would regularly disagree with Jimmy Hill. However, as Jack Campbell said, 'We could argue but we were always good pals; we had some very good meetings and there was never any animosity.'

Personal friendships, in fact, were a key factor in the success of the new committee. For Campbell, the years on the management committee were 'a great experience'. He would pick Cliff Lloyd up from his home near Warrington (in Campbell's car, not Lloyd's, as it would be another 10 years before the union could afford such a luxury) and together they would travel down to London on Saturday night, invariably staying at a bed and breakfast in Earls Court: 'Cliff was always keeping an eye on the expenses and he'd insist we stayed in some right bloody dumps! Rats and all. I'd say, "I know we're only Second Division, Cliff, but this is ridiculous…"'

Harry Hough was also on good personal terms with Cliff Lloyd and, like Campbell, had suffered financial disappointment during his career. A miner during the war, he spent much of his career with Second Division Barnsley whose chairman was none other than Joe Richards, League president. Hough claimed that in all the 12 years he spent at the club, Richards spoke to him just twice – the second time to block a proposed transfer of Hough to Walsall with the words: 'You'll go where I tell you.' Hough eventually moved to Bradford Park Avenue, losing, he claimed, almost £1,200 which the Walsall deal would have guaranteed him.

Hough, Campbell and the rest of the management committee were thus much more of a 'team' than previous groups had been. With Lloyd's administrative shake-up ensuring that lines of communication were simplified and decisions taken rapidly and confidently there was a general sense of involvement, while the old-fashioned virtues of thrift and accountability so dear to Jimmy Fay were reasserted.

The most significant addition to the union's ranks was not a member however. Manchester solicitor George Davies had been invited to give advice during the final days of Jimmy Guthrie and he would serve the union for the next 30 years or more.

Davies and Lloyd were ultimately to form as close a working relationships as Jimmy Fay and Thomas Hinchcliffe had done in the inter-war years, as Davies shared Hinchcliffe's radical zeal for human rights in general and the players' battle for freedom in particular. In addition to his official function he was Lloyd's confidant, strategist and morale booster all in one, a source of reassurance and intellectual strength who would play an important part in winning the many legal and political battles ahead.

The rank-and-file player was less excited by the achievements of the 'strike' year than might at first have been thought, for without freedom of contract such men had little leverage when it came to negotiating a new contract. However, by the time Jimmy Hill had left and Tommy Cummings had taken over as chairman, the management committee had become firmly committed to an alternative line of attack on the retain-and-transfer system – this time through the courts.

It was a step not to be taken lightly. Cliff Lloyd had worked closely with Jimmy Fay for many years and the latter's fears regarding litigation were deep. The last attempt to gain freedom via the courts, the Kingaby case, had almost destroyed the union back in 1912 when Fay had been a member. The vagaries of legal argument and the lack of any secure legal precedent suggested it would be no simple business.

Star players had been straining at the leash where the restrictive contract system was concerned ever since the end of World War Two. In February 1948 a Sunday newspaper revealed that after having asked for a transfer before reluctantly re-signing, Wilf Mannion, Middlesbrough's 'Golden Boy', was having his new house furnished by the club's fans. A local social club was raising money for a 'wedding present' for the superbly talented England inside-forward, who had just moved into a new house with rent paid by the club.

According to Alan Holby of the *Sunday People* this was nothing less than a 'full-blown public subscription fund open to everyone in the town'. Holby felt it revealed the 'humbug' of the game, where subterfuges such as 'wedding gifts' had to be used to pay top players something approaching their true worth. The following season, however, Mannion again refused to re-sign and requested a transfer. This time there was no social club fund; instead, the club issued him a blank refusal. They would not let him go – at any price.

The saga that unfolded and which continued to drag on for the next six months was a strange one. Mannion, it transpired, wanted to move to Oldham where he had been offered a good job outside football. Middlesbrough, although declaring they would not let him go, did the next best thing by putting a £25,000 price tag on his head which they hoped would frighten other clubs away. This failed and both Arsenal and Celtic were to make realistic, if inconvenient, offers for him.

Whether Middlesbrough would have accepted the offers became academic when Mannion declared that he would not be transferred to any club outside of a 20-mile radius of Oldham. He followed this up by announcing that he would refuse to sign for any club that had to pay more than £12,000 for him because he felt the transfer system was a sham. He held out for five months. Legal action was threatened and he was said to have almost signed for Arsenal when a Middlesbrough director turned up on his doorstep with a blank contract – which Mannion, to everyone's surprise, signed. It was said that he was at the end of his tether. He had a chronically ill wife and a newborn child and, in psychological terms, he never really recovered, being a shy and humble man by nature and certainly not one of soccer's 'awkward squad'.

The Mannion case was more about a player's freedom to move than it was about money, although the latter obviously came into it. Mannion was looking to the future and was trying to secure a good job that would relieve him of financial worries. The tenacity of the club's directorate in refusing point-blank in the face of almost universal criticism to allow Mannion the right to such a choice demonstrated how far the system of player control had warped the judgements of those involved in football politics.

It also illustrated other difficult circumstances under which professional footballers laboured. Many Middlesborough fans resented Mannion's decision to ask for a transfer and called him greedy, a 'traitor' and 'disloyal'. The same thing would happen later to Tom Finney when he was similarly presented with a chance to better himself.

Within a year of the Mannion case yet more top players were attempting to break out of the camp. Colombia was temporarily outside the jurisdiction of the world governing body of football, FIFA, and, keen to establish a professional League, had taken to luring foreign nationals to its footballing shores. In 1950 some of the country's top clubs approached England and no fewer than seven top British internationals, among them Trevor Ford, Neil Franklyn and Roy Paul, were tempted to investigate what were, by any standards, lucrative terms.

The Weekly News, Saturday 22 June 1957.

They flew out in farcically secretive fashion, in some cases without even telling their families, but most found the conditions not to their liking and rapidly returned home. Only Charlie Mitten, who had left a Manchester United touring party in America to go to Colombia, decided to stay for a complete season. Most of the players received periods of suspension for their presumption and were transferred by their clubs on their return. The story has been recounted many times but from any angle it was a pathetic event. Professional men scurrying to and fro across the world like boarding school boys breaking out of dorm for a midnight feast and then having to face the headmaster the following morning. In the event they all took their 'six-of-the-best' and shook the hand of the head prefect administering the blows.

Perhaps the most startling of all the furores that preceded George Eastham's challenge in 1963 was the offer made to Preston North End's Tom Finney in 1952. The England team were on a tour of Italy and Tom Finney, then 30 years old but still considered one of the finest wingers of all time, was made an incredible offer.

Prince Roberto Lanza di Trabia, millionaire president of the Sicilian team Palermo, asked to see Finney after a 1–1 draw with Italy. Finney was sharing a room with Ivor Broadis and it was there that the Prince outlined the terms: £7,000 personal signing-on fee; £130 a month in wages; bonuses for results of between £30

George Eastham

An extremely deft and graceful ball-player, George preferred a creative rather than a goalscoring inside-forward role, blessed as he was with tremendous close ball control and the ability to thread a killing pass through a crowded area. He was, however, occasionally erratic, once admitting that he knew within the first five minutes whether he was going to have a good game or not! He had a good pedigree: his father (also George) 'Diddler' Eastham was a Bolton Wanderers and Brentford player between the wars who had won an England cap in 1935. Thus, when George junior won the first of his 19 caps in 1963 they became the first father and son to have played for England. George made football history in another way. When he tried to move from Newcastle United in December 1959 the club refused his request and simply 'retained' him, despite his repeated requests for a transfer. Eastham then left the game after appealing to the Football League Management Committee over his position. One year later, in 1960, Newcastle United and Arsenal finally agreed a transfer deal but, backed by the PFA, George took his case to the High Court in order to test the legality of the retain-and-transfer system and won a significant victory in the fight for players' freedom of contract. A Football League Cup winner in 1972 (he scored the winning goal), George was awarded an OBE in 1973.

and £100; a villa in the Mediterranean; a new, top of the range, continental car; and free travel to Italy for his family.

'I'll never forget Ivor's face when the Prince made the offer,' Finney recalled. 'He went white and kept repeating over and over again that it was a dream and all too good to be true. We talked about nothing else that night but when the Prince came back again the following morning I knew it was more than just pie in the sky. I must admit that the offer began to dominate my thoughts and I remember promising to put the offer to my directors on returning home…'

The Preston North End board of directors refused to consider the offer, even though Palermo offered a £30,000 transfer fee. The board did issue a statement, however, in which the chairman reported that: 'T. Finney had approached him regarding an offer received from an Italian club for his services. Unanimously agreed that the player be informed that we could not accede to this request. This player has been retained with the FA and was expected to re-sign for season 1952–53 on his return from holiday.'

Palermo did not give up, however, and tried to borrow him for a year but the FA declared that 'temporary transfers will not be approved'. The Preston chairman then put a £50,000 transfer fee on Finney's head, effectively ending the affair. What Preston did was illegal and many in the Football League knew it. As far back as the Kingaby case legal soundings had suggested that the retain-and-transfer system would not stand scrutiny in a court of law. It was just a matter of someone, preferably a star player, making a stand.

Finney retired in April 1960, the very same month in which the Professional Footballer's Association was gathering itself to challenge both the retain-and-transfer system and the maximum wage. It was also, by a strange coincidence, at this time that George Eastham of Newcastle United was pressing to be released from his contract. In mid-July he wrote to the League Management Committee applying under rule 26(b) stating that he was unable to arrange his transfer from the club and asking the League's permission to transfer. On 23 July the LMC considered the appeal and decided that the matter was entirely between club and player.

Eastham's original motivation for leaving Newcastle had, he admitted, nothing to do with altruism. 'I wanted to earn more money, so I asked them to get me a job outside football in the afternoons,' he later recalled. 'We only trained in the mornings so I wanted something to occupy me rather than just wasting money or becoming a better snooker player. They said they'd get me a job but nothing was forthcoming, so I went down to London and started selling cork.'

His new employer – offering better wages than £20 a week – turned out to be Ernie Clay, who would later become chairman of Fulham: 'I opened a few doors for him, as my name was in the headlines at the time, and he helped me out.' In the meantime Eastham trained with the amateurs of Reigate and Redhill and played, incongruously, for the TV All-Stars XI alongside Tommy Steele and Mike and Bernie Winters: 'The FA objected strongly to that, so we told them what to do as well. I had no contact with Newcastle at all. The manager was Charlie Mitten, and his attitude was "If you don't play for us, you won't play for anybody".

As the arguments dragged on and the 1960–61 football season began, the PFA saw a rare opportunity to challenge the legal nature of the retain-and-transfer system via a test case in court. Eastham was no controversial firebrand. He had conducted himself with dignity and good sense that contrasted sharply with some of the pronouncements of the Newcastle directors (one of whom declared that he would see Eastham 'shovel coal' before he left Newcastle). Indeed, it was the special nature of the case, the intemperate remarks and questionable actions of certain Newcastle directors that finally convinced expert legal opinion that there was a good possibility of success.

Despite warnings that it might cost a lot of money, Hill, Lloyd and Davies decided to take the chance. On 13 October 1960 a writ was issued on behalf of Eastham alleging that the Newcastle club had deprived him and was still depriving him of the opportunity to earn his living by playing football, and that in doing so the club were acting in unlawful restraint and trade for which Eastham wished to claim damages.

In early November Newcastle United relented and accepted a bid from Arsenal for £47,000 for Eastham who thus re-entered the professional game amid fanfares and glory: 'In the end they just came up to Highbury to sign the transfer forms. There was no signing-on fee, but you were supposed to get a bonus of £150 for each year with the club, so I was due £600, which was omitted from the contract. They said it would be sorted out, so I signed, stupidly, and that was £600 down the drain.'

Understandably, Eastham was no longer interested in legal action. Pressure was put on him to withdraw, particularly as the union 'strike' had seen the maximum wage lifted, but Cliff Lloyd impressed upon him the crucial importance of the action for all footballers and to his credit Eastham consented to allow the action to continue. 'They thought I'd give it up once the transfer went through,' Eastham said, 'but the PFA had spent a lot of money, just about all the funds they had, so I said I would see it through.'

In fact, Eastham's challenge to the system did not occur in a vacuum. Footballers around the world were agitating for change, none more dramatically than the great Raymond Kopa of France. In the summer of 1963 Kopa was suspended by the French FA for making 'indiscreet' remarks concerning the status of professional footballers. Kopa had written in the leading French newspaper, *France Dimanche*, that footballers were 'slaves': 'Today, in the middle of the twentieth century, the professional footballer is the only man who can be bought and sold without any say in the matter.' Kopa's remarks reverberated around the football world. The sporting newspaper *Goles* in Buenos Aires proclaimed: 'In football, plain speaking is a delight to see…Kopa suspended for having denounced the "slave-traders".'

Legal experts in Belgium had also written that the players contract was null and void in the eyes of the law, while in Germany there was unrest among players concerning the 'retaining' clause. A year earlier the England international match against France as well as the entire French Football League programme had been under threat of cancellation unless the French PFA was recognised. Revolution, of a kind, was in the air…

Nevertheless, success in the action that began in the High Court on 11 June 1963 was by no means guaranteed. Eastham's case was a complicated one: he was suing Newcastle United, seven of their directors, manager Charlie Mitten, the Football League and the Football Association.

Cliff Lloyd and George Eastham arrive at the Royal Courts of Justice, London, in the summer of 1963.

Where the charges against the Newcastle club of conspiracy and damages were concerned, the questions and answers revealed a great deal of bitterness. Eastham claimed that Charlie Mitten had made uncomplimentary remarks about him: 'He told me I was big-headed, my hands were too short and pockets too long and that I was unpopular with the other players.' There was even a moment when Eastham had cried when his fiancée had been refused admission to a match. QC Gerald Gardner for Eastham asked Newcastle director William McKeag, 'Did it please you to see him cry?' to which McKeag replied, 'To see anybody cry always cheers me up.' When another director was asked if they thought they might 'starve Eastham out,' he replied, 'I don't like that phrase. Perhaps we might tire him out. That is happening to a lot of players at the moment.'

Where the action against the Football League was concerned, the onus was on the PFA to prove that the Football League was acting in an unlawful way, that the restraint of trade was not justified and that it went further than was necessary to protect their legitimate interests. The League could claim that the restraint of trade was necessary and that without it dire consequences would flow for players and clubs alike, and indirectly for the public.

If the PFA action succeeded the court would formally declare the system unlawful and therefore unenforceable; with such a declaration in hand the union could then force the League to renegotiate the standard contract to bring it in line with recognised principles of English law. In fact, the League had always contended that it would only continue with the retain-and-transfer system unless, or until, a court declared it to be contrary to public policy.

The stakes were extremely high and the sense of personal responsibility caused PFA secretary Cliff Lloyd a great deal of anguish. By nature a worrier, he found the weeks and months of preparation an ordeal. What was more, it soon became apparent that it would be necessary for him to spend a great deal of time in court giving evidence.

Considerable amounts of detail had to be communicated to the judge and a variety of legal officials. In a sense the case, when it was finally heard in June 1963, turned into a complete review of the workings of professional football; all the legal preparation, the submissions, the groundwork and casework could come to naught without a 'star' expert witness to translate it all into something like common sense. It would be Lloyd's responsibility to put forward the arguments, convictions and beliefs for so long ignored, ridiculed and derided by countless League directors and FA administrators whose own points of view had prevailed for over three-quarters of a century simply because there had been no real opportunity to counter them, their ignorance bolstered by myth and crude economic power.

Nervous, sometimes to the point of panic, in the hours before the trial, Lloyd was cool and collected once he stepped into the witness box, so much so that he himself admitted: 'I think I excelled myself, I really do.' He was able, with admirable common sense and convincing logic, to counter the manifest claims by the League that the removal of the retain-and-transfer system would be to the detriment of competition and the professional game as a whole.

That he was the key to the subsequent outcome of the trial was made clear by Justice Wilberforce in his summing up and judgement, given on 4 July 1963, when he made specific reference to Lloyd as 'a witness who seemed to me to be more in touch with the realities of professional football and particularly the considerations affecting the supply and interests of players than any other witness.'

The core of the League's defence of the retain-and-transfer system was that it prevented the powerful clubs from taking all the best players and thus destroying competition. The system protected the weak and this promoted equality, which was good for everyone and thus served the public interest.

Lloyd pointed out, however, that it was open to clubs to offer players longer contracts if they wished (instead of the one-year contracts then insisted upon) and that by staggering contracts clubs could always ensure that at the end of the season they were left with a nucleus of players, thus preventing richer clubs 'snapping up all the best players.' He also pointed to natural checks on player movement – children at local schools for instance – and to the limit on the number of players any club could maintain. A club would employ only so many to fill a particular position and no good forward, for example, would approach a club which already had a number of good forwards on its books.

There were, Lloyd insisted, plenty of good players to go around. Furthermore, he suggested that the removal of the maximum wage made it more likely that players would stay where they were, happy and contented rather than clamouring for a move.

Lloyd's evidence also helped Wilberforce accept the implausibility of other long-held League beliefs: that without the retention system football would be played only in or near large centres of population (in fact, according to Lloyd, the existing system actually worked in favour of the larger towns); that clubs would be discouraged from spending large sums of money 'bringing on' players if they could not recoup that money in transfer fees (here he was able to demonstrate the relatively small amounts of money that clubs actually did spend on developing young players); that the system 'maintained a uniform standard of play between the various divisions' ('rather far-fetched,' commented Wilberforce); that it maintained employment for players ('conjectural,' according to the judge, whereas Lloyd accused the system of driving men *out* of the game); and that it encouraged cooperation between players and clubs and between players and players ('There is no evidence to support this,' Wilberforce concluded).

Thus the retention arguments, repeated ad nauseum down the years with little or no evidence to support them other than various crude assumptions formulated back in the 1890s, were at last reduced to rubble. Wilberforce summed up as follows:

The big question in Soccer this morning: Could Arsenal sign Jimmy Greaves for nothing?

ALL FREE...NOW THE FREE-FOR-ALL

By PETER LORENZO

PROFESSIONAL football in this country has moved into no-man's land.

Nobody — players, officials, clubs, the Football Association, the Football League—knows precisely what is going to happen following yesterday's High Court judgment that the retain and transfer system is illegal.

The players may feel they have won their last and most rewarding battle for complete freedom. But have they?

CONTROL

According to the law of the land this morning a player who has completed his contract is a "free man." Free to sign for any club who wants him. But the laws of the Football League, who control 2,700 professionals, say he is not.

If, for example, Jimmy Greaves, for whom the Spurs paid £100,000 two years ago, has not re-signed then, according to the judgment, he is free to go—but where?

Could Arsenal sign him for nothing? The law of the land would indicate Yes. But in all the jubilation, Regulation 56 of the Football League has been forgotten. It decrees:

ADEQUATE

"No transfer shall be registered until the transferring club has notified the League that the fee has been paid or its payment adequately secured."

In other words, the Football League would still not allow Jimmy Greaves to play for Arsenal unless Spurs had received a satisfactory transfer fee.

So the players have cleared one hurdle and are now faced with another.

The game will, of course, go on.

ACCEPTABLE

I predict there will NOT be the anarchy and chaos that Newcastle's William McKeag anticipates.

Players will not hold clubs at gun-point.

A new system acceptable to all will be evolved.

My solution is a contract realistically related to the value of a player or to the transfer fee paid for him.

In short a star's contract for a star performer. If Tommy Steele is worth £100,000 to an impresario, then he gets rewards in keeping with that value . . . with the impresario making certain in black-and-white legal terms that he has a chance of getting his money back or even making a profit as a result of their association.

So to satisfy the Tommy Steeles of the Soccer world and to protect themselves, the clubs will have to offer players contracts for a minimum of five and maybe even 10 years.

If during that period either club or player wish to end the contract, the unexpired portion of the contract would be sold.

FORGET IT

If any "freed" footballers have been conjuring up thoughts of winging off to pick up fortunes in Italy or any other sunny parts, they can forget about them.

The regulations of the world governing body, FIFA, prevent such moves.

But, perhaps more deterring, is the following information that was given me yesterday by the Italian Federation official responsible for contract agreements:

"A player in Italy is part of his club's heritage. He has no power to leave when he wants. His future and moves are completely dependant on the will of his club.

"This may seem harsh, but it is the only way of protecting a club who have paid our large sums either in transfer fees or in developing a player."

To sum up, our Soccer slaves have been freed yet again . . . but this time with nowhere to go and no-one with whom to play football.

Daily Herald, Friday 5 July 1963.

'It is claimed as evidence that those who know best consider it (the system) to be in the best interests of the game. I do not accept that line of argument. The system is an employer's system set up in an industry where the employers have established a monolithic front and where it is clear for the purposes of negotiation the employers are more strongly organised than the employees…'

Therefore, he was adamant:

'I conclude that the combined retain-and-transfer system as existing at the date of the writ is an unjustifiable restraint of trade…'

The union had thus obtained the sought for declaration and Cliff Lloyd's personal nightmare was over. Gone were the days when he would be driven by taxi to the High Court confessing to George Davies, head in hands, that he was 'worried sick'. Thirty years later he still could not recall those times without a shudder. For in a sense he had done almost single-handedly what the profession he represented had been unwilling to do for itself. In a very real sense Lloyd stood during those crucial few days for all his professional forebears: for Charlie Roberts, Colin Veitch, Billy Meredith, Jimmy Fay and Sammy Crooks – and for Jimmy Guthrie (who could be seen throughout the trial sitting in the press gallery making assiduous notes).

In October 1963 George Eastham, the man whose case had set in motion the dismantling of one of the most Byzantine of employer/employee relationships, stepped on to the Wembley turf to play for England against FIFA in a celebration of one hundred years of the Football Association.

A month later, at the PFA's 53rd AGM in Manchester, George Davies concluded his review of the year with this tribute:

'Cliff Lloyd has always impressed us and we think also impressed those present when he gave evidence as being probably more knowledgeable and more aware of the detailed practical situation of the football industry than perhaps anyone else.

That he manages to be so, and that in addition he manages to be both human and compassionate in all his dealings with everyone without ever losing sight of the need to be tough when necessary and without ever lacking the capacity to be so, is an immense tribute to him. That the PFA has achieved so much in recent years is an acknowledgement of the courage and determination of all members. It is also in great part a tribute to the immense skill of your secretary…'

PART FOUR
MAKING A DIFFERENCE
1964–81

1. 'You Lucky Footballers!' 1964–67

The George Eastham judgement proved to be a significant victory in a very long war. Justice Wilberforce had not condemned the transfer system outright – only when it was combined with the draconian 'retention' clause. He had also dismissed Eastham's claims for damages against Newcastle United and the individuals involved in his transfer wrangle. As a consequence the PFA had to pay substantial costs, though nothing like as catastrophic as Lloyd had feared.

The immediate aftermath saw the PFA in conciliatory mood, prepared to offer an olive branch to the Football League and renegotiate, step by step, a more equitable players' contract.

Cliff Lloyd put it thus in 1964:

> 'If the Football League Ltd want to have transfer fees and a transfer system they must agree to do it in such a way that does not demand of the player an unacceptable tie on him while he is waiting to be transferred…It must be achieved without fettering the players. For it is the fetter that makes it unlawful.'

Jimmy Guthrie accused the Players' Union of making a tactical error at this crucial stage in the game's history by not pressing its advantage harder: 'With the goal wide open and the opposition defence in ruins, the PFA put the ball wide.' The facts suggest otherwise. As solicitor George Davies emphasised in 1963: 'Your Association is in the unhappy position of being opposed by a powerful monopoly employer upon whose power the Eastham decision made a vital but limited impression…'

Negotiations to establish a new contract for professional players began on 19 November 1963 and were to be carried out through a new joint negotiating committee, one of the important gains for the PFA from the 1961 agreement. By April 1964 the details of the new contract were settled and proved acceptable to both clubs and players. In essence, the new rules were as follows. Every player's contract would now be freely negotiated between club and player and would include, along with the basic weekly wage, everything related to bonuses, benefit payments and additional payments on transfer and talent money. Each contract would now include one option in favour of the club for renewal on terms no less advantageous than those in the original contract and for the same period – unless mutually agreed otherwise. If the club did not want to exercise the option at the end of the original period the player was free to go without a fee on his head. At the end of the second period the club had the right to make an offer to renew the contract, once again on the same terms, unless mutually agreed otherwise. If the club wanted to transfer the player the original contract continued to run until the transfer was completed. If, however, the player was unhappy he could appeal to the League Management Committee. If this brought no satisfaction, he could take his case to an independent tribunal consisting of one representative from the Football League and one from the PFA under the chairmanship of the joint negotiating committee chairman.

The independent tribunal, a key element in the new system, decided all aspects of the contract, including the eventual fee. The dates by which clubs had to notify players and by which players had to indicate their acceptance or otherwise remained the same. What was crucial, however, was that whatever the situation a player continued to receive his full wages. As Cliff Lloyd put it: 'The new agreement means that the hardships experienced by players under the old retain-and-transfer system have now been eliminated.'

It meant a great deal more besides. Although the 'option' clauses were quite clearly weighted in favour of the clubs, the fact that an independent tribunal eventually settled matters if the player pressed on with his demand to leave meant that clubs were increasingly inclined to meet the players' demands. As David Green, union solicitor, put it: 'The new contract was a combination of what was written and real life.'

As a player was guaranteed release sooner or later the club often had little to gain by hanging on to him. It had to calculate whether it was worth continuing to pay the player, often a very good wage, or whether a free transfer would be more economic. The new system worked particularly well for men approaching the end of their playing career. Free transfers helped such older players as it was cheaper for new clubs to sign them on. For the highly valuable players the new system substantially increased their bargaining powers.

The clubs were thus able to hold on to what they increasingly saw as a vital element in their financial set-up – the inherent 'worth' of players as realised on the transfer market – while the player now had a mechanism that both ensured his financial well-being and offered freedom if desired. Within a few years the numbers of players held on transfer lists dropped dramatically while the number of free transfers rose. It was a long way from the freedom of contract enjoyed by the majority of the population, but it was a major step away from the conditions of service players had laboured under since the turn of the century.

Predictably, not all club directors were happy with the new conditions. In August 1964 Bob Lord of Burnley spoke for many when he complained, 'the player today has never had it so good.'

The years immediately following the successful battle for the 'two freedoms' saw great changes in the financial and social position of professional footballers, but they were achieved against the backdrop of declining attendances and the ever-present fear of club

Malcolm Musgrove Chairman 1963–66
Malcolm joined West Ham United in December 1953 after national service with the Royal Air Force. At West Ham he soon established himself as a left-winger, making his League debut in 1954 against Brentford. He went on to make 301 League and Cup appearances for the Hammers and was leading goalscorer in both the 1959–60 and 1960–61 seasons when his goals did much to keep relegation worries at bay. He joined Leyton Orient as player-coach in December 1962 before retiring in 1966, after which he held a variety of managerial and coaching positions at Leicester City, Manchester United, Torquay United, NASL sides Connecticut Bicentennials and Chicago Sting, Charlton Athletic, Exeter City, Plymouth Argyle and Shrewsbury Town. Malcolm died in September 2007.

bankruptcy. English football was an increasingly schizophrenic affair. On the one hand there was the relatively new glamour and riches of European club competitions and the successful 1966 World Cup bringing in ever more lucrative sponsorship and TV riches. On the other hand there was a residual bitterness on the behalf of club directorates confronted by players' new freedoms, and the resultant threat to turn the clock back to retention clauses and maximum wages.

In fact, the football authorities reacted at first with a mixture of resentment, fear and sometimes sheer spite. As top players wages started to rise and the distant prospect of freedom of contract loomed, dire predictions were the order of the day. Newspaper headlines declared '1,000 on the scrapheap' as clubs threatened to cut their squads drastically in order to survive. Wolves manager Stan Cullis announced in February 1964: 'This is the moment of truth for the players. After two years of unlimited pay here comes the pay-off.' Tommy Trinder was even more emphatic. Mr '£100 a week' said, while predicting that Fulham would have to reduce its present squad from 26 to 18, 'I think we need to reinstate the maximum wage clause.' Bob Wall, Arsenal secretary, disagreed but felt that fans might have to pay more in the near future. Such doom-laden predictions would accompany every subsequent move towards an equitable contract.

The press, even those papers once sympathetic to the players' cause, could not resist presenting all professionals as incredibly wealthy. There was a tendency to criticise the quality of the product being supplied. With all this money being earned, it was asked, why have skill levels not increased? Why was the game not more attractive? The professional player, having repeatedly claimed the remuneration of show business stars, was now faced with demands for more 'entertainment'.

Typical would be the *Daily Herald* series run in 1964 entitled 'Soccer In The Dock': 'For two seasons players have enjoyed the New Deal. Many of them now earn show-biz wages, drive expensive cars and live it up. For two seasons fans have wondered when the football is going to start…'

According to the *Herald*, the standard of play had not improved, in fact, it had declined. Rough play had increased with more men being sent off, 'Childishness. Gamesmanship. Orthodoxy. They have increased rather than diminished since the New Deal.' Players, meanwhile, were 'raking the money in'. Liverpool players had recently earned £120 in a week (during which time they had also played three games) comprising a basic wage, a crowd bonus, a win bonus, a draw bonus and appearance money. Everton players had earned £200 over the same period. The players were spending it too: 'Centre-forward Alex Young has bought a £3,500 house – cash down. Goalkeeper Gordon West purchased a £500 car – straight from his wallet. He is 19.' Cliff Lloyd appealed for patience and insisted that the higher wages were necessary to entice young talent into the game: 'It takes time, but I think the new deal will attract more youngsters into the profession…'

However, patience has always been a commodity in short supply where professional football is concerned. At the Football League's 1964 AGM a shock decision was taken to unilaterally axe the players' Provident Fund and substitute instead an insurance scheme for clubs and players. Although the League negotiated an increase in the annual sum paid to it by the pools promoters from £250,000 million to £500,000 million per annum within days of the decision, poverty was the excuse for terminating the players' financial safety net.

League chairman Richards explained that the provident fund was being scrapped because clubs simply could not afford it: 'So many clubs now face financial difficulties now that the players can get unlimited pay…' As for consulting the PFA over such a drastic move he was dismissive: 'We can't consult them over every move we make. After all, we are still the employers.'

Worse was to come. On 7 July the FA, also without warning, gave the PFA six months notice that it intended to cease paying the lump sum of £4,000 towards the insurance scheme agreed under the 1956 TV Agreement. It later transpired that the League had put pressure on the FA to withdraw from the scheme in order that its own insurance proposal was accepted as a fait-accompli.

PFA chairman Malcolm Musgrove, expressing shock at the lack of consultation, indicated that the union would be approaching the Ministry of Labour for help as well as raising the whole issue at the joint negotiating committee.

A truce was finally agreed on 29 April 1965 when the union accepted a Football League deal offering £40,000 for the provident fund for players earning under £2,000 per annum, plus a club-administered insurance scheme offering £750 for permanent disablement. Where the FA was concerned, a threatened ban on players appearing on TV including the FA Cup Final produced a change of heart. The TV money would ultimately be redirected to help the PFA set up an Education Society.

More worrying for the image of the professional footballer at this time was the continuing cancer of corruption, in particular the taking of bribes to fix matches. In 1963, just prior to the Eastham case arriving at court, a scandal involving various lower league players and betting was uncovered. Several players were suspended for life. In 1964 an even more disturbing case involving top England players cast a pall over the game and professional players in general.

As the PFA prepared to defend the lifting of the maximum wage against calls to reinstate a wages ceiling, secretary Cliff Lloyd had found it necessary to declare:

> 'Despite the recent bribery allegations I do not think that public opinion would be against us if we have to fight to keep the present wage scale'.

In April 1964 at a special PFA delegates meeting in Manchester to discuss the issue of pay, one of the principal individuals accused of bribery, England international Tony Kay, was present. The PFA Management Committee felt it necessary to issue a warning to all players regarding bribes. The PFA, it said, was 'alarmed and distressed at the allegations. PFA will not tolerate assist or support any player proved to have received any reward for affecting the result of a match.' What with even more sordid stories emerging concerning

Noel Cantwell Chairman 1966–67

Noel joined West Ham as a 20-year-old full-back in 1952. A natural athlete who moved with grace and sure instincts, he was a solid, thoughtful performer who could also play centre-forward, a position he occasionally filled for both the club and the Irish Republic (for whom he also played cricket). After 245 League games for the Hammers, Cantwell joined Manchester United for £30,000 where he followed in a long line of fine captains and led the side to victory in the 1963 FA Cup Final. He even had a song written in his honour, The Great Noel, sung to the tune of The First Noel. On retirement in 1967 he became Coventry manager. After further managerial spells with Peterborough United and the Boston Tea Men, he managed the New Inn public house in Peterborough. Noel died in September 2005.

Terry Neill Chairman 1968–70

Terry joined Arsenal from Bangor, Northern Ireland, in 1959, making his debut as replacement for Tommy Docherty in 1960. Manager Billy Wright soon switched him from wing-half to centre-half, however, and in a 10-year career at Highbury he played 241 League games. As a defender he was strong, intelligent and uncompromising; a player who could be physical or skilful as the situation demanded. He won 59 caps for Northern Ireland, one of the highlights of his career being when he scored the winning goal against England in his 50th international match. After his playing career ended he became Tottenham's youngest-ever manager, a distinction he would later achieve with Arsenal. After leaving the game Terry had a successful business career which included running Terry Neill's sports bar/brasserie on Holborn Viaduct.

the use of pep pills such as benzedrene by Everton players, the image the public was receiving of the professional footballer was as depressingly distorted as ever.

There was little the PFA could do about such issues at this point in its history but it did make significant strides in presenting itself to the public as an intelligent, moderate and responsible body. Management committee members during the 1960s included Malcom Musgrove, Noel Cantwell, Phil Woosnam and Maurice Setters. Musgrove and Cantwell and later Terry Neill – all of whom would serve as PFA chairmen – were examples of the new breed of player-coach in direct line of descent from that great innovator and teacher, Walter Winterbottom. They also played their football for some of the most entertaining and progressive-minded clubs in the land. Phil Woosnam, a business graduate, served on the PFA Management Committee for a year before setting off for the US where he became Commissioner of the North American Soccer League and a champion of progressive ideas where the presentation of the game was concerned.

Nobby Lawton, Nobby Stiles, Bobby Charlton and Terry Venables were also invited to stand for the management committee as secretary Cliff Lloyd made a determined effort to raise the union's profile. His policy of inviting articulate, thoughtful men onto the committee only highlighted the wastage of talent where the game at the very top was concerned. Men such as Musgrove, Woosnam, Cantwell and Neill, along with Freddie Goodwin, Derek Dougan and Bobby Robson – all of whom were elected to the committee between the years 1961 and 1967 – could have played a significant role in changing the way football was governed in the 1970s and beyond, had not both the Football League and the FA closed their ranks to ex-professionals. As it was, PFA committee men either became embroiled in football management or they left the game entirely. Not that club management was always a dead end: witness the changes Jimmy Hill attempted at Coventry City during his tenure as manager there, introducing novel ideas to bring in the crowds that he had learned on his trips to Canada. Derek Dougan would also make an enlightened and enterprising manager and club executive. Such innovation ultimately depended upon directors being prepared to take a gamble and such men were distressingly few and far between.

The battle to keep the provident fund, however, would be the last such open conflict between the PFA and football's employers and administrators for some years. With the staging of the World Cup in 1966 and the false dawn of increased attendances in its wake, not to mention the necessity for a period of reflection on behalf of players then beginning to negotiate their own contracts for the first time, a kind of peace broke out. There was a lot to digest and much with which to come to terms.

Nevertheless, the PFA was broadening its horizons. Solicitor David Green of the George Davies practice reported to the 1966 AGM that his firm, 'have worked with your management committee on the considerable and growing number of questions that arise within the industry as a whole and with its economic and long-term development'. Referring to the 'specialist economic intelligence units that many US unions now employ', Green suggested that while the PFA was not a large union, the Davies law firm had made considerable efforts to ensure that the association 'had adequate briefs in considering current issues both within the industry and with several enquiries now being carried out at national level'.

Increasingly, as economists, government departments and academics began to look more closely at professional football, the emphasis where the PFA was concerned would move away from the militancy of pitched battles into the more studious world of reports and commissions.

In 1967, to celebrate the Diamond Jubilee of the founding of the union in 1907, Cliff Lloyd and secretary Miss Hardman moved into rather more spacious offices at the Corn Exchange. Lloyd, while drawing attention to the anniversary, commented:

'Never in the history of the Association has the organisation been in such a strong financial position and the Association has been successful in achieving several of the objects for which it was formed…'

2. Duncan's on the Dole! 1967–78

'Anything short of total freedom is an imposition on players…All formulas set up were designed for one purpose, to safeguard the financial interest of clubs with literally no concern for the players.'
George Davis, November 1974 AGM

Sir Norman Chester

In 1966, following representations by the Football League and the FA to the Labour government concerning the 'deteriorating financial position of the game and the need for cash for its improvement and administration', the then Secretary of State for Education and Science appointed Mr Norman Chester CBE and Warden of Nuffield College to chair an enquiry.

Its terms of reference were: 'To enquire into the state of Association Football at all levels, including the organisation, management, finance and administration, and the means by which the game may be developed for the public good; and to make recommendations.'

In 1968 it published its recommendations, which must have made hard reading for both parent organisations, in particular the Football League given that it was theoretically committed to implementing many of the report's recommendations in the hope that the government might set up a Football Levy Board similar to the Racing Levy Board to funnel much-needed cash into the game.

Chief among the committee's many wide-ranging recommendations was the suggestion that the existing players' contract system should be swept clean away. While acknowledging that the transfer system was 'deeply rooted' in football, Chester nevertheless insisted that it was 'not consistent with professional players' professional standing and must alter'. The committee recommended various fundamental changes, such as that clubs should issue longer contracts with players free to move on at the end of each contract. There would be a five-year changeover period during which clubs would be able to adjust their finances. As the report said: 'It will provide a better moral basis for the transfer system' while 'the new system would add to the dignity of the professional player'.

The transfer system itself would remain and men could still be bought and sold in the traditional way during the period of the contract. However, Chester called into question the core belief of the Football League that the transfer system provided poorer clubs with the opportunity to raise cash in order to continue trading and that it kept money circulating within the game. In 1963 Justice Wilberforce presiding over the Eastham case had accepted this theory in the absence of facts and figures to prove it otherwise. The Chester committee, by contrast, had carried out some research and confronted the long-held idea head-on.

To the bemusement of many League club directors, facts suggested the very opposite – that the transfer system saw a general movement of players down the divisions rather than up. According to Chester: 'Whatever may have been the position at one time, it is not now the case that lower divisions are the nursery for the First and Second Divisions and that transfer money flows accordingly from the top to the bottom…'

The Chester committee's recommendations were music to the ears of the PFA. Its immediate response was to draw up a list of issues and demands based on the recommendations that touched on all areas of concern upon which serious negotiations with both the League and the FA might be based. At the 1969 PFA AGM Cliff Lloyd outlined the demands as follows: changes in the option clauses in players' contracts so that players were placed on an equal footing with clubs where contract renewal was concerned; a proper pension scheme to replace the provident fund; a new standard form of contract; plus a complete reform of the structure of disciplinary procedures.

Derek Dougan Chairman 1971–78

Derek was one of the great characters of the game, and was probably the most talented player to serve as Players' Union chairman. He was a deadly effective centre-forward, scoring over 120 goals for Wolverhampton Wanderers with whom he won his single medal in their victorious 1974 League Cup side. He also helped Wolves win promotion to the First Division at the end of his first season with the club, scoring nine goals in 11 games including a hat-trick on his Molineux debut on 25 March 1967. He was Wolves's top scorer in 1967–68 with 17 goals and topped the scoring charts again the following season. In 1971–72 he helped Wolves reach the Final of the UEFA Cup. He also won 43 Northern Irish international caps. Known to most supporters as 'The Doog', he also earned the nickname 'Cheyenne' at Blackburn Rovers where, anticipating David Beckham by some 40 years, he shaved his hair into a Mohican style. He later shaved his hair off completely, an outrageous thing to do in the early 1960s. His career would always involve daring and flamboyance during a period when British football could boast many a 'wayward genius'. After leaving the first-class game he managed Kettering Town, then in 1982, seven years after leaving Molineux, he returned as chairman and chief executive. He was the author of a number of books on football, including an impressive novel, The Footballer, and a book about the history of professional players, On The Spot. As chairman Derek was a passionate champion of players' rights, especially contractual freedom, and he worked tirelessly on ways of adapting and reforming the transfer system. He was also instrumental in helping to transform the image of the PFA, developing the PFA Awards event as well as appearing on television as an erudite pundit during the World Cup of 1970. Derek died in June 2007.

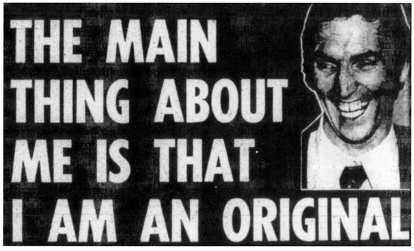

The Sun, Wednesday 28 January 1970.

Once again, however, the very mechanics of negotiation would prove to be the barrier to progress. The arguments might have been won, the facts might seem incontrovertible but without the necessary three-quarters majority of League clubs no reforms would be possible.

A package, agreed upon by both management committees, was put to the League clubs in May 1970. It included four key proposals: abolition of the option clause in players' contracts without mutual agreement; a pension scheme for all players to be paid for by a levy on transfer fees; a £15 minimum wage; and the inclusion of apprentices in the system. However, this far from radical package was thrown out completely by the clubs, a decision that more or less ended the useful life of the national negotiating committee. It would meet only twice more until 1974!

Just as in the mid-1950s when the joint negotiating committee had provided the League with a perfect dead end down which to shunt the Players' Union, now the national negotiating committee would serve no other purpose but to absorb time and energy and nullify all effort. As Cliff Lloyd put it some time afterwards: 'It was plainly a waste of time negotiating with a body that did not have the authority to settle what had been agreed upon.'

By 1971 an impasse had been reached. Progress towards the ultimate goals – freedom of contract and a modern pension scheme – had slowed to a snail's pace. With the PFA ruling out militant action, only a new government bringing with it new union legislation would succeed in getting the process moving again.

Commission on Industrial Relations Report 1973

The Conservative government's Industrial Relations Act of 1971 would cause the trades union movement a great deal of strife. The new laws limited wildcat strikes and placed limitations on legitimate strikes. It also established a National Industrial Relations Court which was empowered to grant injunctions as necessary to prevent injurious strikes as well as settle a variety of labour disputes.

The Trades Union Congress, under the leadership of general secretary Vic Feather, campaigned against the legislation with a nationwide 'Kill the Bill' campaign. On 12 January 1971 the TUC held a 'day of action' in protest with a march through London. In March 1,500,000 members of the Amalgamated Engineering Union staged a one-day strike. After the bill received royal assent in September 1971 the TUC voted to require its member unions not to comply with its provisions (which included registering as a union under the Act). The Transport and General Workers Union was twice fined for contempt of court over its refusal to comply. However, some smaller unions did comply and 32 were suspended from membership of the TUC at the 1972 congress, including the PFA. It would be another 20 years before it would be invited to return.

The move must have broken Jimmy Guthrie's heart, but there were significant gains to be made. For the PFA the act offered the hope that real negotiating machinery might be set up or, failing that, the existing national negotiating committee might be given some 'teeth'. In May 1973, therefore, the management committee approached both the Departments of Employment and Environment with the result that the Ministers of State referred the vexed question of industrial relations between professional footballers and their employers to a commission on industrial relations. This body would 'seek ways to promote any improvements in their relations that appear to be necessary or desirable', and while its recommendations would not be binding they would carry considerable weight in any subsequent case brought before the Industrial Court.

The move, coming as it did after three frustrating years of negotiating stalemate, was not enough to quell growing ripples of discontent with the association's apparent lack of progress. For the first time since the days of Jimmy Guthrie, criticism of the association appeared in print by some who felt a more 'radical' approach was needed.

Foul magazine, an independent periodical modelling itself on *Private Eye*, would provide a radical voice during the 1970s dedicated to opposing what it called the 'greed, vested interests and phoney glamour' that it felt increasingly characterised the British game. In its self-appointed role as guardian of football's soul, *Foul* took an occasional swipe at the PFA, particularly its leadership which it felt was 'feeble' and 'fainthearted' in its approach to football's governing bodies. The association's 'collusion' with 'Tory' legislation, which the rank and file union movement was fighting tooth and nail to rescind, was clearly at the root of some of this ire.

Eamon Dunphy, a professional with Millwall and a future journalist and author of the classic pro-footballer's 'diary' *Only a Game?*, used the columns of *Foul* in August 1973 to personalise the issue. 'Since Jimmy Hill,' Dunphy wrote, 'no one else has emerged with the character to unite the union behind any of its demands.' *Foul* editor Alan Stewart went further and described chairman Derek Dougan as 'smug', suggesting that his real aim in life was to secure a comfortable manager's job. Dunphy wrote, 'Chairmen of the PFA never seem to be men with radical views; and, once there, they use the post for advertising their conformity and responsibility to club chairmen.' Cliff Lloyd was moved to point out that Dougan – like all chairmen – worked extremely hard for no pay, normally during precious free time. The fact that PFA chairmen sometimes became managers was, according to Lloyd, all to their credit: 'This simply confirms that they possess the necessary qualifications which must surely include leadership.'

More damaging for the PFA at this time, however, were criticisms from players growing increasingly frustrated with a contract system that was becoming ever more ill-suited to the times. In the summer of 1974, almost simultaneous with the publication of the CIR report, rising star Duncan McKenzie was hitting the headlines with his one-man stand against Nottingham Forest. McKenzie was a 24-year-old, extremely talented forward with a knack for unusual publicity. He once leapt a mini, could throw a golf ball the length of a football pitch and, in his relations with managers, never suffered fools gladly. Intelligent and eloquent, he had seen his stock rise over the previous year. After a loan spell with Mansfield Town, he had scored 28 goals for Forest and been selected for the full England touring party that toured Eastern Europe. When his contract came up for renewal he felt a pay rise was reasonable and so approached manager Allan Brown in early July. The club's offer was nowhere near his own estimate and stalemate ensued. The club indicated that a transfer request would be turned down and when McKenzie tried to arrange a further meeting he was told by Brown that he would have to wait as he was off for a week's holiday.

Thus far it seemed a typical summer storm in a tea cup, the ritual dance endured by many a player seeking a pay rise and normally settled by the start of the season. However, McKenzie was incensed by his treatment and decided to take a stand. He told reporters: 'I went to the ground yesterday to have a talk with the manager Allan Brown but he wasn't available and getting no satisfaction I asked to be given my cards. Naturally I don't

Mirror Sport, Tuesday 9 July 1974.

PART OF THE UNION

Or, The Mill - Owners' Charter

EAMONN DUNPHY, of Millwall and Eire, on the role of the players' union.

THE IMAGE of the Professional Footballer as a glamorous show-business type, surrounded by pretty girls and flash cars, is firmly implanted in most people's minds. I know him more accurately as the deeply insecure family man or the tearful, failed Apprentice. Getting that image across is what the Professional Footballers Association, the players union, should be all about.

And while it is often said that the Trade Union movement in Britain is too powerful, the equation between Union and power in football contains an element of black comedy.

The PFA is a small organisation comprising two fulltime officials and fifteen hundred largely apathetic members. We have in fact, practically no say in the games' decision-making process, there is no consultation process, and very little consideration of the players' point of view. It is a situation no normal Trade Union or professional body would tolerate for a moment.

Consequently, our conditions of employment are such that a reincarnated 19th century mill owner would be gratified to see that restrictive practices so dear to his heart are alive and well in football.

Men can still be bought and sold in the market place, apprentices (sic), are callously dismissed on completion of their apprenticeship, and the possibility of retirement through injury, without compensation, looms over every game – an additional tension in an already high-risk profession.

The existence of such conditions could be regarded as a massive indictment of the PFA. However, this would be an oversimplification. The unenviable task of securing civilised working conditions falls almost wholly on Cliff Lloyd, the Union secretary. He brings to the job of negotiating with soccer's abrasive bosses a rare dedication, allied to a keen concern with the plight of his members, particularly those in the lower divisions.

He is, however, badly handicapped by the apathy that exists among the superstars employed by the wealthier First Division clubs, most of whom do not bother to attend the AGM, the annual gathering that attempts to gauge the players feelings in order to develop a coherent policy.

It is ironic that those who are the main beneficiaries of the one significant gain achieved by Union militancy, the abolition of the maximum wage, should now cripple the organisation that served their interests so well, by lack of interest. The removal of the maximum wage was only achieved after a long and bitter struggle with soccers' administrators. It took the inspired leadership of Lloyd and Jimmy Hill to overcome the apathetic membership and relentless bosses. Since Hill, no one else has emerged with the character to unite the Union behind any of its demands

That was over a decade ago – since then the rate of progress has been painfully slow. The slave mentality still exists among professional footballers, Despite the powerful weapons at our disposal, among them the Government sponsored Chester Report, which bitterly attacked the term of employment in football, we have failed to mount the militant campaign necessary to achieve real freedom. Given the nature of many of the game's administrators, progress will only be made as a result of sustained pressure.

The PFA cannot move in that direction without the support of all its members, particularly the game's star players. If any of these stars doubt the need for action they should look more closely at the situation in their own clubs Wealthy clubs are frequently the most ruthless exploiters o players, particularly youngsters who sign on as apprentices. Their economic strength allows them to employ the full quota of 15 boys in the freely admitted hope of finding perhaps a couple with First Division potential. What happens to the remaining dozen in terms of educatior and opportunity should provide food for thought for even the most irresponsible superstar.

In their treatment of older and more established players these clubs also leave a lot to be desired. Competent professionals are often retained in reserve teams, for instance, thus being denied the opportunity to seek more fulfilling employment in a lower division.

Obviously, there is no cause for complacency at any leve of football. And it is the job of the PFA to combat apathy where it exists, in any form. I believe this can be done by raising the issues wherever the opportunity occurs.

There must be more discussion of the problems among players, perhaps through Regional Councils. Players' easy, and constant access to the media should be used to present a more realistic picture to the fans who may understandably mistake the high living excesses of the few as typical of the footballer generally. 🌚

The debate that raged in the pages of Foul Magazine, 1973.

DOOG PUTS THE BOOT IN

The Players Union Chairman replies to Eamonn Dunphy

DEREK DOUGAN LTD., 120 WROTTESLEY ROAD,
TETTENHALL, WOLVERHAMPTON

Dear Eamonn

This is an open letter (though I prefer closed letters as a rule) about some scathing things you had to say concerning the P.F.A. in the September issue of FOUL. To say that I am exasperated and frustrated by a few P.F.A. dissenters is an understatement. You give the impression that the P.F.A. committee does absolutely nothing but sit around and idle away the time.

It does not take much research to discover that committee members devote considerable time and energy to improving the welfare and fundamental rights of players. I agree with you that big-name stars are not noted for their active interest in the Association and its affairs. Few of them attend the annual meetings. This is a regrettable example to younger, less celebrated members. But even before the maximum wage was abolished the situation was the same. Perhaps the stars think they don't need the P.F.A. – a short-sighted view.

But for the magnificent team that assists and advises the P.F.A. committee – that is, Cliff Lloyd (Secretary), Miss Hardman, and George Davies (Legal Adviser) – the Association would not be able to operate.

What dismays me about your article is its absence of information about the achievements of the P.F.A. You seem to be under the impression that we are ineffective if not, indeed, wholly impotent.

But since 1961 we have won the George Eastham case, got a percentage of transfer fees for players, and obtained independent tribunals to adjudicate in disputes involving players' contracts. To me this is even more important than the lifting of the maximum wage, which was inevitable anyway.

We fought and won the John Cook case in March, 1972, establishing the right of a player to be re-registered by the F.A. when he returns to England after fulfilling a contract abroad. The Ernie Machin case was won, though it could not have been foreseen that the decision would be reversed on appeal. Having followed that case minutely, I am still baffled by the reversal.

A new disciplinary procedure was introduced a year ago, with a further right of appeal should a case go against a player. This surely was a major step forward.

Two years ago the P.F.A. appointed Bob Kerry as Education Officer, and in a short space of time we are now seeing remarkable progress, because of the response by the vast majority of our members. I must point out that not all the response is coming from the lower divisions. No one can point an accusing finger at the P.F.A. and say that they are not offering to players the opportunity to add another string to their bow.

I would like to point out that in the P.F.A. there are 2,500 members and four not two full-time officers, as you mistakenly say. In the eight years I have been on the committee it has always been P.F.A. policy to treat all members as equal. You know as well as anyone that our professional organisation is different from any other. You should also know that there are many issues regarding players' welfare and rights with which the P.F.A. has dealt. Here obviously I can only mention a few of the more important.

The P.F.A. has not been dragging its feet, as you are trying to make out. The way it is at the moment constituted means that the committee is severely handicapped. What I look forward to is, freedom of contract, and the implementation of a pension scheme for all members of the P.F.A. Then we shall have given you and everyone else a Utopian Association!

I welcome criticism from members if it is constructive and well informed. But I cannot accept you, Eamonn, as a member. Your subscription has lapsed and you appear, therefore, to have disqualified yourself from present membership, and also from the role of critic. I am sure, however, that Cliff Lloyd will be delighted to receive back dues.

Yours sincerely,
Derek Dougan
10th September 1973

want to finish playing but I am still unhappy about the terms which I have been offered for the new season.'

Club secretary Ken Smales said that he had no option but to allow McKenzie to have his cards but insisted that McKenzie would not be joining any other professional club. McKenzie was adamant: 'Unless something drastic happens, I won't be at the City ground when the lads report back for training on Wednesday.'

The *Mirror* ran a headline, 'Duncan on the Dole!' and McKenzie then launched into his association in no uncertain terms:

'My generation will not put up with it. Many things are wrong with the British contract system but the PFA are not militant enough and there is a complete lack of communication with the rank and file. Young as I may be I have discovered just how unjust our system is, not so much to my own cost as to the cost of players who may benefit if I stick out. In any other business I could resign from one company and take a similar job elsewhere. In football you can fail to get on with the manager, but you cannot go and play elsewhere because the club holds your registration. I also question the right of the FA to fix a players share of his transfer fee at five per cent. Somebody has got to make a stand against these iniquities. Professional footballers in general are more intelligent nowadays. My age group will not tolerate the anomalies of the past. I am prepared to seek alternative employment. If necessary I will go on the dole.'

What he was not prepared to do was challenge the system in the courts as Eastham had done back in 1961. His lonely vigil, training in a local park while waiting to see who would come and rescue him, ended a month later when Brian Clough paid £250,000 to take the contract 'rebel' to Leeds United.

McKenzie would not be the only one taking a tilt at the PFA. In August of that year an old friend and active member of the union, Joe Mercer, entered the lists in the *Nottingham Football Post* beneath the headline, 'Players Are Too Greedy!':

I have great admiration for Cliff Lloyd, the Secretary of the Professional Footballer's Association. But I think he's talking through the hole in his hat when he says that players should have freedom of contract. What's going to happen to the game if at the end of the season half a dozen of your best players can walk out and get themselves fixed up with another club? There would be chaos! Football in France has made itself bankrupt by abolishing the retain-and-transfer system. Gates are less than 10,000 in the French First Division. Do we want that here? Players talk about being able to play on the Continent and Continentals playing here. I can't see that happening. I read recently that Bertie Vogts, the 28-year-old German defender who stopped Johann Cruyff in the World Cup Final, was paid £250,000 to sign on by his German club. I certainly don't want to see that here. At least when big money is paid for a player in this country, the money stays in the game. It filters down to the Third and Fourth

Division clubs and enables them to continue their parlous existence. But when these huge sums go to the players, the money goes out of the game. I'm all for players. I'm a player's man. But I think they're going too far. I really mean that.

Mercer was anticipating the imminent findings and recommendations of the CIR report. He was voicing common fears among managers and directors, although CIR would downplay many of them. The final report, issued in September, made four main recommendations:

1. Freedom for players at the end of contracts;
2. Legal representation at disciplinary hearings with the admission of TV evidence;
3. Professional Footballers' Association to represent players during contract negotiations with clubs;
4. PFA to be represented on all committees, Football Association and League, altering the structure or form of competition and major policy in the game.

Within the football world most attention was paid to the suggestion of contractual freedom and the implications this would have on the transfer system and the game in general. The majority of responses were gloomy, reflecting fears of the Football League and the prejudices of the general public; typical being that of respected journalist David Miller in the *Daily Express* whose thoughts appeared beneath the headline 'The Freedom That Can Kill'.

The report, he felt, was compiled by men, 'largely lacking in knowledge of the delicate, special relationship between players and clubs and the unscrupulousness of both…' and what the CIR was proposing was little short of 'Player Power'. He continued that no matter how 'morally desirable or justifiable the report's recommendations, the trend towards player-power may finally wring the neck of the increasingly feeble egg-laying goose.'

Sir Norman Chester also looked at the report and the proposal for freedom of contract and noted that the major difference of opinion between players and administrators was in the way present contracts were renewed, which only allowed for a one-way renewal option at the end – in favour of the club. The player still had a long-winded appeal process to go through to gain a move that was both irksome and undignified. Chester's committee back in 1968 had suggested altering this. He now noted that three quarters of all contracts for professional players in the Football League were still for one year only with an option for a one-year renewal. Why, he asked, did clubs simply not issue longer contracts to players they regarded as being valuable? Despite the scare-stories, players in general did not want to rush from club to club each season. They wanted stability and the security that a four or five-year contract would bring. Managers could surely build their teams with a judicious mix of short and long-term contracts, thus avoiding the 'chaos' Joe Mercer had predicted?

Chester felt that the transfer system itself did not have to be abolished. Players could still be bought and sold while still in contract. A system could be devised to compensate clubs for the loss of a player who decided not to renew his contract at the end of its term. He also noted that, 'Most of those who run football object to a freely negotiated contract because they cannot envisage how a new system would work and they fear it might work to their disadvantage. A case of the devil you know…'

The CIR report had not all been good news for the organisation. It had concluded, after talking to a number of players, that the PFA's situation was 'weakened by its slender income, the ignorance of players of activities on their own behalf, and a general unwillingness to take issue.' The report remarked that 'a substantial proportion of the players we interviewed were ignorant of the PFA's activities on their behalf…[and] it is often seen as being a fairly remote body having little relevance to the daily problems faced by the players…'

Secretary Cliff Lloyd commented: '…to some extent I find it hard to accept the situation as described by the CIR…' His response to the suggestion by critics that the PFA no longer had the 'stomach for the fight' as in the early 1960s was more specific: it was easy, he said, 'to say that our best resort is to use the courts, but it would need another player of the calibre of Eastham, not to mention a considerable amount of cash'.

Lloyd insisted, however, that the long drawn-out negotiations in the two years following the Chester report had proved a point and had led, in turn, to the CIR report. Time had proved the PFA right because 'economically and financially football can ill afford to continue with the system as it is now'.

The CIR report, in fact, confirmed Lloyd's optimism regarding the real possibility of progress through a proper negotiating forum. One of its principal recommendations was for a new body – the Professional Football Negotiating Committee complete with an independent chairman – to be established as soon as possible.

The League's willingness to set up the body and to try to make it work was evidence for Lloyd of its acceptance that fundamental change was long overdue. It was also clear that both sides – players and administrators – would have to face up to certain uncomfortable truths. As Professor John Wood explained at the November 1974 PFA AGM:

> 'The Football League Management Committee were somewhat apprehensive about changes in the contractual position and this had been the reason given by the League for their reluctance to enter negotiations…The Football League were now willing to negotiate but they would need convincing of the necessity for change no matter how strong the PFA's case was morally.'

The CIR report had been helpful in this respect. When examining the transfer system and analysing figures for the years since Chester it had been unable to prove that the system did *not* help smaller clubs. The report had also accepted that there was some economic basis in the fears of clubs about losing the value of players if the transfer system was abolished. Although money could not be raised on the security of players, their presence among the assets of the club meant that money on other assets could be more easily secured.

The willingness of the PFA to recognise these points created a basis upon which the new Professional Football Negotiating Committee was able to begin its work. It would be a long time, however, before it reaped any dividends.

Freedom of a Kind 1974–78

At the 1975 AGM Cliff Lloyd announced that the management committee 'had thought it desirable to compromise on the question of freedom of contract despite the decision taken at the last AGM'. He received enthusiastic backing from the assembled delegates. The reason for this apparent retreat was that the PFA sensed that influence, even power, in the professional game was moving inexorably in its direction. Though the League would delay, prevaricate and resist during the next four years of dogged negotiations, a peaceful revolution was under way.

With the establishment of the Professional Football Negotiating Committee in 1975 progress was initially rapid. Comprising three Football League and three PFA representatives (Derek Dougan, Gordon Taylor and Terry Venables and later Bruce Bannister) with an independent chairman and joint secretaries, the committee's constitution provided for quarterly meetings. As early as the second formal meeting an outline agreement was reached based on four principles:

1. During the currency of the player's contract the familiar transfer procedure would continue;
2. Once a contract had been completed a player would have the right freely to seek employment with another club;

Sun Sport, Friday 16 January 1976.

3. A system should be devised by which the club from which a player left should receive compensation;
4. That compensation system should not be a serious hindrance to better employment.

The word 'compensation' reflected the clubs unshakeable conviction that their very survival depended on the 'value' of a player in their 'possession'. Quite early in the negotiations Football League secretary Alan Hardaker suggested a Dutch system called the 'multiplier' that might be used to compensate clubs in the event that a player opted to move. As Hardaker put it: 'It was time to restore some sanity to the transfer market', and the multiplier was intended to do just that by removing the volatile free market element and thus drastically reduce the amount of individual fees. It involved making calculations of the player's worth based on his age, his present wages, the division he was playing in and whether he was going up or down the game's professional ladder.

The multiplier, enthusiastically backed by Derek Dougan, led to a battle of words between PFA chairmen old and new. Jimmy Hill, now a club chairman, felt that the multiplier was an unnecessary bureaucratic interference in the free market, an artificial construction that would lead to a black market. In June 1977, leading a rebel consortium of Midlands clubs including Aston Villa, Birmingham and West Bromwich Albion, he effectively killed the idea and threatened to provoke the association he had once led into strike action. He claimed that even as PFA chairman he had accepted the need for a transfer system. It was the right of the player to move once his contract had finished that had been the key principle to be established: 'The clubs want to negotiate the going price when a player decides to leave.' He added, however, that he did not believe there would be a strike.

Despite Dougan's insistence that the multiplier must be part of the deal, certain other PFA Management Committee members such as Keith Peacock backed Hill and accepted that smaller clubs still needed the transfer market in order to survive. Alan Gowling felt that without a transfer system the spare cash would find its way into top players' pockets – not necessarily a good thing.

Sun Sport, June 18, 1977.

On 13 April 1978 the Football League clubs finally accepted the bulk of the agreement – while rejecting the multiplier. The PFA consulted members at a series of area meetings up and down the country and received firm backing for the agreement as it stood.

Thus, at the end of a contract a player could now exercise the option to leave his club. If the club offered the player new terms that were at least as attractive as the old ones then the selling club would be entitled to a transfer fee from the buying club. If a fee could not be decided between the two clubs a tribunal would decide an appropriate figure. While a contract was in force, neither the player nor his agent could initiate a move; it was up to a potential buyer to approach the player's present club directly. Contracts would end on 30 June by which time clubs would have notified players as to whether they intended to re-engage them and on what terms. If the terms were less favourable than those the player had been receiving he could move to a new club without compensation being paid. The League would publish a list of players offered terms by their clubs, and as soon as they did so players wishing to move could start negotiations with interested clubs.

At the 1978 PFA AGM, eighty years to the month after professional footballers first met to form the union, the most significant step along that long and weary road was ratified. Cliff Lloyd was predictably positive about the new agreement: 'The right of the player to change clubs at the end of his contract has now been firmly established…' Solicitor George Davies, however, was more circumspect: 'The new regulations do attempt to provide more equality to the bargaining position. Time will tell whether the arrangements spelt out in the new regulations offer a reasonable freedom for your members…Legally, perhaps, we are still only at the half-way house.'

3. Changing the Culture 1968–81

The inability of the clubs in the Football League to maintain themselves in purely physical terms, from their archaic, increasingly dangerous stadiums to their hand to mouth, often corrupt, financial governance, would all be criticised and agonised over in the years to come. Just as shameful was the clubs collective neglect of their own employees at almost every possible level.

Where technical skills were concerned, the widespread scorn by British coaches of modern (usually foreign) coaching and training methods had led to a decline in Britain's standing as a world football power. If undeveloped in terms of their basic skills, no surprise then that professional players had been neglected as human beings.

Over the decades the League had managed to nurture via its restrictive contract system and its often crude management techniques a deferential, largely apathetic workforce, poorly educated, sheltered from all outside influence: a body of men who, thanks to a unique combination of rules and restrictions, threats, fines and punishments had been conditioned to accept as inevitable and even 'natural' the existing power structure in football and their lowly place within it.

From the casual treatment of the scores of young hopefuls lured into the game as ground staff or later as apprentices, right through to the ruthless, often heartless, discarding of players of no further use, the majority of clubs' treatment of their employees had always been marked by a breathtaking ignorance.

Perhaps one ought not to judge the Football League Ltd too harshly. A key aspect of Britain's decline as a world manufacturing power had been its inability to invest in modern technology and training – its tendency to rake off the profits and hope that the customers would always return. Eventually, of course, they turned away. That League football, in its monopoly situation, had perpetuated this disastrous tendency much longer than the outside world was, perhaps, only to be expected.

Nevertheless, the League's cries of woe to various governments since the war were ironic indeed and completely misjudged. After so many years of spurning the involvement and offers of help from 'outsiders' it now regularly proffered a begging bowl. When the response was complex and challenging, the League clubs turned petulantly away. They wanted cash, not ideas. The fact that they could handle neither with much skill only made the situation the more potentially catastrophic.

The Chester report of 1968 bolstered the PFA's growing belief that it had an influential role to play in the future of the game. Chester had concluded that the PFA was, in many ways, a typical trade union, giving advice to members about contracts, dealing with settlements under the Industrial Injuries Act and helping players get engagements upon the expiry of their contracts.

Yet, in certain fundamental ways the organisation differed from other more traditional unions. Players' contracts were now individually negotiated in a highly competitive but limited market. Thus, the role of the PFA was to try to ensure that certain general conditions were observed.

With the professional player's working life tending to be much shorter than in most professions (players often finishing their careers by the age of 35), Chester concluded that the PFA 'has the peculiar problem of watching over the interests of boys at one end and men whose careers finish in the early thirties at the other.'

Most complicated of all, 'many aspects of the rules of the playing of football may affect the remuneration and conditions of professional footballers without the connection being direct or obvious.'

Thus, for the PFA, a report such as that delivered by Chester was seen as an opportunity for it to tackle such diverse yet related problems as the disciplining of players by both ruling bodies; the behaviour of its members on and off the field and their public image; the financial security of members; and their education before, during and after their playing careers.

By doing so, the players' body would address questions that concerned the very health of professional football as a whole –something the game's governing bodies, concerned as they seemed to be with cash and competitions, seemed barely alive to.

Education

Professional football has always been extremely cruel on those seeking to enter its ranks. Certainly it has always had an extremely high wastage rate. In the 1890s only 43 per cent registered to play in 1893–94 were still in League football after a year and only 13 per cent after three years. In the 1990s 50 per cent of trainees taken on by League clubs at 16 years of age were released at the end of the two-year stint and only 25 per cent remained after three years.

The treatment of young men entering the trade was, in many respects, shameful. If they 'made it' and were offered full-time terms their education was generally neglected so that when they finished with the game in their early 30s they had no trade and often very little cash to fall back on. Too often in the early days boys signed on as teenagers were used as manual labour around the club, while their opportunity to train and be coached was severely limited. If they failed they were cast out with little consideration as to how this might affect them psychologically.

The advent of war in 1939 had stifled an initiative upon which Jimmy Fay had placed great store – the chance to provide for players, particularly those approaching the ends of their careers, an opportunity to acquire 'professional' skills such as accountancy or running a business. The post-war struggles to remove the maximum wage and to reform players' contracts had seen such aspirations crowded out, but, prompted by the decision of the FA to pull out of the accident insurance scheme in 1964 and switch the cash into footballers' education, new avenues opened up.

By 1967 the PFA Education Fund had been set up with a view to providing financial assistance to any member or ex-member wishing to undertake vocational training. The fund hoped to be able to provide courses that included basic training in the practical and business side of professional football as a guide to existing players and as training for future managers and managerial staff.

Such a development was in line with changes that had occurred in British society since the war and in the nature of the 'raw material' of the professional game. A significant number of young men signing professional forms at 17 had already begun training for a profession or a skill and many were forced to make a choice either between football or a career in industry or the professions. While some clubs encouraged their apprentices to attend college, most did not and for many full-time professionals peer group pressure plus unofficial club/manager policy tended to banish all thoughts of academic improvement.

Typical of many would have been the experience of PFA chairman Terry Neill who had trained as an engineer before signing for Arsenal in 1960. After continuing with his studies for a time at Regent Street Polytechnic, he had given them up to concentrate on football when he gained a place in the Arsenal first team.

Neill could see the advantages of having some kind of training – either academic or practical – and when he became chairman in 1968 during a relatively peaceful time in the union's history he envisaged its main task as being to help players prepare for the time when they would no longer be able to play. This, he considered, would be good both for players and for the game as a whole. Scores of ex-professionals would ultimately enter club management and, as Chester commented, 'Few have had much, if any, experience or training in managing a commercial enterprise, or indeed, in managing people.'

Progress on the educational front was rapid. In 1969 grants totalling £400 were disbursed (to, among others, future union chairmen Gordon Taylor and Alan Gowling). By 1970 that total had increased to over £1,000 and would continue to rise rapidly as the decade progressed. In January 1971 Bob Kerry, a qualified teacher, was appointed as the union's first education officer from among 150 applicants and the education fund became a separate item on the union accounts with its own budget and charity status.

Kerry established links with colleges up and down the country and began developing courses specifically designed for young professionals, ranging from management accountancy to turf accountancy, and from fisheries management to running fish and chip shops. In 1972 he was able to announce: 'Slowly but surely a situation is being created whereby anyone – especially a youngster – will be able to obtain immediate help from a suitable person at a local college.'

Firms such as brewers Watney Mann began sponsoring short courses, correspondence courses were devised, while at St Helens College of Technology a highly successful residential management course was held for the first time in 1973. Kerry noted that of the 13 who took part, four had obtained managerial posts by the time the course started, two were subsequently appointed assistant managers, one obtained a coaching appointment and another was promoted within his club. Men like Terry Venables, ex-management committee member, and Brian Talbot, future union chairman, plus Tony Book and Alan Durban were among the pioneers.

The Education Society expanded rapidly but in the early 1980s the PFA began an involvement in the education and training of younger players that was to revolutionise and ultimately replace the old apprenticeship system. Though regularly derided and condemned by the TUC as a means of exploiting young people without jobs, Youth Training Schemes, first outlined in a 1980 white paper *A New Training Initiative: A Programme for Action* and introduced in 1983 by the government of Margaret Thatcher, would prove a boon for the football industry.

It was clear to many outside football that the government initiative was, in the first instance, aimed at reducing youth unemployment figures. This was of little concern to football clubs, particularly those clubs in risky financial circumstances. The scheme helped them both recruit young players and provided some much needed income. Whether all clubs used the money to fund the education of their apprentices was difficult to ascertain due to an absence of rigorous monitoring.

For pro-footballers with experience of real exploitation as old-style apprentices confined to sweeping the terraces, cleaning seats and the occasional kickabout at the end of the day, the relatively low weekly wage of £29.50 (in the first year) and £33.50 (in the second year) was also irrelevant. At a time when many clubs were finding it hard to make ends meet and were cutting back on the development of young players, sacking coaches and disbanding youth teams, the YTS meant a chance to gain a foothold in the profession. The clubs did not pay the wages and the PFA saw to the educational side of things. The scheme was immediately successful.

In 1983 Pat Lally, assistant education officer, reported that over 500 YTS boys had been taken on by 82 clubs. The PFA Education Society had been appointed as the managing agency for football schemes and was given the general responsibility for the welfare and training of all trainees. The young men involved were expected to join the PFA at the same rate as apprentice professionals. Trainees were covered by the League Accident Insurance Scheme and PFA delegates were urged to take an interest in both the football and the educational side of trainees' lives, and 'to make sure it [the scheme] is carried out properly'.

The youth policies that had been all but wiped out by the financial depredations of the 1970s and 1980s had been dramatically revived. In 1983 there had only been 33 apprentices in the whole of the Fourth Division. In 1989 Crewe alone had 21 YTS students on their books. By 1984 the Education Society could claim that the scheme had helped to double the average number of schoolboys entering professional football. Some 10 per cent of them had played first team football and half of them had been taken on for a second year. Over £1.5 million had been put into the scheme, and over the next few years that would rise to £3 million. This paid wages, travelling expenses, lodging allowances and reimbursement to clubs for their outlay, as well as the fees for educational courses at local colleges.

By 1989, just six years after the PFA had taken responsibility for the scheme, Doncaster manager Dave Mackay stated, 'The scheme has probably been the saviour of the Third and Fourth Divisions…Without it we couldn't entertain signing apprentices.' In that year six out of eight YTS boys had been signed on by Doncaster as full pros while the whole of the club's Youth Cup Final team were YTS trainees – many of them worth potentially substantial transfer fees. The year 1986 saw predictions of over 1,000 boys being received on to the scheme and in 1987 the Education Society's success was reflected in the award of Approved Training Organisation status from the Manpower Service Commission. In 1991 only one club in the League system –Watford – remained outside the scheme.

Though hardly the stuff of headlines, the impact of YTS can be regarded as one of the most significant developments in the pro-game during the 1980s and as Gordon Taylor commented: 'It's not just about producing players. It gives them the opportunity to learn other skills – coaching, refereeing, administration and commercial enterprises, hotel and catering, communications, computers, first-aid and life-saving…'

Discipline

In 1967 solicitor David Green had told the union AGM that the union was watching 'with particular concern' the functioning of various tribunals involving player discipline, but that action would be postponed until Chester reported. The union's submission to the Chester committee had been based on the contention that disciplinary hearings were like being put on trial in the court of one's employer; players, therefore, should have the automatic right to legal representation.

Chester did not accept the PFA's argument completely, considering a 'special elaborate system for professionals would not be acceptable'. Nevertheless, he felt reforms *were* needed, principally at 'personal hearing' cases where there should be an independent chairman with some legal qualification, where players should have the option of legal representation and where, if the sentence was severe, there should be a right of appeal.

Derek Dougan, no stranger to on-field trouble and its consequences, was particularly forthright about the conditions under which players suffered in this respect: 'Disciplinary procedures in the game cause a great deal of heartburn. The "courts" run by the FA are often no more than the "kangaroo" variety. Justice is not always done nor seen to be done. Players are resentful, feeling that they will not get a fair hearing, and referees are uncomfortable appearing before the disciplinary committees to give evidence. Hearings were often reduced to fiascos, when players feel the evidence is loaded against them and that an official's word will always be preferred to theirs. Independent witnesses are not allowed.'

Extra point was given to the demand for legal representation by the Ernie Machin case which came to the Royal Courts of Justice in October 1972. Machin, a Coventry City player (ironically, one of Jimmy Hill's first signings as Coventry manager) had been sent off in September 1970 for apparently kicking an opponent after both men had fallen to the ground.

TV film of the incident, allowed for the first time in such a case, showed that the referee's report, upon which the whole FA case was based, to be completely at odds with the facts. After viewing the film, however, the FA Commission, spotting something *else* Machin had apparently done wrong, decided to uphold the referee's decision anyway and fined him £50 – not grasping the fact that they were sentencing Machin for another offence entirely, against which he had not been given the opportunity to defend himself.

The judge declared the decision void, saying: 'It would be hard to find a clearer example of a committee failing to conduct a hearing in accordance with the rules of natural justice'. It was the first time a civil court had upset a decision by the FA disciplinary committee. Machin had his original fine of £50 and costs of £43 returned to him.

Quite simply, the FA had got itself into a muddle because it employed no one with legal expertise to point out that it was making basic mistakes. If the case demonstrated anything, it highlighted the inadequacy of the traditional 'paternalistic' system where the men in authority felt free to more or less make up the rules as they went along.

Player resentment and referee discomfort had already been brought to fever pitch in 1971 when the FA decided, without consulting players or clubs, to institute a dramatic 'clean-up' campaign which involved, as the PFA put it, 'changes in the application of the laws governing the game' and resulted in a sudden rise in the number of sendings off and bookings. In the first 15 matches of the season 32 players were cautioned; by the 11th week the number had risen to 700; and by December 1,000 men had received a card of some kind! Doogan complained, 'If this continues we will have eighty-five minutes of stoppages and five minutes of football. It seems that there is no longer any room in the game for physical contact.'

As there had been no warning, everyone had been taken by surprise – which had been the FA's intention. However, the resulting furore saw a truce arranged in early 1971 and a committee of study set up involving all interested parties. Once again the Conservative government's Industrial Relations Act was a key factor. The Act granted employees the right to legal representation, as well as the right of appeal in cases of disciplinary action. The PFA and FA were thus obliged to come to some kind of agreement.

The new system agreed upon in 1972 clarified the procedures and introduced a considerable independent element. Players would now accumulate points for misdemeanours. Fines were eliminated and penalties were made uniform. Players were granted a personal hearing when charged with offences carrying heavy points penalties or when sent off, and they had the right of appeal to an independent chairman whenever the sentence was particularly severe.

On 9 November 1972 Larry Lloyd, Liverpool and England central-defender, made football history by becoming the first player to appear before the new independent disciplinary tribunal. Not only that but he won his appeal against a three-match ban. He had been sent off in the opening game of the season for 'chopping and then kicking' Manchester City centre-forward Wyn Davies. Sir John Lang, a 75-year-old retired civil servant, Stan Cullis, former soccer manager and Norman Hillier, an ex-referee, formed the three-man tribunal which sat for two hours and 10 minutes and watched TV film of the incident.

Sir John Lang later issued a statement: 'The tribunal is satisfied that Lloyd is not free from blame. It does, however, regard his sending off as sufficient punishment and therefore quashes the sentence of a three-match suspension imposed by the Football Association.'

Television

Television would prove to be both a danger and a blessing to the PFA and its members: a danger because its massive economic impact would create unbearable tensions which would ultimately threaten to destroy the existing fabric of the national game; a blessing because the ever-increasing amounts of cash flowing into the PFA's coffers from its share of TV contracts would enable it to transform both itself and the lives of its members.

The first broadcaster to show a regular weekly programme devoted to nothing but football highlights was Anglia TV in 1962, when it offered the Football League £1,000 to screen highlights of 30 matches involving teams in the region 24 hours after they were played. Anglia was followed by ATV who launched *Star Soccer* with Peter Lorenzo as commentator. In 1964 *Match of the Day* made its debut on BBC2, was moved to BBC1 in 1966 and eventually became a national institution. Possibly the most significant development came in 1967 when ex-PFA chairman Jimmy Hill left football management to embark on a new career with London Weekend Television as the new franchise's Head of Sport.

Hill was keen to make changes to what had already become a set format. *The Big Match* was a highlights programme that went out on Sunday afternoons, meaning there was more time to put the show together and, with many more younger viewers watching, more emphasis on sheer entertainment. John Bromley, Jimmy Hill's deputy at the time, explained 'We wanted to attract not just the soccer fan, but the average audience, mum, dad, kids, everyone.'

If the matches chosen turned out to be less than thrilling, the programme would feature silly or unusual soccer moments from around the world. Viewers' letters were invited and big name guests appeared in the studio, not just from the world of football but also celebrity fans such as Freddie Starr and Elton John.

The TV camera also began to poke its nose into previously 'sacrosanct' areas: down the tunnel leading to the pitch, into the dressing rooms, on to the training pitch, even travelling inside the team coach as it headed for Wembley. TV thus began to influence what fans saw and what they expected to see and, in turn, it affected those it exposed. Footballers began to be seen as entertainers, with their personalities being featured rather than just their football prowess. Jimmy Hill also encouraged players to be more outspoken. In 1970, for ITV's World Cup coverage, he recruited a panel of experts to comment on the action – but a panel with a difference, unafraid to spark off some controversy and engage in lively debate. Malcolm Allison, Derek Dougan, Pat Crerand and Bob McNab were the chosen quartet and the results were astounding. For the first time ITV actually beat the BBC in viewing figures.

For one man in particular the TV exposure proved to be a seminal moment in his already colourful career. Derek Dougan, elected PFA chairman a few weeks after the 1970 World Cup, would prove to be a perfect figurehead for this difficult, transitional period when professional football and footballers moved uncertainly into the TV age. Soon after assuming office he became involved in a venture never before attempted in Britain, the setting up of a Football Hall of Fame.

The hall had been created by a private company headed by solicitor and Arsenal fan Gerald Black, along with business associates including Oscar S. Lerman and Raymond Zelker. Lerman was an American film and one-time Broadway musical producer, owner of Tramp discotheque and husband of blockbuster novelist Jackie Collins. Zelker was the founder of rag trade company Polly Peck.

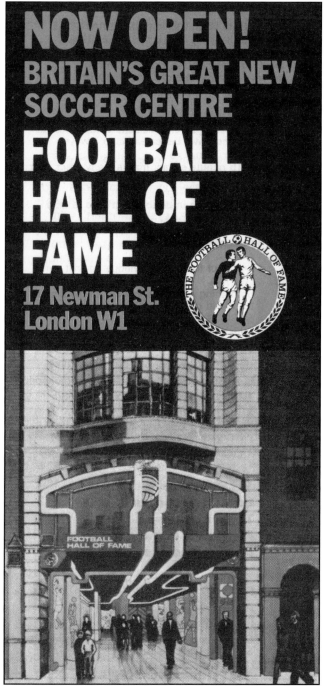

Poster for the Football Hall of Fame, August 1971.

Black had approached Cliff Lloyd in 1968 and asked for advice and co-operation and also for the use of the PFA's name as a sponsor. In return he offered the players' organisation £1,000 a year or 10 per cent of all profits to go to the Players' Benevolent Fund. Lloyd took his place on the board as a managing director along with Sir Matt Busby as chairman, followed by a host of other big names serving on an advisory board: Alf Ramsey, Denis Follows of the FA, Alan Hardaker of the League, plus representatives from London Weekend TV and the BBC.

Situated in Newman Street, off Oxford Street, it appeared perfectly placed to reap the publicity spin-offs from the recent World Cup. The plans were extensive: when it opened in March 1971 it operated on the ground and lower ground floor of the building where football exhibits, wax effigies of football greats and the latest gadgets were on show. 'We have five back-projection sets, each of which will operate continuously on the push-button principle and show 3–4 minute films about football history, FA Cup Finals, international matches, training and coaching subjects and so on,' Black explained to reporters. Trophies, shirts and other ephemera were to be loaned from the famous Hitchen Football Club museum as well as Sir Stanley Rous's personal collection.

For the Hall of Fame itself 12 'greats' including Stanley Matthews and Dixie Dean had already been selected by a panel of 'experts'. Another 12 would soon follow, and each man selected was presented with a special trophy. Later, a restaurant and 'areas for rest, relaxation and games' would be available. Admission was 30p (20p for under-15s) and the hope was that real live footballers would be present to shake hands and sign autographs.

Sadly, despite the occasional appearance of the likes of Geoff Hurst and the promptings of management committee member Terry Venables, star players were as conspicuous by their absence as paying customers and the hall folded in 1972 due to lack of interest. Professionals had not yet woken up to the commercial possibilities of their new status.

Derek Dougan, however, was in no doubt as to their worth. A particular feature of the doomed Hall of Fame that appealed to him was the 'Players' Player of the Year' to have been chosen by the PFA committee. Dougan, along with Lloyd and Eric Woodward of Aston Villa, decided to build an event around the concept and in 1974 the PFA awards dinner was inaugurated.

Dougan would later cite the event, a lavish, black tie occasion held in one of the best hotels in Park Lane and transmitted live by ATV, as one of his proudest achievements:

'The image of the footballer as a thick-headed yokel who needs constant discipline and cannot be trusted to manage his own affairs is a distant throwback. The real image belongs to the PFA Awards night…The television cameras, roaming casually through groups of dinner-jacketed players, waiting to go into dinner, have presented nationwide a more articulate, self-assured image…anyone who doubts the social progress of the modern footballer has only to switch on the Player of the Year Awards on ITV, without doubt the best night on the sporting calendar…'

At times he would find himself being mocked for his attempts to upgrade the image of players in this way, especially by those commentators of a more radical persuasion. The awards dinner only fed the fears and provoked the scorn of critics who realised that professional footballers were no longer content with remaining 'working class heroes'. With its chandeliers and lavish catering, the awards looked like the thin edge of the 'celebrity' wedge. What was more, the first recipient of the Players' Player of the Year in 1974 – Norman Hunter – could hardly have been more of a challenge to the perceptions of friends and foes of the PFA.

At a time when pro-football was coming under increasing criticism for its dour, defensive, not to say violent tendencies, the players picked that arch exponent of the crunching tackle, Norman 'Bite Yer Legs' Hunter. Hunter's selection was not consciously designed to make a point but it certainly represented a public thumbing of the nose to critics at all levels, in particular to those in the press and the media in general. Players were starting to do things for themselves.

Cliff Lloyd retires

The 1978 AGM was a significant milestone as it marked Cliff Lloyd's 25th year of serving the union. He was now 63 years old and contemplating retirement. His successor had already been decided upon. Gordon Taylor, the new chairman, had been asked by the management committee if he would serve as assistant to Lloyd for the next two years before stepping into the latter's shoes. He would thus become the first man since Jimmy Fay to have held both top positions in the union.

Lloyd was preparing for his departure in the same careful, constructive way as he had carried out the union's affairs ever since 1953 when he had taken over from Jimmy Fay. The new standard players' agreement, then in the process of being drawn up, would provide him with the finest of monuments – indeed, with perfect timing it would come into force in November 1981, the year he was destined to step down.

Nevertheless another ambition remained, possibly an even more satisfying one in view of Lloyd's continuing concern for the average professional. A new pension plan, almost achieved in 1969, recommended by the CIR in 1974 and agreed in principle in 1978, had still to be negotiated with the League.

By 1980 the players' cash benefit scheme, as it had come to be known, was being put to area meetings of players for their enthusiastic endorsement. The new scheme provided pro-players with something no other 'industrial' worker, other than deep-sea divers, could boast – a lump sum payment attained on reaching the age of 35, based on years of service multiplied by average earnings which was equivalent to between three and four per cent of a man's total earnings, plus a death-in-service benefit of up to £15,000.

Cliff Lloyd hands over to Gordon Taylor in November 1981.

A five per cent levy on transfer fees provided the premium for the scheme so players contributed nothing to it at all. Ironically, the despised transfer system that had more or less called the union into existence was now paying for each man's security.

Thus, at the 1981 AGM, Cliff Lloyd could look back over 30 years of almost unrelenting toil on behalf of professional footballers and point to successes beyond the wildest dreams of men like Charlie Roberts, Herbert Broomfield, Billy Meredith and Jimmy Fay – even of Jimmy Guthrie, who had died in 1978.

The union had now delivered a measure of financial security for each and every member, limited freedom of contract, a provident fund, accident insurance, an education scheme, legal advice relating to contracts, representation on disciplinary tribunals, representation on numerous committees concerning football's present and future, and, finally, freedom of speech. All this and 100 per cent membership without a closed shop.

Inevitably, George Davies would put into words what most members were feeling:

'Cliff Lloyd's depth of purpose and endeavour, to which must be added his immense standing in the football world and his character as an individual, has provided the PFA with a consistent champion of the rights of footballers. In the period of his secretaryship the lifestyle and standard of living of footballers in the life of the community has taken a very great uplift...and this period has seen what can fairly be described as a revolution in the conditions and financial rewards to players. He has had the loyal support of the succession of management committees during the whole of this period but it must be said that he has been their mainspring and much credit is due to him for the enormous changes which have taken place...'

PART FIVE
TAKING CENTRE STAGE
1982–2002

1. Bucking the Trend 1982–89

Upon taking office in 1982 Gordon Taylor told a national newspaper:

> 'All the battles the players needed to fight, against the maximum wage, for freedom of movement and now freedom of speech, have been won. What we need now is cooperation between all bodies in the game to stop the kind of disputes and mud-slinging that, I'm sure, have helped disillusion the public.'

Gordon Taylor had been brought onto the Professional Football Negotiating Committee along with Bruce Bannister in 1975 where the influence of Professor Sir John Wood had been fundamental to his development as a PFA official. Protracted negotiations, open-ended discussions inching gradually towards some kind of mutually acceptable agreement – this process Taylor professed to enjoy, almost revel in.

Perhaps it is significant that his degree in economics was gained the hard way, by evening classes and correspondence while earning his bread and butter as a pro-footballer rather than enjoying the luxury of three years at university on a student grant. Such an achievement both reflects and reinforces the qualities of perseverance and tenacity, suggesting a personality unlikely to be swayed by those around him and stubbornness belied by his gregarious, almost benign, exterior.

In this latter respect he was straight out of the Cliff Lloyd mould. However, Lloyd had grown up in a harder, more insecure world, he had experienced a world war and the bleak austere years that followed. His was the more cautious, deliberate outlook of the senior civil servant feeling disinclined to risk too much.

Taylor, by contrast, had no such inhibitions. He saw himself and his role increasingly as that of chairman of the board – responsible certainly, but entitled, if not obliged, to take risks in order that the membership should reap the bountiful harvest of the modern world.

Taylor's own father had been a diligent and dedicated Amalgamated Engineering Union official and so he was no stranger to orthodox trade unionism. However, from the outset Taylor eschewed overtly political stances, insisting that the traditional union stance of 'them and us' was irrelevant, if not futile. He would maintain that any conflict can be resolved by discussion, that somewhere a position could be found that

Gordon Taylor OBE Present Chief Executive

Born in December 1944 at Ashton-under-Lyne, Gordon's father worked as a British Rail motor fitter at Gorton Tank in Manchester. As a boy in the 1950s, Gordon cycled into Manchester to collect the autographs of men like Roy Paul and the pre-Munich Busby Babes. His own career began in the early 1960s. Signed by Bolton Wanderers, where one of his heroes – Nat Lofthouse – was second-team manager, Gordon was thrust into Wanderers's 1963–64 relegation struggle at the age of 18 and found himself at Old Trafford confronting the resurgent Manchester United of Law, Best and Chariton. Gordon broke his nose, Bolton lost 5–0 and were eventually relegated after a desperate struggle that almost saw them claw their way to safety. For a decade he would play for Bolton in the Second Division. After clocking up over 250 appearances at both inside-forward and on the wing he was signed by Birmingham City for a fee of £18,000. Bolton were in dire financial straits and Gordon was told, 'We're sorry to see you go but in a way we're glad – we'll get our christmas turkey now.' Playing alongside the young Trevor Francis and Bob Latchford, he helped City gain promotion to the First Division in his second season with the club. He almost reached Wembley on three occasions during his Birmingham days but was transferred to Blackburn Rovers in 1976, only to be seriously injured in the same year. He recuperated by playing in the North American Soccer League during the summer of 1977 alongside the likes of Pele and Beckenbauer. He then returned to England and later moved to Bury where his 20-year football career ended. When he assumed the mantle of secretary of the PFA his keen ambitions both for the union and for himself were to be tempered by a mix of memory and experience, a sense of history as well as an appreciation of the game's commercial possibilities that would serve professional football remarkably well as it plunged into the crises of the 1980s. Over the succeeding years Gordon has overseen a radical transformation of the PFA's role and position while himself becoming a major figure in the national game. In 1992 he became President of FIFPro, the international professional footballers' union, stepping down in 2005. He remains FIFA's honorary president. He is also a member of the Football Foundation, the FIFA Football Committee, UEFA and FA Committees and the Institute of Professional Sport. He received an Honorary Masters Degree for his services to football from Loughborough University and also holds an Honorary Doctorate from De Montfort University. He was appointed officer of the Order of the British Empire (OBE) in the 2008 New Year Honours.

AS A NEW ERA STARTS THE FANS GET A PROFESSIONAL CHAMPION

He's Taylor-made!

By PETER JOHNSON

GORDON TAYLOR inherited yesterday one of English soccer's greatest seats of power. It was from that chair—or, more accurately, its un-padded ancestor—that his predecessor as secretary of the Players' Union, Cliff Lloyd, directed most of the battles which revolutionised the game.

When that polite head-line-maker started work nearly 29 years ago, his dis-contented members were known as the slaves of their clubs.

Nowadays—or so it seems to poor, out-of-work Joe Public—too many of them hide the scars of the manacles under gold bracelets.

Having spent his playing career gainfully, but not extra-vagantly employed by Bolton, Birmingham, Blackburn and Bury, Taylor knows that to be largely a fallacy.

Disputes

And if, on the day of Lloyd's retirement, Taylor has one overriding ambition, it is to push the players closer to their public.

'All the battles the players needed to fight . . . against the maximum wage, for freedom of movement and now freedom of speech . . . have been won,' he says.

'What we need now is co-operation between all bodies in the game to stop the kind of disputes and mud-slinging that, I'm sure, have helped disillu-sion the public.

'There could not be a better time for it. There are new people at the top in the PFA and League, the managers and sec-retaries are working well together and the players realise they have a responsibility to

As Lloyd retires the players' player takes over hot seat

FAREWELL AND WELCOME . . . for Cliff Lloyd and Gordon Taylor

give something back to the game.'

There can be no doubt Taylor will play his own part in fostering the new peace. During his last two years in office, Lloyd chose his successor as carefully as he had selected his words in the previous 26.

His protege first emerged 17 years ago when as a 19-year-old winger at Bolton, he was alarmed that not enough was being done to safeguard the future of youngsters less fortunate than himself.

He, at least, had a grammar school education, 'O' and 'A' levels and, at his parents' insistence, had embarked on a university course that eventu-ally brought him a BSc in economics.

By 1978, his experience of life 'on the shop floor' and his ability to express it in moder-ate, uncluttered language brought him the chairmanship of the PFA in succession to such luminaries as Terry Neill and Derek Dougan.

It was then, with his career nearing its end, that he was left with the choice—politics or management. He was offered two coaching jobs and was to be interviewed for the manager-ship of a Fourth Division club.

'It was Cliff's faith in my ability to do this job that

eventually made up my mind,' he recalls. 'But it was a very hard decision.

'I still miss the day-to-day contact with players. And for a long time after I quit it was agony going to a match just to sit there and watch. Now, at last, I find I'm actually begin-ning to enjoy games.'

That enjoyment is fostered by a belief that football, jolted by falling attendances, is waking up to the fact that it must be entertaining.

Encourage

'There is a danger that as clubs turn more and more to sponsorship, television and the pools for extra money, the man on the terrace will get his nose pushed out.

'We have to realise that these people are the game's bread and butter, the whole reason why it's played.

'That's why we are trying to encourage more men into coach-ing—to cut out the danger of in-breeding among coaches. There has been a tendency to resent interference, a feeling that the public couldn't really be expected to understand what was going on on the field.'

ONE of Gordon Taylor's first tasks is to lead the Players' Union in moves to curb the import of foreign players.

The Union want players to come to England only if: They have gained at least six caps in the last three years, and they are not aged over 28.

Daily Mail, 14 November 1981.

satisfied everyone. Once agreed it was incumbent on all concerned to stick to that agreement.

The PFA would thus remain outside the TUC for some time. It had more to gain by doing so. In many important respects it was a union with a difference, something Gordon Taylor would exploit to the full.

The Conservative government's employment acts of 1980, 1982 and 1988 had the cumulative effect of reducing union power by allowing employers to withhold union recognition, oppose union involvement at the workplace and prohibit the closed shop. As a consequence trade union membership in general fell from a high of 13.2 million in 1979 to 7.8 million in 2000, a 41 per cent decline. There was also a decline in union density, that is the percentage of workers in any firm actually belonging to a union, from 56 per cent to 30 per cent over the same period. Allied to this was a dramatic decrease in union recognition at workplace level from 73 per cent in 1980 and 1984 to 64 per cent in 1990 and 54 per cent in 1998, while between 1984 and 1998 the percentage of workplaces with union recognition that had a union representative on site fell from 80 per cent to 70 per cent.

In stark contrast, the PFA experienced *increases* in membership throughout the 1980s and 1990s and sustained a 100 per cent union density among Premier and Football League clubs. Union recognition at the level of the workplace was also an accepted norm within the industry. There was an appointed PFA representative at each of the 92 Premier League and Football League clubs who received regular information concerning union activities. How did the PFA manage this?

Firstly, PFA members possessed a certain degree of protection from anti-union legislation which was provided by the collective bargaining arrangement that underpinned employee regulations in the football industry. Essentially this meant that a football club had to honour its contract with an individual player and the player had to do likewise. This binding agreement was reinforced by the PFA's decision not to proceed with challenging and ultimately smashing the transfer system, that 'holy grail' of both organisations. In effect the PFA had said to football's employers 'recognise us, and guarantee not to sack our members and we'll let you continue to buy and sell us'.

Added to this the general situation in the football industry was such that derecognition of the PFA by a particular club was simply not workable. PFA recognition existed for a number of reasons: all top professional players were members and, more often than not, senior members of the coaching or management staff would have had playing careers and been members of the PFA. A degree of empathy therefore existed towards the role and importance of the union.

It was also a fact that the clubs acknowledged (albeit grudgingly at times) the role the PFA gradually came to play in supporting the game and the industry in general. These factors would have made it difficult for any football club to use anti-union legislation; there plainly did not exist the material basis for such an approach as it would almost certainly have had negative implications for the club involved.

This somewhat remarkable situation had not been achieved by a closed shop policy, rather it was a function of what is termed a closed union. This means that membership is only available to a concentrated group of workers, in this case skilled Premier League and Football League professionals and youth trainees. A small number of semi-professional players with non-League football clubs have also become members but it remains the case that only a select group of individuals are able to join the PFA.

Membership even for an apprentice brings with it the right to a wide range of services which the union provides. Former PFA members also have the right to certain entitlements that continue for life.

The players' Cash Benefit Scheme agreed with the Football League and FA back in 1980 was the first of many reasons why a player would swear loyalty to his union. The lump sum payment on attaining the age of 35, based on years of service multiplied by average earnings and equivalent to between three and four per cent of a man's total earnings, was non-contributory. Its maximum payout in 2000 was £800,000, and in its first 20 years the scheme paid out almost £33 million to 3,500

Alan Gowling Chairman 1980–82

University educated, Alan started his career at centre-forward and made his debut for Manchester United in September 1969, playing alongside George Best and Bobby Charlton. Described as a tall 'ugly duckling' of a player, Alan was in his element when ploughing through a morass of stamina-sapping mud or scrapping energetically for a loose ball when the efforts of more elegant players came to naught. In all Alan made some 467 League and Cup appearance and scored 139 goals. He also won an England Under-23 cap as captain. He was one of the first players to receive a PFA educational grant (in 1972 of £28 8s) and went on to complete an MA, his thesis being a study of the relationship of professional footballers to their union. He later played for Huddersfield Town, Newcastle, Bolton Wanderers and Preston North End. After his playing days ended Alan chose to leave football entirely and went on to build a successful career in industry.

players and/or dependants. By 2002 the figure had risen to £45 million. The premiums for the scheme are paid for in an ingenious way via a five per cent levy on transfer fees. Players gave up their shares from transfers along with their signing-on fees. Thus the despised transfer system that had more or less called the union into existence would now pay for each man's security.

Further membership benefits followed during the next decade. In 1985 a joint initiative between the PFA and the Football League to provide a private contributory pension scheme for all full-time professional footballers was started, the PFA/Football League Players' Retirement Income Scheme.

In 1986 the Footballers' Further Education and Vocational Training Scheme (FFE+VTS) was initiated, one of three welfare schemes which the PFA operates for members. Today, the reconstituted PFA education department works in partnership with Premier League Learning (PLL) and League Football Education (LFE) to 'promote and enhance' educational and vocational training for apprentices aged 16 to 18. The majority of boys now join what is called the Apprenticeship in Sporting Excellence (ASE) an educational programme that looks to provide a safety net for those who fail to make the grade. Ex-Swansea City, York City and Doncaster Rovers midfielder Pat Lally, Head of PFA Education, also plays a major role in encouraging current and soon-to-be-retired players to take up educational courses in preparation for the days when the contracts end.

PFA Education uses part of its healthy television income to fund courses variously at Warwick Business School, the University of Salford, Staffordshire University, the University of Bath and the Manchester Metropolitan University in subjects such as sports journalism, physiotherapy, football management and coaching science. Typical is the contract for five places at York's St John University reserved for ex-Football Academy and ex-footballers to pursue new career paths in physiotherapy. Tom Wilkinson, who once played for Lincoln City before injury forced him to retire, was one of the first students to participate, hoping, like so many ex-professionals, to return to the game wielding more than just a 'magic sponge'.

Members can apply to the association for grants towards tuition and book costs for courses leading to any recognised qualification. Between July 2006 and June 2007 the department processed a total of 783 such individual grants totalling almost half a million pounds. Players at all levels participated. In 2007 Darren Ferguson, Martin Allen, Les Ferdinand and Steve Hodge successfully completed a Certificate of Applied Management at Warwick University, while Daniel Gabrielson, ex-Wigan Athletic, achieved a first in his BSc in physiotherapy at Salford University. The days when 'graduate footballers' like Steve Heighway could be treated as quaint curios seem to be long gone.

There is now even a PFA magazine devoted to re-education and the possibilities of life beyond the touchline. *New Goals* is devoted to the work of the education department, profiling the many success stories of ex-professionals who have built new careers after injury or retirement, both inside and outside the profession. It showcases the wide range of courses on offer for members and publicises PFA-sponsored events such as Progression 08, held at Manchester City's Eastland Stadium, where representatives from IT, the armed forces, health, construction and retail industries along with universities and business advisers showed players how they might use their unique skills and abilities to find employment when their playing days ended.

Also in 1986, Football in the Community was formed by the FFE+VTS. Through this initiative Football League and Nationwide Conference clubs, supported by the PFA, began developing community schemes which offered a wide range of sports and social based activities. Incorporated as a separate registered charity, the PFA allocated it an annual funding budget and encouraged ex-players to take part. Two years after its formation it had created 350 jobs at 35 clubs helping former players such as Duncan McKenzie, Tony Currie and Alex Williams to keep contributing to local life.

Through PFA coaching, formed in 1994, further assistance is provided to players contemplating a post-football career by offering all members the opportunity to gain formal coaching qualifications. According to the association's own surveys, over 75 per cent of current players wish to remain in the game in some capacity and with the qualifications now needed to coach at the top level being mandatory, many professional players find it necessary to attend coaching courses while they are still playing.

The PFA's concerns with coaching pre-dates World War One. In 1913, in the *Football Players Magazine* under the headline 'Do Players Need More Ball Practice?', Charlie Roberts wrote critically of training sessions:

Jimmy Armfield OBE

On 27 December 1954 Jimmy Armfield made his Blackpool debut at Portsmouth. He would play the whole of his Football League career at Bloomfield Road, usually at right-back. Between 1954 and 1971 he played 627 games in all competitions, scored six goals and spent a decade as the club's captain. He made his international debut on 13 May 1959 against Brazil in front of over 120,000 fans. He won 43 caps for England between 1959 and 1966, captaining the side 15 times. Jimmy was voted Young Player of the Year in 1959. Not long after hanging up his boots he became manager of Bolton Wanderers. He also subsequently took the helm at Leeds United, leading them to the European Cup Final in 1975. He is best known to younger fans as a match summariser for BBC Radio Five Live. A coaching consultant to the FA, Jim is now technical consultant to the PFA coaching department and one of the most respected coaches in the game. In 2000 he was awarded the OBE for his services to football. In 2004 he was appointed a deputy lieutenant in his home county of Lancashire, and in 2005–06 he served as high sheriff of Lancashire. Jimmy won the 2008 PFA Merit Award.

'the players stand about six yards away from the goalkeeper and shoot, which any navvy could do. There is no running about or dribbling, feinting, passing with the inside or outside of the foot, trapping or heading the ball, placing it with the head like you do with your feet, judging distances etc indulged in at all. Players, in my opinion, should try and do the things with the ball they have to do on a Saturday…'
Peter O'Rourke, manager of Bradford City, agreed: 'I am certain that the day will come when ball practice during the week will form a fundamental part of the training of the professional footballer. When that day does dawn there will be far less hustle and more cleverness and combination.'

In 1994 the PFA commissioned an inquiry into coaching practices worldwide, culminating in the 1995 report 'A Kick in the Right Direction' which called for greater consultation between the FA and the PFA in player and coach development. It stressed the need for greater involvement from coaches who have 'played the game at professional level rather than former schoolteachers.' The association was subsequently asked to nominate former players to sit on the five liaison committees of the FA's Centres of Excellence. In 1996 it decided to employ players who had qualified as FA coaches on a full-time basis to provide a coaching service to professional clubs, helping other players and ex-players who wished to become coaches. A year later a free-standing PFA coaching department was established, originally overseen by ex-Manchester City forward Paul Power and subsequently by Jimmy Armfield OBE, who was also the FA's technical consultant.

As only an exclusive minority of players are financially secure at the end of their playing days, many more players are now embarking on coaching qualifications. In 2008 Curzon Ashton FC was the venue for the UEFA Level 3 Coaching Licence Award run exclusively for former professionals by the PFA's coaching department. Ex-professional full-backs, Geoff Lomax (Bolton Wanderers) and Andy Barlow (Oldham Athletic), delivered the course to 24 players – past and present – keen to improve their employability options. They came from all levels of the game: Stephane Henchoz and Bruno Berner from Blackburn Rovers, along with Matt Jackson and Mike Pollitt from Wigan, Terry Dunfield of Macclesfield, Colin Woodthorpe of Bury and Neil Taylor from Wrexham.

Back in 1907, when the idea was first mooted of an organisation to represent players, Billy Meredith was keen to emphasise the role the union should play in safeguarding the rights of the lesser-known players without a voice, those journeymen whose pay packets were small and whose influence negligible. Thus, from the very start, the union's workload would be dominated by cases such as that of Sheffield United's Frank Levitch who had died without leaving adequate provision for his wife and children. From then on a significant aspect of the union's workload would involve similar arrangements being made for players and their families in times of need.

Over the years the PFA has also offered invaluable assistance in relation to personal injury and clinical negligence claims arising out of footballers careers. In 2006 it saw many successful cases being brought with damages recovered amounting to almost £500,000 for the benefit of members.

The PFA's legal department has also provided contract assistance to many others, from Premier League managers to Nationwide Conference players, both in terms of advising upon proposed contracts as well as compromise agreements for the termination of contracts. It has also been instrumental in negotiating monetary settlements for members or has succeeded in having them reinstated to their positions where contracts have been terminated without notice and/or pay.

In 1989 PFA Financial Management Limited, the financial department of the association, was established to handle anything from personal investment to advice on signing contracts. The PFA had thus become football agents.

In these ways and many others the association grew both quantitatively and qualitatively as no other union organisation was able to do. What is more, from the moment Gordon Taylor took command its secondary role as a quasi-guardian and protector of the industry its members worked in would be considerably

Steve Coppell Chairman 1982–84

Steve first played as an amateur with Tranmere Rovers while studying at Liverpool University for a BSc in economics. He turned professional with Rovers in January 1974 and signed for Manchester United in 1975 for a fee of £60,000. Noted mainly for his all-action, never-say-die attitude, he was a wonderful 'line' player, an incisive right-winger who crossed splendidly on the run. He rapidly progressed to full international level and was an England regular between the years 1978 and 1983 when he won 42 full caps, scored seven goals and appeared in the 1982 World Cup Finals in Spain. Tommy Docherty rated Steve the best player he had ever bought. After retirement in 1983 he was appointed team manager of Second Division Crystal Palace, making him the youngest League manager at 28.

enhanced. Much of this was made possible by the association's healthy bank balance, the lion's share of which now came from TV revenues passed on to it by the Football League and the FA. While the latter bodies tended to divide up their shares into relatively insignificant portions, the PFA's share, averaging between £300,000 and £400,000 per annum for many years until it started to dramatically escalate in the 1990s, arrived in one lump. While much of the money was put to good use by the rapidly expanding Education Society and in providing a multitude of services to PFA members, a significant proportion was invested leaving a significant amount left that could be loaned to clubs in need.

As the 1980s began, many clubs would benefit from the PFA's good housekeeping. The onset of a severe economic recession saw an increasing number of smaller clubs facing financial difficulties. With attendance figures plummeting from 24 million in 1980 to 17.8 million in 1985, with hooliganism becoming a serious social problem and with old grounds facing enormous costs in order to meet new safety standards, this was no longer the case of clubs pleading poverty in order to obtain government handouts.

In January 1982 Bristol City suddenly announced that they were sacking eight of their senior players in a bid to avoid bankruptcy and closure. An accountant's report on the club's affairs revealed that it had debts of £1,500,000 pounds, and assets of only £78,000. The eight players' contracts were worth £290,000. Thus, the 'Ashton Gate Eight', as they came to be known, were offered a redundancy package totalling £58,000 between them. The alternative, it was suggested, was the winding up of the club.

The human aspect was not lost on Gordon Taylor:

'The players have been put in a terrible position. The first words I spoke to them were assurances that, no matter what was said, they'd been given contracts they'd worked for and deserved and £58,000 just wasn't acceptable. On the other hand, we all wanted the other players at the club to have a future. It was a very delicate problem.'

Taylor was faced with a sensitive balancing act. The players had refused an initial redundancy package and Geoff Merrick, the club's 31-year-old captain and PFA representative, commented, 'If this happened in a colliery it would have the coal industry up in arms straight away.' There was more than the players' livelihoods at stake. The club itself looked to be on the brink of extinction. Rescue packages were being discussed and a new company in the throes of formation.

For the press, the resulting drama of noon-deadlines and smoke-filled rooms was perfect copy: 'The plush Dragonara Hotel in Bristol was awash yesterday with ashen-faced managers and tight-lipped players…' But for Gordon Taylor and the PFA it was a moment of harsh truth: doom-laden prophesies (his own included) seemed to be coming true:

'We really are in grave danger. Football has been like the South Sea Bubble. The figures frighten me. Clubs have been allowed to build up overdrafts on the strength of players' values going up. In the past, whenever the banks have started asking questions, directors have been able to say: "Oh, Jimmy Smith can go for so much." Now the other clubs haven't got the money to buy Jimmy Smith…We've had warning signs for some time…unless the game changes and there is a strong lead from the top, this is going to be just another contracting industry…'

Financial crises at English football clubs can be dealt with by various measures. In the short term they will typically include wage deferrals or wage cuts agreed to by players, the sale of player registrations (i.e. transfer fees, with valuations often reduced as in a 'fire sale') and involuntary redundancy of staff, including players and commercial staff

Unlike in any other industry, however, involvement by the PFA is almost mandatory due to the privileged position players occupy as 'preferred creditors' under Football League rules. That means that the players' contracts come first in the queue. As a quid pro quo the PFA is allowed to lend the club money in order to keep players in work and ultimately maintain employment prospects for its members. The Football League was more than willing to cooperate. In early March 1982 it even agreed to give the PFA the power of veto over clubs that tried to avoid bankruptcy by forming a new company. It also underwrote PFA loans to clubs by agreeing to channel the club's share of pooled monies directly to the PFA as repayment.

In the Bristol City case the PFA were represented on the creditors committee and eventually a redundancy package for the players involved of approximately £80,000 was obtained. This was tied to a new £1 million share issue in the new club plus the proceeds of a testimonial match between Southampton and Ipswich.

Geoff Merrick persuaded his fellow players to accept the deal:

> 'I am heartbroken. Bitter is not a word I like the sound of. I took my boots into the ground this morning in the hope that things would not turn out the way they have but I shall still be there on Saturday to support the team…We have gained a lot more than we would have done if we had accepted their ultimatum.'

Taylor, though agreeing to tear up the men's contracts, still felt the best deal had been arrived at.

> 'Considering the serious financial state of the club we feel that the eight have been fairly protected. The financial terms, I believe, should be kept personal and private. There have been many changes in the final offer and we have gone through many channels of discussion. The position has been looked at by all other clubs in the country. We want to make sure that this does not happen again.'

Taylor was awarded the *Observer* newspaper's Sports Personality of the Week for his pains, and he took the opportunity to make a crucial point. Asking that the jeroboam of champagne that went with the award be raffled 'for the Bristol lads', he continued,

> 'I tell you, there were a few vultures who'd come to Bristol hoping for a death. There are a few people in football who want a super league, want to see the end of the small town team, but the whole magic of this game is that clubs like Ipswich, Swansea, Northampton and Norwich can come up. Little teams living in hope. To disqualify them from that hope is to begin the end of football.'

Bristol City would not be the last club that would find itself being approached by Taylor and the PFA. The following hectic couple of months saw him rushing from town to town, 'trouble-shooter' style, working out rescue packages, lending cash and looking for ways to keep his members in employment.

At Hereford the PFA and players met with the local council to discuss a renegotiated lease for the club which offered it a crucial lifeline. Hull City and Wolverhampton Wanderers called in the receiver but the newly formed companies honoured the players' contracts. It was, as PFA solicitor George Davies put it, 'a baptism of fire' for Taylor but one from which he emerged triumphant.

At the beginning of March 1982 he was admiringly profiled in the *Daily Mirror*:

> Gordon Taylor stepped into soccer's most unenviable pressure-cooker with his eyes open. Just as well. His big difficulty now is finding the time to close them. 'Yes, the bags underneath are becoming a bit of a fixture,' says the beleaguered PFA secretary. Bristol City, Darlington, Hull, Halifax, the files on his crisis-packed desk are inches thick. And this personable, highly articulate leader of 2,900 playing members knows that every phone-call could be the next SOS. Taylor has driven 77,000 miles in eighteen months from his Lancashire home – plus numerous train-trips to London. 'Playing the game was certainly a lot easier,' says the thirty-seven-year-old who has leaned on his economics degree – and the union's accountants and lawyers – to unravel club balance sheets of doom and gloom in this season of threatened shut-downs…

Apart from giving the PFA a tremendous publicity bonanza, the latest phase of football's ongoing crises and Taylor's pivotal role in it had the effect of putting the Football League and its apologists on the defensive. Clearly, any club going out of business meant a loss of jobs for players but during these frenzied months Taylor managed to present both himself and the PFA as guardians of the original Football League philosophy. He was determined to see the structure survive, despite the shortcomings (or the contrary intentions) of those ostensibly in charge.

For one thing, he doubted that certain clubs threatened with bankruptcy had thought hard enough about how to solve their financial problems. They had not looked around for alternatives involving the local council, the supporters or the local community. He warned of the damage done by simply cutting out 'uneconomic units' in the way that

Brian Talbot Chairman 1984–88

Brian Talbot joined Ipswich Town as an apprentice, turning pro in 1972. After 227 Cup and League appearances he was sold to Arsenal in January 1979 for £450,000. A right-sided, industrious, goalscoring midfielder, he was the type of player for those who like their footballers 'full-blooded'. In the late 1970s Brian would equal Lord Kinnaird's century-old record of collecting Cup-winners' medals in successive seasons in the colours of two different clubs, Ipswich and Arsenal. Brian became a qualified FA coach in 1980, one of the youngest to hold the distinction, and he first tasted management with West Bromwich Albion where he was player-manager. His latest post is with Maltese side Marsaxlokk, whom he guided to the domestic League title and a place in the Champions League.

Lord Beeching as Minister of Transport in the 1960s had closed down railway stations – stations that in the 1980s could have solved critical transport problems. Not enough was being done, he felt, by the larger clubs to persuade smaller clubs not to commit hara-kiri. It was a theme he would virtually make his own, as suddenly he was being presented as the man holding everything together, the man to whom everyone was looking for answers. In a *Daily Mirror* interview in March 1982 Taylor declared he remained optimistic about the future of most of his members:

> 'despite clubs showing a lot of financial irresponsibility and overstretching themselves. I can see some light at the end of the tunnel. Even managers now ring up to seek our advice. And the League cooperates because they know our intentions are genuine.'

In effect, the Football League had no choice but to deal with Taylor and the PFA. With its public image so poor at that point, the League could not afford to be seen obstructing an organisation whose philosophy and practice looked to the public to be so positive and constructive. Even so, it felt that underwriting loans was not the same as lending hard cash: the League Management Committee argued that if it helped one club it would be obliged to help them all. Beneath the surface there remained a disturbing indifference to the fate of smaller clubs in trouble, an attitude that flew in the face of the League's own traditions.

Garth Crooks OBE Chairman 1988–90

A snappy little striker with a blistering turn of pace, and scorer of some memorable goals, Garth scored 53 times for Stoke City before moving on to Tottenham Hotspur in 1980 where he won two FA Cup-winners' medals and a UEFA Cup medal in 1984. Injury ended his career in 1990. In 1988 Garth became the first black chairman of the PFA. Garth's extensive media work included co-host of Top of the Pops, presenting BBC2's late night Despatch Box, while his discussion-cum-record show on Greater London Radio won him a Sony Award. He has produced and presented football programmes on Channel 4 and for BBC's Match of the Day team. Garth has always been very active on a variety of charitable projects. In 1985 he founded SCAR, the Sickle Cell Anaemia Relief Organisation, and is presently chairman of the Football Foundation's Grass Roots Advisory Group. He has worked with the Commission for Racial Equality (CRE) as well as athletic bodies such as the Institute of Professional Sport. In 2003 he became chair of the racism and equality issues committee of the Independent Football Commission.

This was made manifestly clear by Football League president Jack Dunnett. He was later quoted as saying:

> 'It's true I believed in natural wastage. If a community couldn't sustain a football club I didn't see why it should be propped up. We were quite prepared to see the League slimmed down to ninety or even seventy clubs. We certainly weren't going to provide special arrangements under which clubs who were teetering on the edge would have been allowed to avoid paying tax or their creditors.'

No doubt this made sense in crude free market terms but the economic struggle in the early 1980s was a many sided one. Football was under siege. It had an identity crisis of enormous proportions on its hands. This crisis was reflected in the country's crisis too. Clubs in economic trouble were at one with individual industrial towns in similar straits. The economic recession, bringing with it large-scale unemployment, caused widespread despair. Football clubs were often the focal points of such communities and to keep them going was a small but sometimes significant contribution to keeping up people's morale. As Taylor put it: 'The League believes in natural wastage, whereas we think that clubs have a debt to supporters to stay in existence.'

This, according to Taylor, was the true 'identity' of football, confirmed by the fact that on certain occasions he was welcomed more by local supporters and councillors than by the club's directors. Despite, or perhaps because of this, Taylor and the PFA often received little but abuse from certain beleaguered chairmen who persisted in attempting to lay their financial troubles at the feet of players. Sam Rourke, Halifax Town chairman, faced with the collapse of his club, attacked the PFA, 'for the way they have got more and more money for players, many of whom would be on the dole at the end of the season'.

There remained within boardrooms up and down the country a substantial residue of anti-player feeling that blamed 'freedom of contract' and the removal of the maximum wage for all soccer's financial ills. This feeling might well have been exacerbated at the start of 1982–83 when clubs such as Sheffield United, Southend United, Wrexham and Lincoln City attempted to cut incentive pay-schemes without the agreement of players. The PFA challenged all such cost-cutting attempts via the Professional Football Negotiating Committee.

Increasingly, however, it was being realised that the clubs themselves – directors in particular – were the architects of their own destruction. The fact that players could not now be sacked, nor held on the retain-and-transfer list, nor paid on a sliding scale with no bottom rung, merely closed off the traditional avenues of escape for many poorly run, inefficient club administrations. The anger and resentment expressed towards the players' 'massive pay packets' was often the gut reaction of men who were now finding themselves with no alternative but to talk to Gordon Taylor and his specialist insolvency accountant as part of the price of survival.

From saving minnows, however, the PFA was soon pitched into a battle with the behemoths…

Super League is Coming! 1982–88

The concept of a Super League had first been mooted by various top club directors in that troubled year of 1982 when the PFA had rejected the notion out of hand. Taylor caught the mood of the average supporter when suggesting that the idea 'would kill off the future of the Watfords, the Swanseas and all the small town clubs.' He added, 'such sentiments betray the traditions of our game, the underlying strength of the Football League acknowledged as the most competitive throughout the world.'

His sentiments were laced with pragmatism, however. At the PFA's 1982 AGM it was decided that if the Super League idea was put forward seriously by the top clubs then the PFA would press ahead for complete contractual freedom for players and thus 'smash' the transfer system: 'Complete contractual freedom would effectively abolish the transfer system – and provide a complete deterrent to a breakaway.' Taylor added:

> 'We could have gone for this in 1978 but voted not to because we committed ourselves to upholding the present ninety-two club structure of the Football League'.

The 1978 FA/Football League/PFA agreement on players' contracts had been considered by some to have 'legalised' the transfer system but it was no more than a compromise between the players and the clubs. As the Kerry Packer case proved when professional cricketers successfully freed themselves from restrictive contracts with the Test and County Cricket Board, the opportunity remained for professional football players to resort to the courts if their 'right to work' appeared in danger of being infringed by a monopoly employer such as the Football League.

However, financial pressures were now building within the game that would render such compromises irrelevant. In 1985 the Football League was arguing with itself and various TV companies over new broadcasting deals. Many topics were under discussion: how much would be paid; whether the number of live matches would be increased; whether sponsors' names should be prominently displayed on shirts. Personalities clouded the issue as Oxford United chairman Robert Maxwell clashed with Everton's chairman Philip Carter, while accusations of vested interests abounded.

At this point the PFA was very much on the sidelines though continuing to lend substantial amounts of money to smaller clubs who were quite clearly not going to gain much from the increased TV revenue. The eventual collapse of the TV negotiations, however, sent ominous reverberations through the game. The PFA's income for television therefore temporarily ceased and at the 1985 AGM Mike Birch, accountant and auditor, suggested that a substantial increase in membership subscriptions was advisable (from £15 to £20 a year). After all, 'subs' contributed a mere £27,000 to the association's funds while expenditure on education, accident insurance, hardship grants and general administration amounted to almost £350,000.

By then, however, unforeseen tragedy had struck. Fire at the Bradford City ground, collapsing walls at Birmingham City's ground and a hooligan-inspired riot at the Heysel Stadium in Brussels caused over a hundred supporter deaths. The lethal combination of decaying superstructures and declining standards of public behaviour was dragging professional football in Great Britain to its knees.

The response from the larger clubs was predictable. Excluded from European competition indefinitely by UEFA, banned from selling alcohol in grounds by government order, saddled with ever-increasing costs to modernise and make safe outdated stadiums and now deprived of TV revenues, they decided that their future lay in a Super League. The PFA was immediately propelled into the argument. This time, however, it was not simply a matter of announcing opposition to the Super League concept and hoping the idea would eventually blow over. As the secret meetings and negotiations between the chairmen of the biggest League clubs continued into late 1985 it became clear that the idea was being taken very seriously. Clubs such as Manchester United, Everton, Liverpool, Tottenham and Arsenal – the 'Big Five' as they were called – appeared to be in deadly earnest. The League system had, according to chairmen like Philip Carter of Everton and Martin Edwards of Manchester United, to be radically altered. The Third and Fourth Divisions had to be cut adrift. Top clubs could no longer afford to be part of an unwieldy obstructive out of date organisation like the Football League. Everyone was being dragged down into bankruptcy and ruin.

Daily Mail, 26 November 1985.

Gradually, however, a pattern emerged from the welter of rumour and panic-inducing headlines. The initial Super League idea was shelved and new plans began to be developed. The First Division clubs issued an ultimatum to those in the Second Division to join them in a breakaway, or the First Division clubs would go it alone. Discussions began between the two parties, the nub of which concerned money. The top clubs wanted to keep the entire TV revenue, along with all sponsorship monies. They also wanted an abolition of gate levies; in short, it would be a complete financial break with the lower clubs. The Third and Fourth Division clubs were understandably alarmed and frightened. However, realising that little could be done without the players' consent and that the plans were a clear threat to players' jobs, they turned to Gordon Taylor who, in November 1985, began to act as unofficial arbitrator, go-between and catalyst.

Taylor was once again doing what he did best: searching for a solution and slowly edging suspicious and essentially antagonistic parties closer together. However, he was not just a peacemaker. He carried with him a substantial mandate from his membership that committed him to hold out for certain minimum criteria, the most fundamental of which was the retention of all 92 Football League clubs within the existing League structure:

'If the players in the First and Second Division clubs are prepared to support their Third and Fourth Division colleagues then we can influence the changes for the benefit of all members and the game. Remember that many of today's top players either started or will finish in the Third and Fourth Divisions…'

The Star, Tuesday 12 July 1988.

Gradually, by exerting pressure on the 'associate members' of the Third and Fourth Division and extracting concessions from them, Taylor was able to bring the bigger clubs back into the fold. He convinced the lower clubs that they must agree to promotion and relegation in and out of the Football League itself, something they had consistently opposed. In fact, the two clubs involved in proposing and seconding the change – Rochdale and Halifax – could well have been in danger of relegation themselves.

It was conceded that the larger clubs ought to have a bigger slice of the TV money but a system of potentially lucrative play-offs was suggested to settle certain promotion places to help compensate the smaller clubs for the sacrifice. A reduction in the number of Division One teams also meant more clubs and more matches in Division Two. Taylor also calculated that TV money ought to be divided according to the percentage of spectator support each division attracted. Thus, the First Division roughly accounted for 50 per cent of total support and should therefore receive 50 per cent of the TV revenues. The remainder would be divided as 25 per cent to the Second Division and 25 per cent jointly for the Third and Fourth Division clubs.

By 26 November Everton chairman Carter was backtracking on earlier comments emphasising: 'There has never been any intention on our part to cut the Third and Fourth Divisions away…'

Once again Gordon Taylor and the PFA were being presented in the best possible light, with headlines such as 'Gordon Battles For The Minnows' and 'The Voice of Reason' bearing eloquent testimony to the influence he was able to bring to bear on events. Finally, on 18 December, at an hotel near Heathrow Airport, agreement was reached on a restructuring package that achieved Taylor's major objective: the survival of the traditional 92 club League system. A slightly reduced First Division would now receive more money (and pay less in the end of season gate levy) and would enjoy increased power to influence future events on a restructured League Management Committee. Significantly, however, the PFA agreed to accept a cut in its own share of the TV money to facilitate the agreement.

The Super League concept would, however, refuse to die. The arrival of satellite TV in 1988 – in this case BSB – saw the bidding for football television rights raised to dramatic heights. A long-running BBC/ITV 'cartel' had kept television fees artificially low for decades, now the lid was lifted. In fact a lucrative deal with BSB and BBC seemed to have satisfied most parties, but then the smaller clubs voted to end the payment of 'compensation' money to clubs (usually the biggest clubs) featured on live matches (in case their actual attendances fell significantly). Once again the Super League idea was raised. ITV, excluded from the original deal, approached several of the larger clubs and offered each £1 million for exclusive live coverage. With cash like that on offer the break up of the Football League seemed inevitable once again.

Accusations of secret deals and the involvement of key League Management Committee figures only increased the intrigue and hastened the deadlock. At a Football League Management Committee meeting in Plymouth on Friday 8 July,

Philip Carter of Everton, David Dein of Arsenal and Gordon McKeag of Newcastle were requested to leave the meeting when television rights were under discussion. The remaining members of the committee then asked Taylor and his deputy, Brendon Batson, to travel down to Plymouth as they believed an emergency had arisen which they saw as a threat to the very existence of the Football League.

It was 1986 all over again, even to the extent that the ultimate settlement whereby the First Division clubs took 75 per cent of all TV revenues leaving 25 per cent for the remaining three divisions, was once again facilitated by the PFA agreeing to accept yet another cut in *its* percentage share. Although it actually meant more money in cash terms for the association (the deal with BBC/BSB was eventually worth £44 million over four years, with the PFA receiving £550,000 per year, more than double what it had received during the previous two-year deal) the percentage of what it received overall had been reduced from 10 to almost five per cent. Gordon Taylor justified the cut to delegates at the 1988 AGM as necessary because: 'I considered that it was essential for the clubs to come to an agreement before the start of the season and put an end to the bickering and bad publicity which the game had received.' Significantly it was also agreed that no club could break away from the League in future without giving three years notice and being subject to financial penalties

Ironically, having played a major part in sustaining the fabric of the professional game and, in the process, enhancing his own profile, Taylor would now suddenly find himself at the centre of controversy and speculation. The departure of Graham Kelly, secretary of the Football League, in early 1989 to

The Mail on Sunday, 13 August 1989.

become chief executive of the FA led to moves for Gordon Taylor to replace him. At first he insisted the job was not for him and signed a five-year contract with the PFA but in August 1989 he appeared to have changed his mind. When Bill Fox was elected as the new President of the Football League Gordon Taylor appeared to be part of his plans, 'I made it clear before I was elected that the appointment of Gordon as chief executive was on the same ticket. Gordon has always been the right man for the job...' At the same time, Taylor told Joe Melling of the *Daily Mail*, 'The task which awaits me at the Football League may prove impossible but at least I'll know I had a go.' Given the crucial importance of such a move it seemed strange that neither man appeared to have persuaded, nor even informed, their respective management committees. There was an immediate outcry. Three League Management Committee members – John Smith of Liverpool, Doug Ellis of Aston Villa and Robert Chase of Norwich – were determined to oppose Taylor's appointment even though Fox insisted that he had the backing of the clubs ('I have been elected by the 92 League clubs and my platform included Gordon Taylor').

His opponents, however, insisted that he had acted unconstitutionally by negotiating secretly with Taylor before he had the authority to do so. They were also annoyed that the expensive and sensitive 'shortlist' process had been scuppered. Taylor, they pointed out, had refused to apply before and thus had disqualified himself. What was more, the suggestions by Fox that Taylor would have extra 'far-reaching' powers that had not been included in the earlier job description made various members of the management committee nervous and suspicious, particularly when Taylor himself outlined those powers:

> 'I see my role as running the League from day-to-day, making financial and commercial decisions and influencing policy with reference to the management committee but answerable only to the president and having complete security of tenure.'

This opposition to Taylor's appointment presented the PFA Management Committee with the opportunity it had apparently been waiting for to prevent Taylor from leaving. In a sense, Fox had attempted a publicity coup: by suddenly announcing Taylor's appointment he had gambled that any opposition would be swept aside on a tide of enthusiasm and, had the decision been greeted with unanimity, the PFA would have found it hard to resist. However, once Fox's opponents had demonstrated their determination not to be 'steamrollered', Garth Crooks, PFA chairman, was quick to act.

A management committee meeting was called in London on Monday 14 August, and what was to have been a press conference endorsing the move became a meeting to stop it. The management committee asked Taylor to honour the agreement he had signed less than a year previously.

Garth Crooks later confessed to having been shocked when Taylor had first informed him of his decision to leave and join the League should Fox win the election. While recognising that Taylor was struggling with a difficult decision which could involve an opportunity for him to have a greater control over the game's destiny, Crooks was nevertheless angry that Fox had not considered it necessary to consult with the PFA or even to ask permission to approach their chief executive. Furthermore, the response to Fox's victory from defeated opponents had convinced him that the prospect of unity at the Football League was now remote.

Thus, the hastily convened PFA Management Committee attended by Nigel Spackman, Colin Gibson, Trevor Morgan, Crooks and David Mercer, the PFA lawyer, were adamant: Taylor must stay. Crooks explained:

> 'Events since last Friday have satisfied the committee that Gordon could not be guaranteed the support and backing he enjoys at the PFA if he joined the League. Gordon fully understands and accepts our reasoning. He has set a marvellous example to everyone in football that contracts are there to be honoured by all…'

Their decision dealt a body blow to Fox's strategy and placed Taylor in an awkward situation: 'I accept the reasons and the decision because I don't want to go and leave bad blood behind me. I am not going to say I am disappointed, but I would have relished the challenge, given the opportunity by both sides…'

With Fox left battling on alone to secure his own position, questions were now asked about Gordon Taylor's judgement in allowing both himself and the PFA to become embroiled in such a fiasco. It was suggested in the press that he had been naïve. It was even said that he must now 'contemplate his sparkling career stagnating for the foreseeable future.'

The determination by the PFA Management Committee to categorically insist that Taylor serve out his contract was, in many ways, a surprise but demonstrated its independence and even safeguarded its integrity. Gordon Taylor's rapid rise to prominence in British football during the 1980s had tended to eclipse the rest of the management committee. His successful style entailed taking personal initiatives while counting on the support of a membership that trusted him implicitly. He considered regular, detailed consultation with the membership and management committee to be unnecessary and even a hindrance to effective decision making. Thus, it had appeared at times Gordon Taylor *was* the PFA. Now the management committee had asserted itself. Crooks would later add that Taylor was 'our man – we're keeping him because we believe that the players need him and we believe that we are the most important body in football, representing the players that play the game.'

Over the next decade and more, this decision by the players would be seen as a turning point in English football history.

2. Bosman and Beyond 1990–2009

'I would have preferred someone else had taken part in all this. I would have liked to have been just a young player on the verge of a good career.'
Jean Marc Bosman, 2005.

At about the same time that Gordon Taylor was committing himself to the PFA, an obscure Belgian midfield player called Jean Marc Bosman was signing a two-year contract with RFC Liege on a monthly salary of approximately 120,000 Belgian francs. Shortly before this contract expired in the spring of 1990, he was offered a new one-year contract but with his wages slashed to 30,000 francs – the lowest wage the club could offer under the rules of the Belgian Football Association. Bosman refused to sign and was placed on the club's transfer list. From that point on he would come to dominate professional football's worldwide agenda like no other player before or since.

In cases such as Bosman's, the Belgian Football Association used a complex mathematical formula to determine what fee might be placed on his head. Unfortunately for Jean Marc, the figure was almost 12 million francs, more than any Belgian club was willing to pay. Thus, in May 1990 he negotiated a one-year transfer to a French Second Division club, Dunkirk, for a 10th of that figure. Dunkirk had an option to sign him permanently if they paid another 4,800,000 Belgian francs by the beginning of August, but the deal collapsed and Bosman was suspended without pay.

In late 1990 he started court proceedings to force Liege to pay him a salary until he found a new club while also at the same time asking the court to prohibit the club from seeking a transfer fee for him. He also requested that the case be transferred to the European Court of Justice (ECJ) for determination of the ultimate issue – the legality or otherwise of the Belgian transfer system.

Bosman caused football's leaders headaches galore. At a press conference in 1997 Phillipe Piat, Gordon Taylor (Fifpro President) and Sepp Blatter (FIFA President) share their concerns with the Press.

Over the next three years Bosman plied his trade at three lower division clubs in France and Belgium on a succession of one-year contracts while his legal proceedings dragged on. In April 1992 he amended his claim so as to seek an order that neither the Belgian FA's transfer rules nor the UEFA rules concerning overseas player 'quotas' were applicable to him. In June 1992 he was granted permission to take his case to the ECJ to seek a ruling on the compatibility of both the Belgian transfer system and UEFA's rules on overseas player quotas with the Treaty of Rome provisions under Article 48 guaranteeing 'freedom of movement' for all EC citizens in search of work.

Finally, in 1995, the ECJ ruled in his favour, deciding that the existing football transfer rules were in breach of European law guaranteeing free movement for workers between member states. As a result the European Union demanded that the regulations concerning players' transfers and limitations on foreign players be amended almost immediately. The judgment was not greeted with universal hosannahs.

In fact, as Bosman had doggedly pursued his rights through the legal labyrinth of the Belgian justice system, the PFA, rather than rush to help, had instead attempted to persuade those in power to do a deal with him. Gordon Taylor was by that time also President of FIFPro, the International Federation of Football Unions, and was following events closely:

> 'We had initially warned UEFA of the Bosman case and that FIFPro was prepared to support it through to the European Court of Justice and that it was up to them to put pressure on the Belgian authorities to compensate Bosman and change their rules which had not allowed Bosman to transfer to Dunkirk and had kept him at his club in Belgium at a reduced wage. Clearly this was not acceptable legally and took us back to the situation in England before the George Eastham case which had already set a precedent with regard to the retain-and-transfer system.'

FIFPro had been formed at a meeting in Paris on 15 December 1965 and was made up of representatives of French, Scottish, English, Italian and Dutch players' associations. Its first congress took place in London in June 1966, just before the start of the World Cup, its original objective being to coordinate the activities of the different players' associations and to pursue and defend the rights of professional football players worldwide. By the 1990s it had begun to assume critical importance in world football affairs. Between 1998 and 2001 FIFPro grew from a European organisation into a global network boasting over 40 affiliates in Europe, South America, Africa, North America, as well as Australia, Asia and the Middle East. In 1994 a permanent secretariat was established and, following the Bosman ruling in 1995, it was accepted as the official players' representative in all negotiations by UEFA and FIFA. The European Commission also officially recognised FIFPro in 1998.

As chance would have it Gordon Taylor had been appointed FIFPro president in 1992 and would thus be at the heart of the subsequent negotiations that would dramatically transform the status of professional footballers. He would find it a difficult task in many ways, not least because FIFPro's affiliates would be divided as to what their position should be in establishing new employment rules, particularly where changes to the transfer system were concerned. To put it simply, certain European unions would be more militant than others, reflecting their different histories and status. At this point in the game's history, the English PFA, being the senior organisation in terms of longevity and experience and having enjoyed almost 20 years of peace and prosperity, was not inclined towards the radical end of the spectrum.

In fact, the European Court's judgement threatened what had, until then, been a mutually beneficial relationship between the PFA and its English employers where players' contracts were concerned. Unlike other national football unions, the PFA had a collective bargaining agreement with the Premier League and the Football League recognised by the Football Association under which unilateral breaches of contract by either players or clubs was prohibited. Underpinning the agreement was an acceptance by both players and employers that professional football, although increasingly big business, was still different to everyday life. As Premier League chief executive Richard Scudamore put it:

> 'If you look at what happens to a normal employee and what happens to a footballer the whole system is very different in football and therefore it does need a specific set of rules. It's an exchange; it's a bargain between consenting parties. They have far more protections than the rest of us have, in terms of when they are injured and unavailable for work. They also have a protected contract where they can sit and get paid even when they are not working. It's also worth noting that the players, particularly the players in this country, are not unhappy with the system.'

Gordon Taylor agreed. In the autumn of 1995, following Advocate General Lenz's Bosman ruling, Taylor an published an article in *Football Management* that was critical of Lenz. The transfer system, he said, had worked well in England. He added: 'It was perhaps significant that the English system was not referred to as a model by the [EU] Advocate General as clearly this gives a player the right to move at the end of a contract with an independent transfer tribunal to settle the fee should there be any dispute. Our system has also enabled many millions of pounds of transfer income to go to lower division clubs to help keep them alive on a full-time basis.'

The PFA now appeared to be supporting the transfer system in terms that had once been the prerogative of the employers, the Football League. Ending the system, Taylor considered, 'could have a devastating effect on football. The weaker, smaller clubs must be protected, youth training schemes must be preserved and clubs encouraged to develop better youth development programmes. Home-grown talent must be allowed to develop and prosper, so protecting the future of our international team. To find a new system that meets these needs as the present one does is a difficult challenge. We feel the system that we have in being has enabled our leading players to capitalise on their ability but has also encouraged a record number of full-time clubs (92), full-time players (2,300) and youth trainees (1,250) in a footballing country with the highest aggregate attendances of over 20 million a year.'

Literal freedom at the end of a contract which the Bosman judgement appeared to provide threatened rather than enhanced the interests of his members. He was fearful that if clubs were afraid that players might leave at the end of the (then traditional) one-year contract, they would seek to place them on longer-term contracts. This would 'deny players the flexibility and freedom to move and lend to dissatisfaction for both parties. It [the present system] has the support of the employers and the employees and there is little reason to abandon it. If it ain't broke, don't mend it.' As for Bosman himself, Taylor said, 'Whilst we had every sympathy with [him] with regard to his situation, his circumstances could not have occurred in England.'

Although the Bosman judgement addressed only international transfers and did not affect transfer fees for players still in contract, England's governing bodies, along with the PFA, felt it prudent to agree on a new, more flexible internal contract system in the hope that more drastic changes would not be demanded by the European Commission.

A couple of years after the Bosman decision, therefore, a new set of contract arrangements was agreed in England that drastically increased the contractual freedom of players. By the end of June 1998 players who were aged 24 or over and at the end of their contracts had literal freedom to join any club of their choosing in the UK or abroad. It also introduced a system of compensation for clubs releasing younger players. If a player was under 24 and found himself out of contract he would still have the right to move on but compensation would now be payable to his old club, the amount being based on the training and development he had received while at the club. This 'compensation' was designed to ensure that the parent club did not lose out if a player they had nurtured chose to sign for someone else. It was also introduced, according to Taylor, to encourage all clubs throughout the four divisions of the Premier League and the Football League to continue developing youth systems, something the PFA had spent a great deal of time and money promoting and supporting.

Thus, with practically little fanfare and no overt celebrations, professional footballers in England gained a measure of self-determination unheard of since the turn of the century. It cut both ways, of course. Clubs could now offload players when they no longer needed them and the number of players out of work rose sharply in the immediate aftermath of the new contract's introduction. In November 1998 it was announced that 341 players in the Football League had been given 'free' transfers while in the Premier League the figure was 103.

Inevitably, however, all the attention centred on the stars. Suddenly top players saw a wide world of financial possibilities opening up before them. With the end of his contract approaching, a sought after player could now choose to wait until it expired and then negotiate a lucrative new deal with another interested club. The latter, freed of having to stump up a massive transfer fee, could offer most of the money to the player by way of wages. The phrase 'doing a Bosman' now entered football's lexicon to be illustrated perfectly by Liverpool's Steve McManaman. McManaman became the most lucrative 'Bosman' transfer in history when Real Madrid offered him a £14 million contract package over five years. His old club Liverpool, who might once have expected to sell him on for a similar sum, looked on helpless, gaining nothing from his departure. In July 2000 it was estimated that within the Premier League 24 per cent of players were planning a 'Bosman' transfer and a further nine per cent were considering it. In the First and Second Divisions the percentages were almost the same.

The timing of the new contractual freedom could not have been better. Players in England had assumed control over their own destinies at a time when the game in England was awash with cash. A £670 million, five-year television deal with Sky TV was secured for the FA Premier League rights in 1997, thereby providing clubs with a bigger pot of money to spend than ever before. This had crucial consequences: clubs offered radically improved salaries not only to out-of-contract 'Bosman'-type players but also to currently contracted players in an effort to stave off 'Bosmans'; long term contracts became the norm; transfer fees rocketed radically as clubs tried to purchase players currently *in* contract; and significant numbers of overseas players, many on 'Bosman'-type contracts, now began to arrive in England.

Lower down the divisions, 'Bosman' transfers hit smaller football clubs hard. Clubs were having to negotiate longer and costlier contracts to their youngest players or risk losing them to bigger clubs for nothing. Transfer fees filtering down from the Premier League slowed to a trickle because top flight clubs now shopped mainly overseas for 'ready-made' players. Meanwhile, older players, chasing more pay via 'Bosman' moves as their contracts were getting shorter, were increasingly fearful for their jobs.

However, the Bosman case had affected only the transfers of players whose contracts had come to an end. It did not address the potentially more serious issue of the legality of the payment of transfer fees for players who were still under contract. It was a situation that would not last forever.

'I was a nobody but I stood up to the major powers in football and I'm proud of it. But the judge went further than any of us imagined in allowing any out-of-contract player to move for nothing. That's not my fault. I don't make the rules.'
Jean Marc Bosman, 2005.

When, in 1997, Italian club Perugia took legal action alleging that they were being hindered in their attempts to sign a Swiss international player, Massimo Lombardo, who was still under contract with the Grasshoppers Zurich club, the European

Commission's competition commissioners were moved to intervene. Concerned that players in contract could not exercise their desire to move on in the same way that other workers could, EC commissioner Mario Monti maintained that footballers and professional sports people in general should have the same entitlement to freedom of movement as anyone else. Football should not, he felt, be granted special exemption status from EU law in this regard.

In 2000 the moment arrived that many in the game had been fearing ever since the Bosman judgement. The European Commission issued a statement of objections to the international transfer system for contracted players and, seeing no discernible voluntary movement towards change on behalf of football's authorities, declared that the international transfer system was incompatible with the EU Treaty. Obliged under Declaration 29 of the Treaty of Amsterdam 'to listen to sports associations when important questions affecting sport are at issue', the commission entered into negotiations with the football authorities to 'reform' the system and bring it in line with the Treaty, a tortuous and, at times, seemingly interminable saga that has still not reached a satisfactory conclusion.

From the very outset the commission accepted that a player could not simply give a month's notice to his current club and then move to local rivals as this had the potential to devalue and unbalance competitions. Instead, it called for a compromise that would bring the international football transfer system more in line with EU law without devaluing the competitions themselves.

What troubled the commission most was the inordinate size of certain transfer fees. In August 1999 Nicolas Anelka of Arsenal moved to Real Madrid mid-contract for £23.5 million following a protracted row over what he was actually worth. Anelka's lawyers had suggested that the real value of the 'compensation' owed to Arsenal for Anelka breaking his contract should be around £900,000, that is, the value remaining on his contract. Fortunately for Arsenal, the case did not go to court and they received the fee they demanded.

The commission reasoned that such enormous amounts of money demanded by selling clubs – should the buying clubs refuse to meet them – had the potential to severely restrict a players' freedom of movement between EU states. The even larger £37 million price tag put on Barcelona's Luis Figo meant that it was only Real Madrid and perhaps a couple of the larger Italian clubs that could *realistically* afford to buy him. If Figo had wished to return to Portugal he would have to wait until the end of his contract as no Portuguese club could have afforded him.

Thus, the commission wanted the compensation payable for 'contract breaches' on the part of a player to be objectively and impartially determined so that it more accurately reflected the actual loss suffered by the club. The amount decided upon should also not prevent players moving between EU states.

Football's governing bodies had initially reacted to such challenges to the transfer system with expressions of horror and outrage. FIFA president Sepp Blatter announced that the payment of transfer fees would soon be 'a thing of the past' while

FIFA general secretary Michel Zen-Ruffinen declared, somewhat prematurely, that it was 'the end of football'. It seemed inconceivable to those in authority that the EC could ever understand the complexities of the game. The Bayern Munich president, Franz Beckenbauer, hardly helped football's cause by declaring: 'You've got a bunch of failures sitting in Brussels. All failed existences, shoved off to Brussels by their governments. It is Europe's biggest gang of dead losers.'

However, Mario Monti, or 'Super Mario' as he was known in Brussels after the Nintendo character, was no pushover. With his Brussels-based Merger Task Force – a 75-strong group of lawyers and economists that reviewed and occasionally disallowed proposed mergers in the European Union – he was acquiring a reputation as a fearless 'trustbuster' who had blocked General Electric Co's bid to buy Honeywell International and had taken on software giant Microsoft Corp. Fairly soon some of the football industries pet shibboleths were being called into question.

For instance, when FIFA suggested that transfer fees were a free market form of re-distribution of monies and that smaller clubs sold players to bigger clubs as a form of income-generation, the commission retorted that, according to *its* figures the reverse was the case. Most 'big money' transfers now took place between the richer clubs for already proven players, particularly in the UK. At the same time the EC noted, just as many small clubs were getting into financial difficulties through overspending in the transfer market as were being bailed out by being able to sell their best players to larger clubs. If the football industry wanted to redistribute wealth then why not share out its television revenues more fairly?

In September 2000 a six-man Transfer Task Force was appointed by FIFA to lead talks with the European Commission in the attempt to find a legal solution to the problem. The task force was led by UEFA vice-president Per Omdal and also included Gerhard Aigner (UEFA chief executive), Michel Zen-Ruffinen (FIFA general secretary), Pedro Tomas (Spanish League general secretary), Gerhard Mayer-Vorfelder (German FA vice-president) and – on the insistence of Monti – Gordon Taylor (of the English PFA and chairman of FIFPro).

As the months passed it became clear that the task force, set up to represent the whole 'football family' and to present a united front to the EC, was anything but united. As the wearer of two hats, Gordon Taylor had the difficult task of reflecting the conflicting interests of FIFPro's various member countries.

Smaller unions were opposed to transfer fees on principle. Instead of clubs having to sell players they had often trained and nurtured from a young age, union's such as Greece's Panhellenic Professional Football Players' Association and Sweden's SFS Svenska Fotboll Spelare felt broadcasting rights revenues should be shared out more equitably. If a player moved on then the parent club should receive money from a central fund to which all clubs had contributed. This was also the declared position of the EC.

Furthermore, they contended that transfer fees restricted a player's economic freedom. Encouraged by the European Commission's requirement that any new regulations had to have the blessing of FIFPro, they also felt the players possessed a unique opportunity to pursue a forceful collective bargaining agenda.

Gordon Taylor, however, disagreed with the idea of a central fund: 'I could not see how this had any credibility for being established on a practical basis.' As for abolishing transfer fees, he wrote at the time, 'It goes without saying that the abolition of the transfer system as we know it, as proposed by the EC, will cause absolute chaos.' If players were to be treated no differently to any other employee in any industry and be allowed to leave their employment under a set notice period, 'players would be able to walk out on their clubs and young players at smaller clubs will be cherry-picked by the big boys.'

Mads Oland, of the Danish players' association, quickly took Taylor to task claiming, 'Gordon Taylor's viewpoints are new to us and have certainly not been discussed at the congresses of FIFPro and therefore it cannot be the policy of FIFPro at this moment of time.'

Such internal differences among the players would make Taylor's negotiating position difficult. As the arguments continued within the 'football family' and with FIFPro threatening to pull out of the task force talks in October 2000 amid accusations that the clubs were trying to 'bend the rules' to restrict the freedom of players, it was noticeable that UEFA's spokesman exonerated Taylor from responsibility for the friction. Taylor's work within the task force, it was claimed, was being undermined by 'hard-line' French players' union chairman Philippe Piat, who was trying to force more concessions out of the employers in terms of freedom of movement.

However, tensions within the players' group were nothing compared to those that eventually surfaced between the two main governing bodies and FIFPro itself. Rows, misunderstandings and public spats culminated in late October with the players' proposals not being incorporated in the final task force submission to the EC.

Taylor and FIFPro had been encouraged to think that the EU was broadly sympathetic towards the players and their demands for greater freedom of movement. Mario Monti assured them that, 'I have taken good note that FIFA does not have the support of FIFPro on the subject of the propositions which I have received and I very much regret this.' All parties had to agree to the proposals, otherwise what was the point of the task force in the first place?

Ominously, after examining the task force proposals that were being put forward Taylor announced, 'they are ambiguous and look as though they have been drafted with the hidden agenda of maintaining the status quo. We have had lengthy discussions with Commissioner Monti and his staff, over a period of months, and if this goes through they have been giving us completely the wrong information. We will wait to see what the EC think of the task force's proposals, but I would personally be astounded if they found them acceptable.'

What had upset Taylor, and FIFPro in particular, were attempts by UEFA and those representing the employers to insert into the new transfer/contract proposals various penalties, both financial and sporting, for the breaching of contracts as well as 'compensation' fees to be paid for the transfer of players under the age of 23.

Relations between the employers and FIFPro were now at breaking point. With FIFPro threatening to go to court if the rights of their members were not protected in any new deal, Richard Scudamore, speaking for the Premier League, was scathing, claiming that FIFPro had altered their earlier position and had added extra demands at the last minute. He began to question FIFPro's right to speak for the players: 'Few players in this country have ever heard of FIFPro and Gordon has put himself in a very difficult position. It's completely hypocritical.' David Dein of Arsenal also tried to suggest that Taylor and FIFPro did not represent the majority of players. He claimed to have approached some of the senior players at Arsenal who stated categorically that they had not been consulted and were totally unaware of the issues: 'FIFPro are playing a dangerous game. The way they are going could administer the kiss of death to many of their members.' He also suggested that a rival trade union called ProProf, based in Holland, was also claiming to represent players abroad. FIFPro, he said, had little grass roots support.

In early 2001 FIFPro looked increasingly isolated. Excluded from the main negotiating rooms in Brussels on 16 February as FIFA and UEFA spent several hours locked in talks with commission officials, Taylor and his team eventually gave up and left for home, explaining to the waiting press, 'We have been sitting around drinking coffee all afternoon waiting for FIFA and the EC to finish, and now we have planes to catch, it's time to go home.' Told that the players had departed, a FIFA/UEFA source quipped, 'I suppose they must because they could not find anybody to talk to.'

On 5 March 2001 EC Commissioners Anna Diamantopoulou, Vivianne Reding and Mario Monti finalised discussions with Sepp Blatter, president of FIFA, and Lennart Johansson, the president of UEFA, announcing an agreed resolution on the international transfer system.

For FIFPro the terms of the agreement came as something of a shock: smaller clubs would be compensated for developing young players; there would be one transfer period per season plus a limited mid-season window and a limit of one transfer per player per season; contracts would last from one year to a maximum of five; and financial compensation would be paid if a contract was breached unilaterally, whether by player or club. There were to be sporting penalties for players unilaterally breaching contracts, with bans for up to six months in certain cases. Where the much criticised transfer system was concerned, if player and bargaining clubs agreed then transfer fees were to be left undisturbed!

The Premier League appeared particularly pleased with the new regulations. Richard Scudamore defended 'sporting sanctions' on players who left a club in mid-contract 'without just cause': 'There has to be some form of sanction because unilateral breaches are unacceptable. There will be some more discussion about how long this should be but there has to be an incentive for players not to unilaterally breach.'

FIFPro's assessment was understandably downbeat. One moment players were glimpsing total freedom, with the end of transfer fees and the start of an equitable redistribution of TV revenues, the next they were looking at fines and suspensions if they exercised their rights as European citizens, while clubs were free to spend ever more of their massive TV revenues on headline-grabbing transfer deals.

It refuted the European Commission's claims that the new rules gave players the technical right to unilaterally break a contract. In actual fact, they claimed, the conditions were so restrictive and intimidated by sanctions that it would prove far from easy to do so. Gordon Taylor went so far as to claim that the new agreement was not 'just pre-Bosman, it's pre-George Eastham and the dark days of 1963. It violates fundamental rights.'

FIFPro spokesman Laurent Dennis also condemned the deal as a 'very black day for European sport and footballers,' while the vice-president of the French players' union declared, 'They are treating players like imbeciles. We have been taken for turkeys.'

'People are blaming me for what is happening now but that's unfair. I never, ever broke my contract with a club and I don't think it should happen…I believe players should remain with their first club for at least three years in order for that club to reap some of the benefits.'
Jean Marc Bosman, 2005.

It seemed to many that FIFPro had been outflanked by the diplomatic wiles of FIFA's Sepp Blatter, who, by courting heads of state such as Tony Blair, German chancellor Schroder (who made a joint plea to the European Commission outlining the 'potentially catastrophic consequence' of scrapping the transfer system), French President Jacques Chirac and many more, had managed to put pressure on Commissioner Monti and his team to reverse their earlier pledges. How else to explain the apparent volte-face of the commission which had completely backed down in its attempt to control transfer fees as well as comprehensively dumped the idea of using some of the vast sums accrued via the sale of TV rights to compensate clubs for the loss of players? Why would Mario Monti, who had insisted for years that there could be no special case for soccer, at the very last moment made an exception? Monti's reputation was of someone who could resist political pressure and who was imperious to high-level lobbying.

What had been overlooked when the 'settlement' had been announced in March had been the statement that 'The Commissioners pointed out that the discussions do not prejudge the question of compatibility of such regulations with national law. The Commissioners invited FIFA and UEFA to encourage clubs to start or pursue the social dialogue with the representative bodies of football players…'

It was clear that a window of opportunity remained for FIFPro to influence the fine detail of the new regulations.

Much of FIFPro's unhappiness had stemmed from the penalties likely to be meted out to a player 'unilaterally breaching' his contract before it had reached its end. Under the agreement, if he chose to walk out on his club in the middle of his contract he would not be allowed to play until four months into the start of the following season. According to various calculations, depending on when he actually left his original club that could mean being sidelined for as long as 12 months after his move to a new club. FIFPro were adamantly opposed to such 'sporting' sanctions, preferring financial penalties instead. FIFPro general secretary Theo Van Seggelen explained, 'It's not good when a player has a short career – the average career of a player is 10 years. So it's not good for a player to be missing half a year.'

Equally problematic was the question of the amount a club might receive for training its young players. Under the new regulations, if a player under 23 years of age left the club where he had received his training, the club could receive some money even if it had not been prepared to give him a new contract. FIFPro regarded such compensation as an unreasonable bar to a move.

For these and various other reasons, FIFPro were adamant that the new contract regulations could not be allowed to stand. In May 2001 it initiated legal action, challenging the competence of the European Commission to allow a private body such as FIFA to establish rules that, in FIFPro's opinion, deviated from European law. Theo van Siggelen threatened, 'Even if the new rules are implemented, we will call on players all over Europe who want to break their contracts to go to their national courts. There be will enormous instability.'

The stage was thus set for one more twist in the seemingly endless saga. On 17 July Sepp Blatter agreed to a top secret meeting in Zurich involving only himself, his special adviser Jerome Champagne, plus Gordon Taylor and a FIFPro colleague. Not even Michael Zen-Ruffinen, FIFA general secretary, was involved.

Blatter was, at that particular moment, under immense pressure. He was being questioned about the collapse of FIFA's World Cup marketing agents, ISL, with debts estimated at £300 million; there had been the disclosure of a secret ISL account containing £40 million of television revenue; and on top of that had come the shock postponement of the 2001 summer World Club Championship – Blatter's own creation – which saw FIFA forced to pay each of the 12 participants a minimum of $500,000 in compensation. He may well have been seeking allies; he might also have been heeding the original calls from the commission to ensure that the players' representatives be kept on board. There was also the fact that Blatter had previously suggested he was happy to abolish the transfer system and had been criticised for having initially appeared to be ready to concede far more than the commissioners had been demanding back when the process had first commenced.

Whatever his reasons, Blatter offered the players representatives an olive branch as reward for withdrawing the court case. Taylor explained: 'Blatter told us he could not change the regulations but he would send a circular on the *interpretation* of the regulations and the interpretation would be a lot more "practical". There was an initial stand-off but after Commissioner Monti rang me at home one evening to impress upon me the need to achieve agreement between all parties, I then dictated a letter to FIFA which I signed as President of FIFPro in order to bring matters to a conclusion.'

Blatter's promise of a more 'practical' interpretation of the new regulations emerged in September as FIFA Circular 769 'Regulations for the Status and Transfer of Players'. It proved to be a controversial document as it seemed to grant players who signed contracts after 1 September 2001 almost total freedom of movement. For instance, the new regulations stipulated that the first three years of any contract would be 'protected'. That is, both player and club would agreed not to 'unilaterally' force a transfer. This would guarantee 'stability' for clubs and players alike. However, if a player, for whatever reason, decided to force the issue and breach his contract before the protected period ended, the maximum he would have to spend kicking his heels before being allowed to play elsewhere would be just four months. Thus, if he left his club in August he could be playing for someone else by December, not the following season as had originally seemed likely. If he chose to leave *after* the first three 'protected' years of his contract, no penalties at all would apply.

Although FIFPro agreed to accept the idea of compensation, this was because the amounts to be paid would be determined by a new Dispute Resolution Chamber. This would have an independent chairman and equal representatives for both the player and the club. FIFPro could also nominate representatives for the new Arbitration Tribunal for Football, to which decisions of the Dispute Resolution Chamber would be appealed. The understanding was that decisions would generally be favourable for the player.

Football's employers were taken aback at the development, not least because it had been arrived at in total secrecy. Premier League spokesman Philip French complained: 'FIFA did not inform us that this whole sideshow was taking place. It seems that yet again some unsavoury deal has been cooked up behind the scenes between FIFA and FIFPro.'

Despite the agonising gestation of the new regulations and the apparent new freedoms they offered players, not one player would attempt to take advantage of them for almost five years! Part of the reason was that FIFA embarked on yet another long process of 'refining' the new system, a process that culminated in a 'final' set of revised 'Regulations for the Status and Transfer of Players' which came into force on 1 July 2005. Included in the new arrangements was Article 17.

In simple terms there were now what would be called contractual 'stability' periods for players under the age of 28. Once a player completed three years of a contract then he would have the right to move, with compensation being paid to the original club based on the remaining value of his contract as a priority and 'possible consideration of any transfer fee'. It had been formulated as a bargaining tool between FIFA and the European Union to try to bring the rights of footballers

Jean Marc Bosman, the man who precipitated the greatest transformation in professional footballers' lives.

into line with other EU workers. Article 17, in effect, appeared to go some way towards abolishing huge transfer fees.

In September 2006 Andy Webster, a 24-year-old Scotland defender, became the first player to exploit the new rule. Webster left Heart of Midlothian for Wigan Athletic with 12 months of a four-year deal remaining, unhappy after Hearts' Russian owner Romanov refused to play him in the first team. Hearts, valuing Webster at some £4–5 million, entered a complaint with FIFA and demanded compensation. In May 2007 FIFA's Dispute Resolution Chamber decided that Webster had certainly broken his contract 'without just cause' – and that he had to pay compensation to Hearts of £625,000. Webster was also suspended for the first two matches of the new season with his new club.

However, Wil van Megen, the Dutch lawyer acting on behalf of FIFPro, felt that £625,000 was 'a strange sum' and far higher than they had expected: 'Under the FIFA guidelines we felt that it would be a maximum of one and a half times his annual salary with add-ons. Webster's salary at Hearts was £150,000 per year so we felt the compensation was going to be at around the £300,000 mark.'

Webster thus appealed to the Court for Arbitration in Sport (which now heard appeals from the DRC) in October 2007 while Hearts simultaneously sought considerable compensation, including monies for sporting and commercial losses, legal expenses etc. In February 2008 the CAS decided Webster would only have to pay up the final year of his contract to secure his release, a mere £150,000.

Tony Higgins of FIFPro said: 'Basically, Article 17 gives footballers the sort of employee rights that anyone else would expect in the workplace. What it means is that any footballer can now serve notice on his club [in mid-contract] and move on to a new club.' FIFA president Sepp Blatter, however, described the Webster case as 'a pyrrhic victory for players and their agents who toy with the idea of rescinding contracts before they have been fulfilled.'

Not so Arsenal manager Arsene Wenger, who would lose two star players against his wishes in the summer of 2008. He felt that the lure of inflated wages would tempt players to routinely break their contracts. 'A team sport needs time and stability and all the rules in our game go against that,' he said. Wenger felt that it would only be a matter of time before players could buy out their contracts after just a year, destroying any hope of squad building. 'At the moment it's either three years or two but believe me, soon someone will challenge that and ask why at 28 years old and not, say, at 27,' he said. 'And then it will be why after two years and not one? Once you get to that stage, the transfer system is dead. You'd have a team built for a year – then you are in big trouble.'

Nothing is ever that simple in football. Following a summer of intrigue and endless headlines featuring some of England's most expensive stars, the integrity of the contract would appear to have been upheld – at least for now. Manchester United's Christiano Ronaldo was unable to talk his way into a world-record move to Real Madrid, due largely to the obduracy of United manager Alex Ferguson, backed up by the security of a five-year contract Ronaldo had only just signed. At Chelsea, Frank Lampard's threats to use FIFA rules to buy his way out of *his* contract in order to be reunited with José Mourinho at Inter Milan also proved to be groundless. In fact, the lesson seemed to be for the bigger clubs to tie down their best players to long contracts and dig their heels in.

Peter Crouch's agent, Jonathan Barnett, emphasised the alternative view: that players were still regarded as assets and that more clubs wanted to get rid of players than the other way round. 'In real terms, it's the clubs who invariably force players to break contracts,' he said, 'Every time a club decides to sell a player they, too, are guilty of breaking a contract. Peter, for instance, has never asked to leave Liverpool.' Crouch was sold that summer to Portsmouth.

3. TV Revenue Wars 1991–2002

Premier League Arrival
The campaign led by the cheaply vilified Gordon Taylor must go down as epic resistance to the idea that the process of the football rich getting richer – and the poorer finally being pushed over the cliff edge – is inexorable.
James Lawton in *The Independent*

Control of the English professional game became the most contentious issue of the early 1990s as relations between its two governing bodies, the Football League and the Football Association, descended into outright hostility. In October 1990 the Football League unveiled a comprehensive plan for fundamental change entitled 'One game, one team, one voice' calling for an historic amalgamation of the two bodies.

From the outset the scheme looked doomed, not least because the FA's initial lukewarm response brought forth threats on behalf of certain League Management Committee members that they would withdraw their clubs from the FA Cup and their players from the England squad if the FA were not cooperative.

Billboards state the PFA case in October 2001.

David Busst billboard 2001.

In April 1991 the FA then launched its own reorganisation plan after being encouraged by a number of leading clubs unhappy with their own organisation entitled, 'Blue-print For Football'. The work of FA chief executive Graham Kelly and FA coaching director Charles Hughes, it took the radical step of proposing the creation of a Premier League of 18 top teams to be run by an independent management committee but ultimately under the control of the FA. The Football League, far from being an equal partner, would be left to run the Second, Third and Fourth Divisions.

The Football Association's motives for such drastic surgery were, on the surface at least, altruistic enough. The Football League's decision to revert to a 22-team First Division after having earlier agreed the opposite angered those who felt that too much football was hampering the England team's ability to compete effectively. The League's decision was also evidence of its inability to govern consistently and deliver what it promised. The FA had thus decided to reassert itself as the supreme ruler of football in England.

Taylor's own proposals for structural reform were unambiguous:

'I really feel there needs to be a flexible structure including the PFA because without our involvement the chances of success would be non-existent. I would support moves by the FA to implement a football "cabinet", comprising the heads of different spheres of influence within the game and providing an effective response without being bogged down by red tape and sectional interests. Each would represent his own autonomous body but each would have to accept the authority of the "cabinet".

The truth was, however, that the bigger clubs, having tried to break away before, remained unhappy and were increasingly concerned to retain more of pro-football's overall income, in particular to retain a bigger share of match receipts, television and sponsorship income. Unlike in the 1980s, the PFA would be kept well out of the negotiations. Taylor was as much in the dark as the man on the terrace: 'Everybody's firing shots and nobody can see where we are going because of the smoke. I'm waiting for the smoke to clear.'

In the event the formation of the Premiership [later the Premier League] involved the PFA in some tough negotiating. By July 1991, with the players still not having been consulted, the possibility of a strike loomed. 'Strike is not a word that is in my vocabulary,' Taylor announced, 'but if it looks as though we are being ignored, and the players interests not taken into account, our reaction will be particularly fierce.' To the question of whether top players might ditch the PFA and go with a breakaway Premier League he said, 'Anyone who doubts the loyalty of the players will find they are mistaken.' By August the FA had gained a legal victory in the High Court over the Football League, paving the way for the formation of a breakaway. It now had to secure the PFA's assent and agreement with regard to the PFA's share of TV money. The Premier League's formation had been driven principally by the prospect of lucrative new TV deals. It clearly had no intention of sharing the bonanza with the players' organisation. In March 1992 it offered five per cent with a minimum guarantee of £1 million. Sir John Quinton, the Premier League chairman and formerly the chairman of Barclays Bank, called it a fair and reasonable offer but Taylor disagreed. The PFA had wanted 10 per cent of any new deal up to £15 million and five per cent above that figure. He commented, 'The only conclusion I can draw is that they want a confrontation. They are being deliberately provocative and it looks like war.'

All 594 First Division players were balloted and returned a 90 per cent support for whatever action Taylor deemed necessary. Sir John Quinton was unimpressed. He

Dean Holdsworth billboard 2001.

ASTON VILLA THE Villa players have had no representation since their former PFA rep, Gareth Southgate, joined Middlesbrough. The mood in the dressing room, however, must surely be heavily influenced by their vocal chairman, Doug Ellis, who has warned his players against striking. Ellis said: 'I've written to each player at his home address pointing out the conditions of his contract.'

LEEDS UNITED Rep: David Batty. Chairman Peter Ridsdale has warned his players he would have 'no choice' but to withhold their pay if they strike. Batty holidays in a caravan rather than do anything as ostentatious as go abroad. The traditional flat cap union man or can appearances deceive?

ARSENAL PFA rep: Martin Keown. The players will discuss the issues today for the first time after being given the day off yesterday following their midweek Champions League game. Guidance from the PFA will be sought before any decision over whether to back strike action is made.

LEICESTER CITY Rep: Gary Rowett. He said: 'We were ballotted at a time when the offer was less than £8million. We don't know the exact figures on the table now but in many players' minds they could be more than acceptable. I know that a few players are starting to become reluctant to strike.'

BLACKBURN ROVERS Rep: Stig Bjornebye. He said: 'Hopefully things will move in the right direction before it gets to a strike. But the PFA ballot and the turn-out speak volumes. There's a lot of people out there who need help, and it's important we make a stand.'

LIVERPOOL Rep: Jamie Redknapp. Veteran midfielder Gary McAllister said: 'What other players put on the ballot paper is their business. But I would back Gordon Taylor in whatever he decides to do, and that's always been the case. I'm a big supporter of the PFA.'

BOLTON WANDERERS Rep: Dean Holdsworth. He said: 'Nobody wanted strike action, but we've had a ballot and there was never any doubt that the players would stick together. I spoke to our chairman and he was adamant that we wouldn't fall out over it, which is good.'

MANCHESTER UNITED Rep: Gary Neville. Brother Phil said: 'The PFA chairman will guide us on what he wants us to do and we're fully behind him. I'm not sure I agree with the idea of a second ballot. We've voted once and that should be enough, but whatever he says we'll stand by him.'

CHARLTON ATHLETIC Rep: Chris Powell. Powell pointedly refused to discuss the proposed action yesterday after his manager, Alan Curbishley, gave a broad hint that he believes support for a strike among his players is beginning to waver.

MIDDLESBROUGH Rep: Steve Vickers. Midfielder Dean Windass said: 'When it comes to the crunch it will be interesting to see if the players go through with it. I don't want it to go to a strike but the PFA has done a lot for us all. If we are told to strike, we will all stick together at Middlesbrough.'

CHELSEA Rep: Graeme Le Saux. Le Saux has been reluctant to talk, but Chelsea chairman Ken Bates said yesterday that he would be meeting 'a senior player' who had expressed disquiet over the way the PFA had not kept its members informed about recent developments.

NEWCASTLE UNITED Rep: Warren Barton. He said: 'I'm hoping and expecting the strike won't take place. I believe all our players went with the PFA as we wanted to look after our members but, hopefully, it won't come to a strike. There is still plenty of time to sort it all out.'

DERBY COUNTY Rep: Darryl Powell. Derby's chief executive Keith Loring believes that players at another Premiership club are pushing for a second PFA ballot but, significantly, there have been no voices of agreement from his own players.

SOUTHAMPTON Rep: Paul Jones. Striker James Beattie said: 'The big issue is not to upset the clubs. We may have to strike to get more bargaining power. We don't know what's happening at the moment. Paul had a meeting with the chairman today but we're not sure what came out of it.'

EVERTON Reps: David Unsworth (left) and David Weir. Weir said: 'At some stage there has got to be a compromise. No-one wants to strike. The game has got to be the most important thing.'

SUNDERLAND Rep: Jody Craddock. Club captain Niall Quinn said: 'There has been a dirty tricks campaign by one or two chairmen, but there are a lot of silent chairmen who also believe in the greater good. We are not miles away from a solution and I think it will be resolved.'

FULHAM Rep: Andy Melville. He said: 'It's simple. The players have all had their vote and everybody knows the percentage that came out. The PFA said no to the latest offer and they're supposed to have a percentage and they're sticking by their guns. Now hopefully other people can sort it out.'

TOTTENHAM HOTSPUR Rep: Chris Perry. Conciliatory words from Les Ferdinand about avoiding the strike sum up the feelings across the nation. He said: 'Perhaps if the leagues up their offer some more there will be a second ballot on that offer. That would not be a bad thing.'

IPSWICH TOWN Rep: Matt Holland. Chairman David Sheepshanks' role as one of the strike's chief opponents may make his players feel the pressure. But the prospect of those who decided to strike being sacked by a family club such as Ipswich seems impossible.

WEST HAM UNITED Rep: Steve Lomas. Goalkeeper David James said: 'There is no need for a strike. I wasn't happy with the initial reasons for striking and I am even more against it, the more I hear. The PFA gave its version and the Premier League has not. We've only got one side of the story.'

The union men in the middle of football's crisis. *The Sun*, 23 November 2001.

had originally made his feelings clear as to the place of unions in general when announcing that the PFA would have no place in the Premier League's new management board: 'The FA will be at our meetings but the PFA will not be represented, just as at Barclays board meetings, I have my directors present but not the unions.' As for the strike threat: 'it's just a ritual dance. One expects that from a union. I see it in the banking world.'

Taylor was angry: 'If he feels that he can treat footballers like his bank tellers then he is in for a serious surprise.' He accused Quinton of knowing nothing about the role the PFA had played in the past decade or more, such as setting up 60 club community schemes and saving clubs from going under. He pointed to Quinton's 'poor record in industrial relations and one that has been associated in South Africa with the inhuman and discredited system of apartheid.'

Despite the harsh words, however, agreement was reached by 27 April 1992 on a whole range of issues including the guarantee of both the present contributory and non-contributory pension schemes, an increase in the minimum wage for registered professional players from £75 to £90 a week, plus an increase in permanent total disability cover for all players in the Football League and FA Premier League from £2,250 to £5,000.

The new Premier League and the Football Association agreed to join a new Professional Football Negotiating and Consultative Committee which had authority to cover all issues affecting the professional game, not just those affecting players. A fundamental cornerstone of the newly formed PFNCC was that nothing could be changed which affected players conditions of service without their approval. A new Executive Officers Committee was also formed to meet quarterly prior to the PFNCC to discuss and agree on all agenda items. The newly reformed Football League also invited Taylor to attend all their management committee board meetings and play a part in their policy making process.

Most significant of all, however, for what was about to happen, the PFA share of TV income was agreed with a minimum guarantee (index linked) of £1.5 million, consisting of 10 per cent of the first £10 million income band and five per cent thereon, the money to be used to fund education, youth training, football club, community, accident and benevolent fund programmes.

TV cash: the history

The payment of TV monies to the PFA had begun in 1956 with Jimmy Guthie's successful campaign that had included the cancelling of a floodlit match between Wolves and Athletic Bilboa. Agreement had then been reached whereby a percentage of all TV income was paid to the PFA for its provident fund and specific fees went to all individual players who appeared. The percentage had amounted to roughly seven and a half per cent and players received 5 guineas 'appearance money' per televised match.

In 1967 the percentage of TV income paid to the PFA had risen to 10 per cent, the players' fee to 10 guineas and the agreement had been written into the Regulations of the League. (Regulation 69 read:… 'ten per cent of all fees received by the League for the filming of League matches shall be paid to the Professional Footballers Association for educational, insurance and benevolent purposes…')

The FA's TV contribution helped pay premiums for the players' joint insurance policy, but there was no written agreement similar to that with the League. In 1964 the FA's contribution had been diverted to help fund a PFA Education Society. In 1983 there had been an attempt by the FA to cut the amount by 60 per cent, from £100,000 to £40,000. With more contractual freedom and ever-rising salaries there had been resentment within the parent body at having to hand over relatively huge sums to an organisation, many of whose members appeared to be perfectly capable of looking after themselves. FA chief at the time, Bert Millichip, commented that pro players' freedom of contract had been 'a disaster', 'it has changed the whole balance of power. The word "loyalty" is no longer in [a] football's dictionary.' A threatened ban on PFA members' appearances in televised Cup ties with top players such as Kevin Keegan of Newcastle and Phil Thompson of Liverpool pledging their teams' support took the FA by surprise. They agreed to talk and eventually reinstated their TV contributions.

In 1985 the monies the PFA received as its share of television revenues from the Football League stood at £100,000 per year. A year on it had doubled via a new ITV deal. In 1989 the share amounted to over £500,000, in 1991 it had reached £750,000 and in 1992, the year the Premier League was established, it leapt to £2.5 million from the Premier League plus £500,000 from the Football League. With yet another massive TV deal secured in 1998, the biggest ever television deal in the history of UK sport, the PFA's combined income from TV monies stood at almost £9 million.

There had been moves by football's governing bodies to rein in this income. In 1996 the Football League attempted to change the regulation to make the payment discretionary. As Taylor put it to the union AGM in November 1996: 'We were met with a very intransigent attitude and clearly the Football League were looking to test our resolve and may well have been supported in this action by the Premier League.'

With another union strike ballot reaping a 91.8 per cent vote of support, agreement was reached on a payout of just over five per cent of the League's TV income. The FA Premier League subsequently matched the League's offer. Things would not be so simple the next time around.

The Big Struggle: October 2001–November 2001

In June 2000 football's governing bodies once again negotiated new financial deals with the various TV companies. The figures were staggering: £1,500 million to the Premier League and £315 million to the Football League over three years.

The old PFA agreement had ended in mid-2001 and negotiations were assumed to start on a new deal six months prior to this, but, rather ominously, the Premier League stalled. Eventually, on 11 September 2001 (and without having been shown the extent of the new TV deal football's authorities had agreed) the PFA were offered £150,000 on top of their previous deal! Within days Gordon Taylor announced that he would be consulting his membership on possible strike action unless the Premier League came up with a proper offer, one 'that respected previous agreements'.

A number of factors would make the ensuing struggle completely different to any that had gone before. Firstly, the vast amounts of money involved meant that sentimental feelings of any kind could be discounted. The maximisation of income was, after all, the reason why the Premier League had been formed in the first place. Second, the chief executive of the Premier League, and the man responsible for negotiating the League's broadcast and commercial contracts, Richard Scudamore, had been in the post for just two years, following a two year period as chief executive of the Football League. Prior to that he had worked for the Thomson Corporation in the United States running their newspaper publishing division, managing advertising, sales and marketing activities. He thus came to the job largely unencumbered with any sense of football history, and certainly with no illusions concerning what FIFA chief Sepp Blatter would term the 'football family'.

It was later suggested that one of the stumbling blocks in the subsequent talks between the two bodies had been the fact that Taylor and Scudamore do not personally get on. Taylor refuted this but added, 'In the past we've been dealing with those who respect the history of the game – and that has not been happening of late.' He suggested that Scudamore did not fully understand the issues. 'We come from different backgrounds.' said Taylor. 'I have been in football for a long time, but Richard is not the same. He is a businessman and he didn't want to talk about any of the history of our agreements or the situation of the PFA, so I am not quite sure he fully understood in the beginning.'

The TV contract negotiations were due to begin at almost exactly the same time as the fractious argument concerning the new players' contracts had reached its dramatic finale. Gordon Taylor, in his role as FIFPro president, had angered many Premier League chairmen with his astute backstairs deal with Blatter and FIFA. There was thus a general feeling within the Premier League that it was time the PFA was taught a lesson. Taylor later wrote, 'We believed the football bodies had political agenda to diminish if not extinguish the status of the PFA and its very existence.'

From the outset the PFA found itself backed by the mainstream union movement. John Monks of the TUC declared:

> 'The TUC recognises the valuable work which the PFA does on behalf of its members. While the public rightly take a tremendous interest in the small number of successful footballers who reap the rewards of success with their clubs and country, the fact is that professional football is a precarious profession in which only a few can achieve celebrity status. For every star player there are many young men who are forced to look elsewhere for a living at a time when many of their contemporaries can look forward to a career that stretches ahead for decades. The PFA does a great job in seeing that the increasing wealth that is now coming into the game is shared among those

WHO ARE IN THE POWER SEATS AT THE PFA?

GORDON TAYLOR
Chief executive

THE 56-year-old former Bolton, Birmingham, Blackburn and Bury player is Britain's highest-paid union boss with an annual package worth £458,000. He has been tireless in shoring up support among players and sees this contest as a struggle for the PFA's very existence.

BARRY HORNE
Chairman

Not yet 40, the former Wales captain is a familiar face at training grounds around the country, where he has been testing opinion during the dispute. Seen by some on the Premier League side as a dove to Taylor's hawk, leaning towards settlement rather than strike.

BRENDON BATSON
Deputy chief executive

THE business brain behind the union muscle. The former Arsenal, Cambridge and West Bromwich player turned to the PFA after injury ended career at 31. Now 48, the licensed agent is an obvious candidate to succeed Taylor. He heads the union's financial management arm.

MICK McGUIRE
Asst. chief executive

INVOLVED mainly in the players' agency arm of the union, acting for players who do not have representatives. McGuire, a former Coventry, Norwich, Barnsley and Oldham player, was involved in setting up the Platinum Group which advises top youth players.

JOHN BRAMHALL
Executive

PLAYED for Scunthorpe, Rochdale, Bury, Halifax and Tranmere, so understands hardship. Like most of the 250-plus employees, his role is to support and advise members — from current players in dispute with clubs to old-timers in need of emergency funding.

MICK BURNS
Further education and vocational training chief

AS the PFA reminds us, this is where the money goes. Burns' department is in charge of helping players train for new careers, giving those who have left the game, either through injury or rejection, a second chance of gainful employment.

For the first time, the football public is introduced to the men at the helm of the PFA. *The Sun,* 23 November 2001.

who have given more to professional football than they have got out of it. It is right that as more money comes in from television the PFA should get a fair share of it. I am sure that trade unionists who are also football fans will recognise the justice of the PFA case and will support them in this dispute.'

Ex-pros also chipped in. Tommy Banks, the abrasive former Bolton and England defender, told the *Bolton Evening News*, 'Those who begrudge the players their contracted rights in this TV argument should have their argument turned against them and the people at the top in football should be asked where is all this money going that has been flooding into the game in the last few years?' Sam Allardyce, then Bolton Wanderers' manager, was one of a few managers, Alex Ferguson included, who backed the players: 'I know the PFA does a lot of important work, and one day I might even need to call on their services myself. It's reassuring for those of us who are relatively well off to know that if things go wrong there is a safety net we can rely on. You can never be sure what the future holds for you.'

Countdown to the TV Blackout

The 2001 dispute would be different in many ways, not least for the efforts the PFA made in making their case known to the general public. In the past the association had limited its public relations to press conferences. Now it decided to take the initiative from the start. A key feature would be the use of its newly established website, www.givemefootball.com. Here the management committee could issue updates and publicity aimed both at its own members and the general public. The press, too, had a regular source of up-to-the-minute information. Beyond that there was also a billboard campaign, and even space purchased on the side of buses!

On 1 October the Premier League offered a further £1 million which was rejected and two weeks later another 2.5 per cent was proposed, but this too was turned down. For the PFA, at stake was the 10 per cent agreement it claimed was embedded in all agreements between the association and the employers. The war of words then began in earnest.

From the very beginning Richard Scudamore made it clear that, not only did he not want the PFA's money tied to any future commercially negotiated TV deals, he did not feel the PFA had any right to such a percentage: 'We don't have an agreement. He (Gordon Taylor) talks about a percentage right to our TV money for the last four years – that agreement has now run out. It is a little bit of a myth, and we need to absolutely nail the fact, that there is no right to five per cent or any percentage of our TV money. A long time ago, when the TV deals were down in the tens and twenties of millions, it was expressed as a percentage.' 'Now,' he felt, 'because of the sums involved, it was "inappropriate" to tie it to a percentage.'

Taylor countered: 'He (Scudamore) is trying to cut the umbilical cord between the PFA and the historic TV deal. He said that I am under an illusion to think there is a link. This is rewriting history. He is insulting all the previous administrators of the game by saying that.'

Taylor was even more angered by Scudamore's reference to 'our' TV money. He felt that it was 'an insult' to suggest that the union was being 'funded' by the governing bodies. The money was not some grace and favour handout for 'good works'. It was, according to Taylor, a 'matter of rights.'

Where the players' 'image rights' were concerned, Scudamore was equally emphatic:

> 'Another myth that needs destroying is that the players, through their union, are bringing something to the table by waiving their "right" to television revenue and allowing it all to go to the clubs. Footballers are not opera singers or pop stars and when they pull on the jersey, there is no such thing in law as a performance right, so this is another misconception that has been allowed to grow unchecked. "Image rights?" There is no legal basis for this idea of performance rights. That's something reserved for ballerinas and artists, although you could describe many of our players as artists.'
>
> The Football League's Ken Nagle also questioned why payments to the PFA 'should be the same per cent every time. It should be an agreed figure that supports the work the PFA does, not the same percentage of every television deal. There is a recognition within the Football League that the PFA does a lot of good work. But the majority of Gordon's members are already earning over £50,000 a year.'

Scudamore also paid lip service to the PFA's work: 'I have said to Gordon that it's a good job the union do what they do because it is hard to see the mechanism by which much of what they do would get done. It's much easier that they sort out the welfare, the education on behalf of the game.'

Adverts on the sides of buses!

Brian Tinnion billboard 2001.

However, the PFA's previous good housekeeping was then used against it, with Scudamore claiming that 'the (Premier League) offer was reasonable because of the ability of the PFA to raise money elsewhere and the current funds they have. Plus, it was more than what they got before. The Premier League has to fund a lot of other things: £20 million to Football Foundation, Football League youth development (£25 million), £20 million to relegated clubs as "parachute payments". In one sense, Gordon runs a better business than we do; he's actually got some assets.'

As one football administrator anxiously put it, 'the PFA are acting more like a commercial organisation trying to drive revenue and less like a trade union.'

The countdown to a strike continued with a remorseless logic. Ballot papers were sent out to all members on the 23 October for a final return on 9 November.

Taylor then announced, not without a hint of pride, that the players had voted almost unanimously in favour of a resolution for a boycott of matches played in front of television cameras, either for live games or for recorded highlights. It was, Taylor declared, 'unprecedented in any industrial action.' Of 2,496 ballot papers sent out to members, 2,315 were returned, with 2,290 in favour. 'We can pick and choose,' he said, 'We will have options of individual games, of groups of games, or even whole blanket coverage. That strategy will have to be decided this week if we don't make any progress.'

Unusually, some of the Premier League's top players were quick to get involved. Arsenal skipper Tony Adams put their case: 'The money is not for me but I am the sort of player who might have to strike for everyone to sit up and take notice. It's so that youngsters – and 75 per cent of them are out of the game by the age of 21 – can get re-education funding.' Manchester United's Ryan Giggs was also clear as to his intentions. 'Every footballer has friends who have suffered through injury, not made it as a professional and gone on to coaching or physio work,' he said, 'The PFA provides a priceless safety net for these people.' Bolton Wanderers striker Dean Holdsworth believed the players would be solidly behind any action if the two parties could not come to an agreement: 'Not everyone's rich and not everyone's in the position of being able to pack up and go and sit on a yacht for the rest of their lives. We're not talking about the rich footballers here. It's about the majority of players who have to carry on after football, those who have to retire through injury and so many other ex-players who need the union's support.'

West Ham's David James, however, as one of only 20 players to vote against, struck a discordant note. He had already expressed the view that a strike was 'hurting the wrong people': the TV companies stumping up the money in the first place. He also questioned the 'mythical' five per cent and then went on to suggest that players had voted to strike having only heard one side of the story.

On 15 November a further 'final offer' was made of £50 million, which was officially rejected. A day later came another offer: £52.5 million over three years which was again rejected as it was still less than two and a half per cent and only one per cent of extra TV money the Premier League had negotiated with TV. The PFA then asked for 3.75 per cent over 10 years, which was in turn refused.

By now some of the Premier League's directors had started to weigh in. Ken Bates of Chelsea was typically outspoken: 'If the PFA can afford to buy a £2 million Lowry painting and invest in Bobby Charlton's soccer schools, why do they need any more money – if indeed, anything at all?' Birmingham City's chairman David Gold added: 'We have to stand up to this bully. In the Third Division people are earning thirty, forty, fifty thousand pounds a year. They don't need help from the union when their career finishes, they should just go out and get a proper job.' Southampton chairman Rupert Lowe accused Gordon Taylor of 'empire-building'. 'I'm amazed he can justify a strike,' said Lowe, 'It's highly unusual for employers to even be funding a union, the members usually fund it. Gordon Taylor and the PFA are confusing the interests of their members with the greater interests of football.'

David Dein of Arsenal stated that the PFA got far more than its equivalents in other countries: 'In Germany their union gets nothing, in Italy likewise they get nothing, in Spain about £500,000 and in France just over £1 million.' However, Italian, French and Spanish football players based in England were solidly behind the PFA.

The Italian players' union, ACI, sent a letter of support to Italian nationals plying their trade in England and urged them to support the strike. Gerardo Gonzalez, president of the Spanish players' union AFE, said: 'The PFA are defending football. They have important aims as it is a social service provided for football, and the players who need the support.' France's Philippe Piat, head of the UNFP, also gave his full support to the proposed industrial action: 'I fully back them. What is happening is not normal at all.'

With the first high profile game scheduled to be affected, Arsenal against Manchester United on 25 November, the Premier League suddenly asked the PFA for a meeting on the preceding Monday to try to agree a compromise. They offered £20 million for three years but with provisos as to how the money might be spent. This was rejected, and to the League chairmen's astonishment Gordon Taylor suddenly issued strike notices to his players. A Premier League official was later quoted as saying,

'We kept our powder dry until the last moment and honestly thought that Gordon would accept the offer. We were amazed when he reacted as he did.'

It was at this point, late on Tuesday night, that Richard Scudamore says he recognised that 'exceptional tactics' were called for. Having secured the support of the Football Association's chief executive, Adam Crozier, who previously had been acting purely as a mediator with the PFA, Scudamore held a press conference the following day and laid the details of the offer the PFA had rejected out for all to see.

This was followed by what Scudamore later described as 'a massive sea change in public opinion'. With one or two exceptions the media turned on Taylor and transformed the course of events. The Premier League followed this up by starting legal proceedings seeking an injunction for the following Tuesday to prevent the strike scheduled for the following weekend.

The Premier League's room for manoeuvre has always been limited. Scudamore and other top club directors was aware that a legal battle could have devastating consequences for the game. A court ruling in the League's favour would see a lengthy appeals procedure and no doubt cause untold bad will from the PFA in the future. A ruling against could see industrial action commence that might threaten the collapse of existing television deals. TV companies could well have seized on the breach of contract to renegotiate what were suddenly looking like overpriced deals. ITV Digital was already in trouble and trying to renegotiate the deal that would eventually lead to its demise.

For the PFA the implications were also stark. To some legal experts, the injunction sought by the Premier League looked to have a good chance of succeeding which would lead to the dispute being outlawed under the 1992 Trades Union and Labour Relations Act. In the first instance because clubs are the employers of players and players cannot strike in an action against the Leagues, and secondly, that it was not actually a trade dispute because it did not involve wages and conditions of employment.

Taylor contended that the clubs made up the Premier League and the Football League, while the players were members of the PFA. The PFA negotiated a whole range of collective agreements on the standard contract, including pensions and insurance, and thus it was within its rights to take industrial action.

However, if the injunction did succeed and a judge ruled that the PFA could not lead its players out on strike, that such a step was illegal under current legislation, then the PFA's 'ultimate weapon' would have been lost. It was the fourth time in 12 years that such a threat had been made to good effect. To lose it would be a catastrophe.

The reactions in the football world at this moment of truth were mixed. Charlton manager Alan Curbishly was of the opinion that many players had not fully understood the implications when they first voted: 'They all voted for a strike but some of them don't even know what industrial action actually means – they've only ever seen the words in the papers. I think they thought the whole thing might just go away…' Richard Scudamore opined: 'I cannot think there is a Premier League player who wants to strike.'

Ungrateful, selfish and greedy!

Robert Hardman delivers his verdict on the threatened footballers' strike

An ancient cliché is wheeled out once more. *Daily Mail,* 23 November 2001.

We were only given one side of the story SAYS DAVID JAMES

STRIKE THREAT / Curbishley believes support for action is ebbing away

They didn't know what they were voting for

Fearing for the future: Charlton boss Curbishley

The press onslaught against the PFA's case reached its climax in late November 2001. Headlines in *The Sun* and the *Daily Mail,* 23 November 2001.

In the press there were suggestions that players were now bewildered and uneasy and that 'self-preservation' had taken over as they were suddenly confronted with the very real prospect of risking wages and upsetting supporters through the first strike in the history of England's national sport. Headlines appeared declaring the players as 'Ungrateful, Selfish and Greedy' with no idea what they were voting for, 'We Were Only Given One Side Of The Story' and in *The Sun*, 'PFA ARE PATHETIC', as PFA Management Committee members gathered for an emergency meeting on Thursday evening to consider their options

Nick Cusack, Richard Jobson, Andy Marriott, Gary Neville, Paul Raven, Phil Chapple and Barry Horne were present along with Brendon Batson and Mick McGuire.

Neville would later refute suggestions that 'the players were on the brink of caving in'. When they met, he insisted that all they were concerned with was 'coming to a sensible conclusion'. He also pointed out that players like Richard Jobson, Andy Marriot and Nick Cusack were 'not household names' and so the issue was not about rich players trying to make themselves richer.

However, Gordon Taylor realised that the sudden barrage of bad publicity had affected some of them: 'I told them, it's par for the course when you're a union, this is to be expected, this is what you get, this is where you hold firm, it's the essence of negotiations. Experience had taught me that that was a crucial time. The newspapers I never worried about because one knew, what with Sky and the TV deal where their interest would lie. They were a relatively new management committee and they were very good and supportive but they'd started to get a bit twitchy because their own managers were saying, "come on, are you getting this thing sorted or what?" They were big name players with big name clubs and they had their own situations to look at.' For Taylor it was important at that point not to show any weakness: 'I've always been of the mind that you are not going to succeed unless you risk failing.'

Taylor was convinced that they would be okay: 'The ballot was a tremendous negotiating tool. But it was only a vote in favour of doing whatever you thought was right. That was a judgement up until the last minute. It was no time for suddenly bottling it.' He felt that the PFA could have got more money: 'The Premier League had moved from £5 million to £17 million, although nowhere near the original £50 million or so demanded, so it looked very good, having moved so far. Because we'd started so low, it wasn't bad at all, we could live on that, but more importantly it was a watershed, we had to protect ourselves for the future.'

So when his management committee suggested that they did not want to strike when so much money had been offered, that it would not look good, he decided to acquiesce: 'I took that view on board because I could understand it, but because the deal hadn't been done it was no time to be letting word out that we're all okay now, because there were key issues that I wanted to protect for the future.'

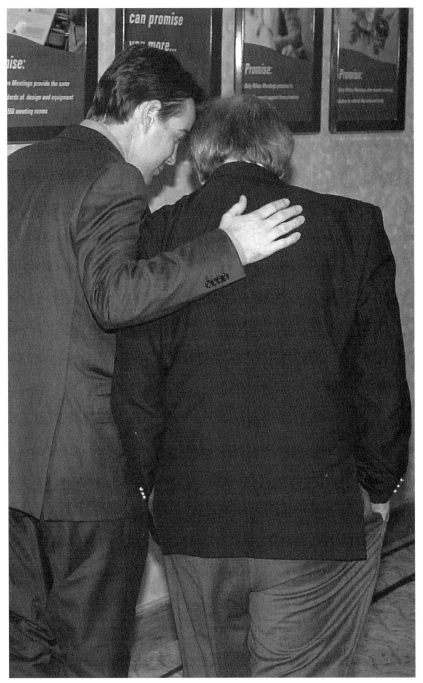

As the negotiations become tense, FA Chief Executive Adam Crozier and Gordon Taylor confer.

The press gather to hear the announcement of the settlement and afterwards Premier League Chief Executive Richard Scudamore and Gordon Taylor shake on the agreement, with Adam Crozier as peacemaker.

A secret meeting was arranged for the following day at the Hilton Hotel at Manchester Airport. It began at 10am. Three meeting rooms were in place. In one were Brendan Batson, Mick McGuire, Barry Horne, Nicky Cusack and John Hewison, the PFA solicitor. Next door was Richard Scudamore, Maurice Watkins and a Premier League solicitor. In a third, Adam Crozier for the FA and David Burns for the Football League.

Watkins and Taylor met in a fourth room to try and finalise an agreement. The Premier League offer was £52.5 million over three years with a possible extension to six years and with no change in discretionary amount. Taylor wanted a 10-year agreement, and for every one per cent increase in television revenue during the 10 years the PFA would receive an extra 0.75 per cent of that figure, and for every one per cent that TV revenue went down the PFA's share would fall by 0.5 per cent. No strings were to be attached to this money, thus underpinning the position of the PFA as an independent body, beholden to no one.

Watkins returned to say such an arrangement was not possible. Taylor intimated that the matter would therefore go to court. Watkins went back to the Premier League room and returned 40 minutes later to say an agreement could be reached. The PFA would receive £52.5 million over 10 years with full discretion as long as the Football League received £10,000 per club for player-related benefits. The PFA agreed. After some time, during which Richard Scudamore tried to contact most of the Premier League chairmen, there was a pause. An attempt was made by the Premier League to reduce the time period to six years, which was rejected. By 5.30pm that very evening the agreement was concluded.

The Settlement

Taylor announced afterwards: 'It was a day of celebration really and everyone is absolutely delighted. We have been able to protect the existence of the PFA and its future. I hope we have got our message through loud and clear, for we know we had to fight hard to get this message across.'

As for the personalities involved, it had been a rude awakening for many of them, although Richard Scudamore claimed, 'There was no bitterness on either side. In fact, after the negotiations were concluded, we sat in the bar of a Manchester hotel with Barry Horne and deputy PFA chairman Brendan Batson and other members of the PFA negotiating team and enjoyed a good drink.'

It had certainly been a remarkable episode, one that had seen the PFA emerge victorious in financial terms, but also not a little chastened at the apparent sea change in sentiment that had largely forced a conclusion to the endless wrangling. Taylor admitted afterwards: 'I don't want to damage this game. I would have failed as a negotiator if we had called a strike. As a union leader I don't want to do that as it causes so many problems to the football public. As for it being a victory for the PFA, I leave you to draw your own conclusions. We are very satisfied. It was an opportunity to make people much more aware of what the PFA does. I think this is an extremely

Ballot result.

seminal moment in the history of football and the players' association and, hopefully, a new dawn for the game.'

Taylor had certainly managed to secure a fine deal with the Premier League and Football League to finance the administration of the association. However, as *The Independent's* Nick Townsend pointed out, 'Though many deserving causes exist – both those players who fail to make the grade and those who retire early because of injury – they also do in many other industries, whose union members have to accept support from their fellow members, not their employers.'

The extraordinary wealth of the PFA in relative terms, allied to the fact that the players themselves contribute so little to what is now an extremely generous raft of benefits and rewards on offer to each and every one of them, had caused the general public to temper their hitherto unqualified support. Serious doubts had begun to permeate the players' minds. Townsend commented that PFA chairman Barry Horne's contribution had been cited as a major reason for a successful conclusion to the dispute, 'Barry was a credit to the negotiations, he realised that enough was enough.'

The 2001 TV monies dispute saw the PFA emerge from the battle as an acknowledged permanent player on the English football political scene. No one could now be in any doubt as to what it did and what it stood for. It had, moreover, secured its independence and its right to a share of the vast sums of money flowing into the game. No amount of huffing and puffing on behalf of various football club directors could blow its house down.

PART SIX
WHOLE NEW BALLGAME
1999–2009

1. Money Matters 1999–2007

*U*ncertainty is, then, a pervasive feature of a professional footballer's life because in this highly physical entertainment industry they have to learn to live with the possibility that one's career can end abruptly at any moment and this fear casts a long shadow.
Martin Roderick, *Work, Employment & Society*, Vol. 20, No. 2, 245–265 (2006)

The PFA had been accused of being 'greedy' in its battle for TV monies; no great leap as it represented a body of working men who had been tarred with the same brush ever since professionalism began back in the 1880s. No surprise then that, in 2001 when financial chaos engulfed the Football League with the collapse of the TV company ITV Digital, it would be players and their 'excessive wage demands' rather than poor financial management by football clubs that would be considered largely culpable for the distress many clubs found themselves in.

Footballers' pay was certainly reaching new and surprising levels. Accountancy firm Deloitte & Touche's annual report on football's finances for the 1999–2000 season confirmed that wages in the four English divisions had risen by 20 per cent in just one year, from £620 million to £747 million a year and that 16 of the 92 League clubs had wage bills that exceeded turnover. Mushrooming TV revenues had clearly encouraged many club directors to gamble on success.

ITV Digital's failure, however, meant that its £315 million contract to broadcast Nationwide League and Worthington Cup matches simply disappeared overnight. Scores of clubs were left exposed and teetering on the brink of administration, while hundreds of players found themselves holding worthless contracts. Up to 30 football clubs claimed they could go out of business and former sports minister Tony Banks warned that League football was facing the 'greatest crisis' in its history. John Colquhoun, an agent with Key Sports Management who boasted clients across the four English divisions, said: 'This is a reality check for everyone involved. The clubs will say that the market has been overprovided, that there have been too many footballers getting too much money with not enough coming in. It's simple economics for them.'

Wage costs were clearly threatening to bankrupt many clubs. On average First Division clubs spent 95 per cent of their turnover on players' pay. In the Second Division it was 85 per cent and in the Third 82 per cent, yet the 'safe' level, according to accountants, was no more than 65 per cent.

Barry Hearn, chairman of Third Division Leyton Orient, saw the solution in reducing the number of players on the club's books and announced that he was going to cut his staff from 34 players to 24: 'At our level we have a surplus of players and the market is awash with available footballers. That will become a monsoon this summer because everyone will cut their squads. We've had as many as 37 pros this season but I've told my manager that the maximum number we'll have next season is 24. Other chairmen are planning to do the same.'

It was predicted that clubs in all divisions would be forced to slash their budgets by introducing lower wages, performance-related pay, shorter contracts and smaller squads. It was, according to various commentators, the end of a decade of rapidly rising wages for England's full-time professional players. While the most talented handful would continue to enjoy lucrative contracts, for hundreds of others it would mean pay cuts and the dole queue. Neil Warnock, the Sheffield United manager, opined: 'I think the players have had the good times. This is it, the peak of their wages. The directors want me to trim wages and I can't blame them.'

Gordon Taylor, while acknowledging that there would be cost-cutting and redundancies, nevertheless defended players' wages: 'It's a competitive game and it's a short career. When you're no longer wanted as a player, you're shown the door. Wages

Brian Marwood Chairman 1990–93
Brian served his footballing apprenticeship at Hull City and developed into a fine right-winger, his speed and trickery being crucial components in the success enjoyed by the club during the 1980s. He moved to Arsenal in 1987 for £600,000 from Sheffield Wednesday, winning a Championship medal in 1989. Very much a two-footed player who could accurately centre from either touchline, he scored in each of the first five games in that Championship season. It was with Arsenal that Brian won his only England cap, coming on as a late substitution against Saudi Arabia in Riyadh. An articulate and intelligent man, he worked for a time overseeing the PFA's commercial department. After spells with Sheffield United and Swindon Town, he subsequently became a soccer pundit with BBC's Radio Five Live and Sky Sports. He now works as a marketing manager for Nike.

Pat Nevin Chairman 1993–97

Pat Nevin's 20-year, 750-game football career saw him play for Clyde, Chelsea, Everton, Tranmere Rovers, Kilmarnock and Motherwell. Pat joined Chelsea in 1983 for £95,000, where his skill and pace made him a pivotal player and a firm favourite with the fans. In 1988 he moved to Everton for £925,000, scoring 20 goals in 138 appearances for the club and winning an FA Cup runners'-up medal. After his playing days were over he served as chief executive of Motherwell FC for a time but now works as a television pundit for BBC Scotland and Channel Five, a co-commentator for BBC Radio Five Live and has written for the Independent, the Times and the Sunday Telegraph among others. His autobiography In Ma Head, Son was written in conjunction with psychologist Dr George Sik. Pat has an arts degree from Glasgow Caledonian University.

are bound to be a big proportion of a club's spending. The PFA believes no club should be spending money they don't have. We want clubs to stay in business.'

The Football League put forward various possible solutions including, inevitably, salary-capping and squad-capping but Gordon Taylor was adamant: 'It may surprise some people to know that, while we are against salary-capping, we are not against clubs having to limit their salary bill to, say, 60 or 65 per cent of their income. The term salary-capping is emotive because people think of a maximum wage. But we do not want clubs to be spending more than they have. If they started talking about a ceiling on the amount that goes out to players then we would talk about it. We are not against good accounting.'

Taylor's argument was that certain clubs had simply been grossly mismanaged. Some had mortgaged their futures trying to get into or trying to stay in the Premier League. Credit had been easy to come by in football. Finance houses had advanced monies to clubs on future transfer receipts; others had 'bought' and leased back players, incurring prohibitive interest repayments; future TV distribution monies and season ticket sales had been offered as security for loans, most of which had quickly been spent; any traditional assets such as grounds were mortgaged to the hilt. By the time directors at certain struggling clubs had called in the administrators, there had been little left to sell.

With typical shortsightedness, however, the very people who had been responsible for misdirecting the clubs then proceeded to lay the blame squarely on the players. Cutting salaries, in their opinion, would bring their clubs back into a solvent position, but it was a false hypothesis. As evidence Taylor pointed to Leicester City whose debts at the time amounted to £74 million. Cancelling all their players' contracts valued at £19 million would still leave their overall debt in excess of £50 million: 'Salary-capping appears to be a knee-jerk reaction to the financial mess in which a number of clubs find themselves. Common sense needs to prevail and clubs need to live within their means, which may well result in players' wages falling, squad numbers reducing and hopefully less expensive credit being taken on board.'

Dean Smith, then a central defender at Barry Hearn's Leyton Orient, was the club's captain and PFA representative, a position he had held at his previous clubs Walsall and Hereford United. He was sceptical about salary-capping: 'I can understand where the idea's coming from with all the money that's being spent, but there isn't really a great deal of resentment within squads over different wage levels. Ultimately, we're all footballers and everyone has the same understanding – if you're offered extra money, and you can get a deal you're happy with, you take it. If you're not, then don't sign. It's a short career and you've just got to try to do as well as you can.' Times had certainly changed, however: 'You're seeing experienced players at the end of contracts having to go for trials at other clubs, whereas before they would have just been snapped up straight away. This used to be unheard of. So that has an effect. And there are going to be maybe 600 or 700 people out on free transfers in the summer.'

Inevitably, the ITV Digital crisis saw the PFA heavily involved in various club 'rescue' packages. In August 2002 Bradford City's players, for instance, had not been paid in nearly four months until the club struck a deal with the association. The debt-ridden Division One side would receive financial help from the PFA for the next two years as they sought to clear an estimated debt of £36 million. Managing director Shaun Harvey said: 'We're delighted the club's future is now secure and we can stop treading water and move forward. The deal has been finalised with the PFA and consequently we can come out of administration.'

In previous years the association had supported around 10 clubs per season. However, following Bradford City's well-documented financial plight, over 40 clubs approached the PFA for support and advice in the 2002–03 season alone. Of these, some borrowed funds to survive, others asked for advice and a number requested deferrals on contracts from their players. The PFA eventually announced that it could not afford to hand out any more emergency loans to meet struggling clubs' wage bills. Taylor explained, 'We have absolutely stretched ourselves and we couldn't do it again. We certainly couldn't cope with another 10 Bradfords.' In the end, the PFA probably had a clearer picture than the Football League itself of the financial position of most of the latter organisation's clubs.

Barry Horne Chairman 1997–2002

A defensive midfielder with a reputation for a crunching tackle, Barry began his career with non-League Rhyl Town before signing for Wrexham where he made 168 appearances scoring 23 goals. He moved to Portsmouth for £60,000 and two years later moved again, this time along the south coast to Southampton for £700,000. Everton then signed him for £675,000 and, after winning an FA Cup-winners' medal in 1995 with the Toffees, he joined Birmingham City for £250,000 in 1996. A year later he moved to Huddersfield Town, and, following spells at Kidderminster Harriers, Walsall and Belper Town, he hung up his boots in 1992. In all Barry captained and played 59 times for Wales. By 2003 he was a regular Radio Five Live summariser. He has also worked on Match of the Day, as well as commentary and punditry for Sky Sports. Barry also writes a football column for the Liverpool Daily Post.

The following summer, according to PFA figures, of the nearly 600 players out of work, a figure which equated to roughly 20 per cent of professional footballers in the country, as many as 200 were not expected to find new clubs. Taylor warned: 'We could lose a third of the 586. Our job is to try to get them fixed up, but I'd be pleased if two-thirds stayed [in football].' Deputy Mick McGuire opined:

> 'In what other industry is 20 per cent of its workforce technically out of work at the end of each year? Whilst we constantly read about the multi-million pound plus deals of the Premier League elite who have the security of four or five-year contracts, the fact remains that 75 per cent of our members play in the Football League and a great many of those are playing with no longer security than a one, or at best, two-year contract.'

In the event, no club went out of business and, although for a time the pool of players seeking engagements was uncomfortably large, the numbers of full-time professionals did not decrease. Television revenues were soon flowing again and players' salaries were once more rising. Exactly *why* their salaries were rising so rapidly again was soon to be another bone of contention between clubs and the PFA.

Brendon Batson MBE
Assistant Secretary/Deputy Chief Executive 1984–2002

Born in Grenada, Brendon moved to Trinidad when he was six and came to England three years later, having never even seen a football match let alone played in one. Brendon was signed as a schoolboy by Arsenal, becoming the first black player to play for the Gunners. He then moved to Cambridge United in 1974 where he captained the side to the Fourth Division Championship before West Bromwich Albion bought him in 1978. There he teamed up with fellow black players Cyrille Regis and Laurie Cunningham. Never before had an English team simultaneously fielded three black players. The Three Degrees as they came to be known, after the American soul trio of the same name, came to symbolise the fundamental changes then occurring in the national game. At the time, however, Brendon was simply happy to be playing in a team that produced such entertaining football. 'The shame of it was that we didn't win anything during that spell,' he later recalled. A cultured defender, Brendon's career was cut short by a serious playing injury in 1982. It was at the Abbey Stadium he first became interested in the workings of the PFA, taking on the role of delegate. Contemplating a career in coaching, a call came 'completely out of the blue' from Gordon Taylor who asked Brendon to be his deputy. For the next 18 years Brendon served as Taylor's right hand man. Whether taking up disciplinary issues on behalf of members or advising them on financial matters and their futures, Brendon always went about his tasks with the calm assurance of a man in control. He was instrumental in setting up PFA Financial Management Ltd in 1989, acting for Nigel Martyn when he helped broker the first £1 million goalkeeping transfer. He has also been a driving force behind the national campaign to eradicate racism from football, his services to football being recognised in 2001 when he was awarded an MBE. After leaving the PFA Brendon became managing director (responsible for football) with West Bromwich Albion and now works for the FA in a consultancy role, providing a key link between the 'Football for All' Division and coaching within the FA's Football Development Division. Brendon is now chairman of the Professional Players Federation. He is surely one the the PFA's modern 'greats' and deserves to take his place alongside Meredith, Fay and Lloyd as one the most influential of the association's servants.

Emile Heskey supporting Kick It Out's anti-racism campaign during their national week of action, October 2008.

Agents

'If we'd handled all transfers in the first place, there would never have been any need for an inquiry into bungs or anything like that.'
Gordon Taylor

As the first decade of the new century unfolded, footballers wages continued to rise at a staggering rate. In 2006 the average basic salary of a footballer in the English Premier League was £676,000 a year, or £13,000 per week, a figure that could rise by between 60 and 100 per cent when performance-related bonuses were added. Where basic pay was concerned, this represented an average rise in earnings of 65 per cent since 2000, when the average was £409,000 a year, or almost £8,000 a week. In 2007, Deloitte's annual review of football finances showed that Premier League wages had risen by yet another nine per cent to £854 million.

It was not just at the very top that such increases had occurred. The average basic annual Championship salary in 2006 was £195,750, up from £128,000 six years before, an increase of 53 per cent. The average in League One was £67,850 (up from £54,600, a rise of 24 per cent), and in League Two £49,600 (up from £38,800, a rise of 28 per cent).

Such wage escalation had been fuelled by the ever-increasing amounts of money flowing into club coffers from television contracts, but there was another element that disturbed many club directors. With the Bosman ruling of 1995 securing almost total freedom for players once their contracts had expired, the employment opportunities for football agents, once something of a rarity in the English game, expanded dramatically. Within a short period of time agents would become central figures in the football transfer market, in some ways replacing the club scout in the football recruitment market. They were certainly paid considerably more than a scout, who was usually an ex-player existing largely on expenses, driving the length and breadth of the country in a clapped-out car trying to spot unearthed talent before someone else beat them to it. It was revealed that during the last six months of 2005 Football League clubs had spent £4.4 million on payment to agents while the 20 Premier League clubs who choose not to release such figures were thought to have spent at least five times as much! Many in the game blamed them, rather than their clients, for the subsequent wage and transfer fee 'inflation'.

Although happy to employ agents, many clubs were resentful of their increasing influence. In August 2007 Middlesbrough chairman Steve Gibson complained of a recent transfer involving striker Mark Viduka: 'Mark Viduka is 32 on his next birthday and he was asking for a three-year contract for a figure which, over a year, would equate to over half of our gate income. We spoke to him and his agent and I was told very early that it was about money and that Mark would go to the highest bidder. The wages went up by many millions and I felt almost tainted by it.' Viduka subsequently moved to Newcastle United.

Much of the unease, however, stemmed from what appeared to be the unscrupulous methods of agents, not to mention their lack of proper legal skills and financial accountability. The problem was not

PFA on the March. Gordon Taylor with ETUC General Secretary John Monks, March 1994.

a new one. Back in 1989, following similar complaints that players were being unsettled and manipulated by unscrupulous men interested only in earning massive cuts from transfer fees and other 'external' payments, FIFA established a code of conduct for agents.

Coincidentally, in that same year PFA Financial Management Ltd was established to provide the organisation's members with an all-embracing financial advice service and to explain to younger members in particular the comprehensive range of benefits that flowed from PFA membership. Brendon Batson (then PFA deputy chief executive) demonstrated the advantages of the new company when, along with the association's financial experts, he was instrumental in arranging the first £1 million goalkeeping transfer of Nigel Martyn from Bristol Rovers to Crystal Palace. It cost Martyn no more than £200, a fraction of what most agents charged. Gradually, however, the emphasis was placed on representing the association's younger, more vulnerable members. As Taylor explained:

'The PMA tends to be very attractive to the younger player. Many parents recognise that when a 17 or 18-year-old negotiates his first contract, he is, for the first time, entering an area where advice is required. Without wishing to in anyway denigrate the service offered by all agents, I think these parents see the PMA as offering a safer and a more ethical approach.'

By the mid-1990s the PFA was forced to rethink its strategy. Members' complaints concerning devious agents were now manifold: their huge charges; the regular conflicts of interest, with agents representing a player and club simultaneously without telling the player; large amounts of monies going astray without explanation; plus a lack of contact or assistance despite the charging of large annual invoices.

The association decided that the best way to protect its members would be to assume a monitoring role alongside the Football Association to help stamp out corruption in the business. The FA, however, proved unresponsive and in the summer of 2004 the PFA decided to relaunch the Players' Management Agency (PMA). Orient's Dean Smith was one of many 'journeymen' players who found their approach more suited to his needs: 'I've never had an agent myself – I've always been happy to go through the PFA – but there are about 10-12 players at the [Orient] club who do. I'd imagine agents are more likely to be seeking different clubs for their clients, that they'll always be phoning and saying "I can get you this club, or that club", but the PFA know the details of contracts and the overall running of the game better.'

For Taylor, it made simple common sense: 'We feel this is a job that it is essential for us to do because the PFA is there to serve the players. A professional footballer's career is a short one and thus it is important to maximise all potential earning opportunities, both inside and outside the game. Having played the game themselves at the highest level, the PMA's staff are well aware of the problems and pitfalls that 'pro' football can present. They have the expertise and experience to

Gordon Taylor as President of FIFPro visiting townships in Johannesburg while at a FIFPro congress in October 2004.

conduct contract and transfer negotiations effectively and to ensure that their client's interests are protected and remain central when considering any move. With the permission of a player's football club, the PMA can also source loan moves to other clubs to help players fulfill their potential and gain playing experience. Loan moves can provide an opportunity for a younger player from a Premier League club to gain experience or allow a player who is lacking opportunities at his current club to gain playing time.'

Every PMA client is assigned a primary FIFA licensed agent. In conjunction with a player liaison officer, the agent deals with the day-to-day aspects of the player's career. They attend a player's matches, source football and equipment supplies, offer media training and the opportunity to gain coaching qualifications and enhance his general education.

By 2006 the agency was looking after 70 professionals in England, including Premier League players at Newcastle, Wigan and West Ham as well as an array of upcoming talent in the Championship such as West Bromwich Albion defender Curtis Davies, James Milner – when he moved as an 18-year-old from Leeds to Newcastle for £3.75 million – Marlon Harewood, Rob Hulse, Craig Gardner and many others. Lower fees and greater transparency in dealings were cited as reasons why an increasing number of players were turning to the PFA. In 2006 an independent newspaper survey revealed that almost 60 per cent of players in England said that they had changed agent or never had one because they were unhappy with them, while three quarters of those asked said they wanted the PFA to develop its management agency and would consider using it.

Not everyone within the game was as convinced as the players, however. In December 2006, following allegations by two League managers that 'parasitic' agents were offering 'bungs' [unofficial payments] to managers, Premier League chief executive Richard Scudamore announced an independent inquiry 'simply to find out where money in football transfers went – to clubs, players or agents – and if there were illicit payments to managers.' Scudamore explained: 'I think the clubs are fed up with the continued speculation that goes on unchecked. It will be up to the chairman of the inquiry to then take the information and convert it from investigation into evidence.'

Ex-Met chief Lord Stephens and his Quest team looked into the probity of all transfers during a two year period between January 2004 and the end of 2006. When his report was unveiled, although naming 17 transfers and five Premier League clubs, no evidence of irregular payments to club officials or players was apparently discovered.

Quite unexpectedly, however, one of the reports key recommendations was that the PFA should no longer continue to act as players' agents. To do so, Stephens declared, involved [the PFA] in a conflict of interests. He believed it should not act as players' agents' in transfers, merely 'educate and advise' on 'their dealings with clubs'.

Stephens offered no further explanation. His Quest team had made no attempt to involve the PFA in its investigation nor sought its opinion and experience of faults with the transfer system. Gordon Taylor felt that:

> 'For [Stevens] to subsequently conclude that there should be no role for the PFA in acting as players' representatives is unprofessional, patronising and arrogant. From a supposedly independent investigation, where no names are given, he [Stephens] has suddenly tarred the name of the PFA…'

Graham Courtney, chief officer of the Independent Football Commission, would later praise the work of the PFA in a report on football agents:

> 'During our investigations, we spoke to loads of clubs, and every one of them felt that the PFA was doing a great job and that, if anything, [its] influence should be increased. Many would like to see the PFA as a transfer clearing house.'

The FA also confirmed that it too was happy that the PFA should continue its role with regard to its Player Management Agency and disassociated itself from the remarks of the Quest committee.

The mystery remains as to why the Stephens Report came to the conclusion it did. The answer might lie in the fact that, although clearing Premier League clubs of any wrongdoing, there were suspicions that the Quest team were keen not to tread on powerful toes. Richard Scudamore had certainly made it clear to Stevens that the big clubs he represented would not welcome a report that would place them at a 'competitive disadvantage' with other European clubs and Stephens himself agreed that too much 'extra regulation' might handicap the English Premier League. Keeping the PFA out of the picture would certainly ensure that clubs and agents could continue with their mutually beneficial murky transactions untrammelled.

The FA's endorsement of the PFA's involvement, however, was one of a number of signs that the two bodies, once at loggerheads, were now finding themselves ever more closely aligned in the fight to wrest control of the national game from the hands of clubs whose interests were exclusively commercial.

Following a structural review by Lord Burns in May 2007, the FA voted to implement a new constitution. The following month the PFA was invited to nominate a representative to the new FA council who was eligible to attend FA council meetings and events. Gordon Taylor, noting that the invitation had come during the PFA's centenary year, accepted the invitation, hoping that the successful relationship the two organisations now enjoyed 'will continue to flourish for the betterment of the game in the future.'

2. A Young Man's Game 2007

'I want to caution the perception that footballers are overly fortunate, too highly paid and arrogant. I believe footballers are some of the most vulnerable people in society.'
Gordon Taylor to Mohammad Bhana of Ethnic Now website, June 2007.

The PFA's long history of dealing with the consequences of many young men lured into a game that promises everything but which delivers very little, places it at the heart of many of the modern game's most pressing issues. As Taylor has said: 'If we [the football industry] were an educational system, we'd face the risk of being closed down because of the failure-rate: 600 boys come into the game every year, 500 are out of it by the time they are 21.'

Having been historically responsible for reorganising the general education of football apprentices back in the 1980s, the association and its education department understand all too well the human cost involved and the plight of thousands of youngsters whose career hopes are regularly dashed and who need help to re-establish themselves, whether inside or outside the game.

The concern shown by the PFA for the development of youngsters reflects the fact that it represents a group of predominantly young, sometimes immature, occasionally extremely wealthy men. Countering the negative public image that some of these young stars have managed to acquire for themselves in recent years has proved a problem. After a century of struggling to deal with the consequences of player penury, it has had to develop strategies for coping with the consequences of untold wealth and privilege.

For various complex cultural and historic reasons, footballers have never been allowed to flaunt their wealth without finding themselves either mocked or resented in some way, particularly since players stepped out of the shadows in the 1960s to become fully fledged 'celebrities'. As far back as 1963, just two years after the lifting of the maximum wage, the *Daily Herald* ran a back page picture of Chelsea players on holiday with their wives in Cannes, a reward for gaining promotion to Division One. Beneath a banner headline 'MEET THE SOCCER SLAVES…and their girls,' the feature was aimed at all fans 'who believe soccer players are hard done by'. Ever since then sniping at footballers' home furnishings, not to mention their 'significant others', has become a major alternative spectator sport, while the affluence, glamour and status of the average Premier League player produces longing and contempt in equal measure.

Perhaps this explains, in a small way, why large numbers of fans indulge in the disgraceful barracking of players, hurling ugly, often racist, abuse at particular individuals, managers included? Graham Le Saux, a one-time PFA representative and long-time target of such behaviour, ostensibly for his mythical 'gay' status, wrote in October 2008: 'Our national sport is one of the biggest industries in this country and projects our image around the world. But it is also the last bastion of this kind of abuse. If you look at how far we have come in the rest of our society in terms of multi-culturism and tolerance, you see football is still a million miles behind.' Questioning some fans about it, he discovered their excuse was that as footballers were paid handsomely to do something which is a privilege, they have to 'put up with the stick' they get. Clearly, some fans were happier when their heroes were shackled to restrictive contracts, treated like chattels, paid a derisory wage and expected to show eternal thanks for the privilege. To be healthy, supremely fit and in possession of a sublime talent to succeed in a game that millions of working class men and boys consider their own is considered recompense enough. To be a millionaire into the bargain – it is simply too much! No surprise then when tales of wild player orgies and drunken violence dominate the tabloid's front pages that the profession as a whole finds itself tarred with the same brush.

When, in December 2007, Manchester United's players hired out an entire 30-room four-star hotel, where rooms cost £325-a-night, for a private event attended by around 150 guests, including 'dozens of models', there was always liable to be some unpleasant fallout. Sure enough, a 19-year-old forward was accused of rape. Three months later he was cleared but in the meantime newspapers both high and lowbrow covered the case in immense, sometimes prurient, detail. It was just one in a string of similar cases stretching back many years in which professional players have been accused of gross sexual behaviour.

Life after football. Ashley Fickling (ex-Grimsby Town and Scunthorpe United) and Paul Teather (ex-Manchester United) each gain a BSc in Physiotherapy at the University of Salford, 2007.

James Beaumont (ex-Nottingham Forest and Northwich Victoria), course co-ordinator Lawrie Madden (ex-Sheffield Wednesday, Charlton and Wolves) and Matt Baker (ex-Hereford United and Milton Keynes Dons) each earn a BA in sports journalism at Staffordshire University, 2008.

Germaine Greer has written:

All athletes (and managers) live on a knife edge. All are only as good as their last performance. All are incessantly reminded that there is only one way to go after reaching the top, and that's down. The situation of footballers is the most precarious of all. As the last in the pecking order, after club owners, directors and managers, players are denied adult status. They are "lads" or "boys" to be bought and sold, transferred or dropped or left on the bench; as they are denied autonomy, we can't be surprised if they lack responsibility. Their survival depends on luck and is as fragile as a hamstring. Much of the concerted misbehaviour that ends in catastrophe begins as an attempt to discharge accumulated tension, which is no excuse.

As long ago as 1995 Gordon Taylor insisted:

'We have more than 2,000 members and it is unrealistic to expect them all to be choirboys. The vast majority are a credit to their profession.

Players are expected to be role models and it is a burden for some. They are young men who are under intense pressure and are expected to have old heads on young shoulders. Men of much more senior stature, politicians and businessmen, fall by the wayside. The illumination of off-field activities is the price football pays for its increased stature. It is an indication of just how much football is part of the fabric of our society. Players are centre stage, everything is on television now.'

The PFA does what it can where player behaviour *on* the pitch is concerned. For almost 20 years it has bestowed the PFA Bobby Moore Fair Play Award upon the team with the best disciplinary record throughout the Premier League and the Football League. In April 2007 Crewe Alexandra won it for the 11th time, along with a donation of £7,500 for the benefit of the players, management and coaching staff and £7,500 for the benefit of the club's community programme. Crewe Manager Dario Gradi put the award in its 'professional' context, however, when receiving it:

'We are delighted to win this award although it's not something we consciously set out to win every year. Getting this award is not the incentive – we just feel it's in the best interests of the football club to try and get the

Nick Cusack Chairman 2002

A university graduate, after spells with Leicester City, Peterborough United, Motherwell, Darlington, Oxford United, Wycombe Wanderers and Fulham (where he was captain of the team that won the Third Division Championship under Mickey Adams and Alan Cork's leadership) Nick joined Swansea City in October 1997. He immediately established himself in the Swansea first team and after a string of good performances was voted Player of the Season that year by club members. Joining the PFA Management Committee in 1996, he served as chair briefly before a period as player-coach of Swansea City in April 2002, but after just 17 games in charge he was replaced by Brian Flynn and left in September 2002. He joined the PFA on a full-time basis with PFA Financial Management Ltd in 2002 and is now one of the PFA's delegate liason executives.

Richard Jobson Chairman 2002–03

Richard began his long career with non-League Burton Albion in 1980 before leaving civil engineering studies to join Watford. In 1985 Hull City paid £40,000 for him and he spent five successful seasons and over 250 games at the heart of Hull's defence, helping the Tigers gain promotion to Division Two in his first season. Oldham then bought him for £500,000 in August 1990. After helping them earn promotion to the top flight, a move to Leeds United in 1995 for £1 million was followed by spells at Huddersfield and Southend before he joined Manchester City on free transfer in early 1998 to play in 44 of the 46 games of the promotion season of 1999–2000! A return to Watford in 2000 followed by spells at Tranmere Rovers and Rochdale saw Richard complete a career of almost 700 first-team appearances in all competitions with nine different clubs! Since retiring Richard returned to football as a PFA executive.

least number of players suspended as possible. We teach the players, at every level from youth team upwards, the benefits of not giving away unnecessary free kicks and cautions.'

The association also has an agreed code of on-field discipline with the FA, the Premier League, the Football League and the League Managers Association of which all PFA members are made aware. Poster campaigns such as the recent *Respect the Game…Respect the Referee* highlighted the need for players to act in a responsible manner on the field of play with regard to the use of foul and abusive language, elbowing and mass confrontations of the referee. As a member of the Professional Game Match Officials Technical Liaison Group along with representatives from the other governing bodies, the association takes part in discussions on current refereeing topics, law changes and the performances of the officials, along with issues regarding player and manager behaviour both on and off the field. Thus, it has an input and can make its voice heard. Just how many players are actually listening, of course, is debateable. Raising the issue of simulating injury during a match in an attempt to gain an advantage was claimed by the association to have led to a decrease in such behaviour. Stricter refereeing might also have had an influence…

Inevitably, however, the PFA is drawn into the defence of players, young and old, whose off-field behaviour sometimes suggests they have more money than sense. In November 1997 Shane Nicholson, a West Bromwich Albion mid-fielder, was suspended after testing positive for traces of amphetamines, a performance-enhancing drug. He was sacked by the club and suspended by the FA. The PFA sent him to a rehabilitation clinic and, six months later, following an appeal to the FA, he returned to play with Chesterfield. Nicholson is now currently rehabilitation and fitness coach at Chesterfield, educating young players about the dangers of drink and drugs.

Since then, with its substantial sponsorship of Tony Adams' Sporting Chance Clinic, a charity set up in 2000 following the ex-Arsenal captain's own struggle to recover from alcoholism, the association has been swift to offer support and guidance to even the most wayward of its members. Sporting Chance's Preventative Education

Mick McGuire Deputy Chief Executive
Mick was born in Blackpool on 4 September 1952. An English Youth international central midfielder, he joined the professional ranks directly from Blackpool Grammar School at just 17 years old without serving an apprenticeship, signing for Coventry City in November 1969. An exceptional young player, he starred alongside Trevor Francis in the England Youth team that won the 'Mini World Cup' in Czechoslovakia in 1971, and he made his first-team debut the same year at the age of 18. After 72 League matches for the 'Sky Blues', John Bond, Norwich City manager, paid £60,000 for him in January 1975. Mick stayed at Carrow Road until March 1983, scoring 11 goals in 182 matches. He then moved on to Barnsley for two more years and while there he studied for a degree through the Open University. He ended his football career in May 1987 at Oldham Athletic after 69 matches, thus completing a career total of 370 League matches. He also had experience of playing in the United States as a teammate of Rodney Marsh, helping the Rowdies to Soccer Bowl '78, scoring two goals. Mick has been involved with the Association for 21 years, five years as a member of the PFA Management Committee and 16 years working as assistant chief executive. Following Brendon Batson's departure, Mick was appointed primary deputy chief executive to Gordon Taylor. He has been a FIFPro board member since 2005.

Gordon Taylor introduces the PFA team at the TUC Congress to receive the inaugural TUC award for promoting equality and diversity. Left to right: Bobby Barnes, Chris Powell, Simone Pound and John Hudson, September 2004.

Programme is designed to give young athletes 'the information and tools they need to avoid the pitfalls and destructive behaviour patterns which can develop in the pressure cooker world of professional sport.' Many prominent players have availed themselves of its services, including former Chelsea striker Adrian Mutu, Paul Gascoigne, Warren Aspinall, Glasgow Rangers defender Fernando Ricksen, ex-Bolton star Noel Whelan and England Under-21s and QPR star Clarke Carlisle.

Unfortunately, the case of Joey Barton, whose repetitive, violent off-field outbursts eventually led to a term of imprisonment, illustrates how ultimately powerless the association is in curbing or altering its members' deviant behaviour. By directing Barton to 'anger-management sessions' at the clinic the association ran the risk of leaving itself open to accusations that it was being overindulgent towards a character who, in everyday life, would probably have lost his job and a lot more besides. Gordon Taylor, in claiming 'I try not to give up on people,' remained unrepentant. Barton appeared less so. On release he refused to accept a fine or a reduction in his £65,000-a-week salary, safe in the knowledge that Newcastle would not sack him – having paid some £5 million for him, they knew he could not be replaced cheaply and that they risked losing all that they had paid for him.

The contrasting fates of Barton, a top Premier League player, and Nicholson, one of soccer's journeymen, illustrates another unique difficulty the PFA faces in representing its members: simultaneously addressing the aspirations and needs of young men wildly disparate in skill and financial wherewithal. It is a dichotomy reflected in one of the association's own publications, *The Players Club*, a glossy 'lifestyle' magazine published by PFA Enterprises, the PFA's commercial arm.

Replete with articles on expensive (second) homes in Dubai and Morocco, adverts for 52ft powerboats, luxurious health resorts, Jaguar and Mercedes cars and Rolex watches, *The Players Club* is, as Graham Le Saux declared, 'the voice of conspicuous consumption,' conveying a lifestyle 'to which only a tiny proportion of our members could relate.' He went on:

> 'Imagine being a lower division player struggling to survive and, in some cases, lacking even the certainty that you will be paid every week. You pick up the magazine and read about houses costing millions. You are advised on the dos and don'ts of buying racehorse.'

It was, Le Saux suggested, difficult to blame the media for portraying professional footballers as rich, materialistic and arrogant, 'when our own magazine so effectively perpetuates the myth.'

Yet, it can be argued that star players probably deserve the attention given to them by *The Players Club*. Without their high-profile support during times of dispute, the association might never have achieved the status it now enjoys. It is also largely thanks to the stars that television companies pay the enormous sums they do to screen football, thus providing a major source of PFA income. On top of that, the five per cent levy on all transfer fees that goes into the players' pension scheme means that it is the highest-valued players who contribute the most towards a scheme that benefits all. The fact that everyone, star player or first-year scholar, pays the same modest subscription to be a member, only underlines the philosophy that, within the union, everyone is treated equally.

Gordon Taylor handing the Bobby Moore Fair Play Award to Dario Gradi in 2007.

Gordon Taylor acknowledges great professionals both old and new. Top: Sir Tom Finney; bottom: Eric Cantona.

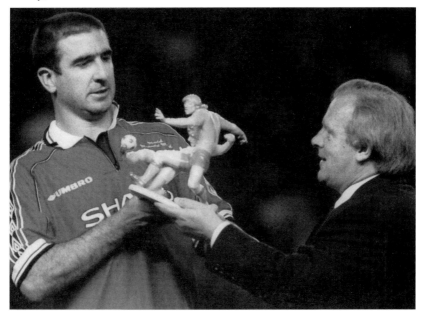

3. Meltdown 2006–09

'While the FA, as the formal governing body, is supposed to be responsible for the overall game, it hasn't got the power to perform that role. We need a strong independent-minded governing body that can make decisions for the general good of the game rather than owners viewing their clubs as businesses and only voting for what is in their own best interests.'
Gordon Taylor, 2006.

In late 2007 Richard Scudamore admitted that the 2002 TV monies dispute with the PFA had been the worst moment he had experienced thus far as Premier League chief executive. 'I never felt under so much pressure,' he revealed. Since its foundation, the Premier League has been used to getting its own way. The jolt it experienced when facing an obdurate players' organisation was painful and much resented. Had it been more aware of the professional game's long history, however, it might have treated the dispute as rather more than a squabble over cash. It might have realised that one of the reasons why the original Players' Union had come into existence was because professionals were afraid of the ever-increasing power of the Football League to make rules that suited it at the expense of players and supporters alike. Back then, the union had hoped to find the FA sympathetic and had appealed to it for help, especially where the transfer system was concerned. Unfortunately, being too wary of 'professionalism', the FA had turned out to be the union's principal opponent.

Today, 100 years on, the PFA finds itself in an uncannily similar position, grappling with the consequences of an all-too-powerful Premier League, trying to ensure the game in this country remains healthy at all levels and that the original essence of competition is not eroded by the demands of those interested purely in profit. Just as it did at the turn of the 19th century, it is seeking to galvanise the FA into more positive action. When necessary, it has been unafraid to court controversy in this quest.

In December 2006 journalist Chris Lightbown joined forces with statistician Mike Joyce to investigate some startling developments in the English game. Aided by a small team of researchers including David Walls, Steve Griggs and Chris Hill, Lightbown compiled an exhaustive report, a number crunching exposé of personnel changes that had occurred in first-team line ups in the decade or so since the establishment of the Premier League. Feeling that the PFA would be sympathetic to the underlying philosophy of the report, they took it to Gordon Taylor who arranged that it be published. The report was called Meltdown. To the consternation of some in the game it appeared to be calling for quotas to restrict the numbers of foreign players operating in the English game.

Back in 1930 there had been little controversy or disagreement where such issues were concerned. Charles Sutcliffe, Football League official and FA councillor, considered importing foreign players to play in English League football 'repulsive to the clubs, offensive to British players and a terrible confession of weakness in the management of a club.' His stance had been fully supported by the Players' Union at the time, who were keen to protect the jobs of British workers. When, in that same year, Arsenal tried to sign an Austrian goalkeeper, the union and the FA made representations to the Ministry of Labour to deny him a work permit, before coming to a formal agreement opposing foreign professionals. A clause was inserted into the FA's rules stating: 'A professional player who is not a British-born subject is not eligible to take part in any competition under the jurisdiction of this Association unless he possesses a two-year residential qualification within the jurisdiction of the Association.' Foreign professionals were thus effectively banned from earning a living in this country until 1978 when Britain entered the European Community and had to accept the principle of free movement of workers enshrined in the Treaty of Rome.

However, the situation did not change much, partly because of a UEFA quota system which restricted the number of foreign players who could play in any particular match. In the UEFA club competitions only three foreign players plus two 'assimilated' foreign players could be selected. When Jean Marc Bosman began his fight for justice back in 1995, Gordon Taylor had been uneasy about its wider implications, what he termed the 'sting in the tail' of the case: the lifting of restrictions on entry of non-national EU players within the European Union and the ending of the 3+2 quota system. Sure enough, once the Bosman judgement was delivered, Manchester City immediately approached the Premier League to remove this rule and the floodgates opened.

The PFA Awards, soccers big night 1996 winners. Left to right: Robbie Fowler (Young Player), Pele (Special Merit) and Les Ferdinand (Player of the Year).

Michael 'Micky' Burns

Micky was a former England amateur international signed by Blackpool from Skelmersdale United in 1969. He was a striker with pace who could score goals and was the Seasiders' top scorer in three of his five seasons at Bloomfield Road. In the summer of 1974 Newcastle United bought him for £175,000 and it was with the Magpies that he reached the 1976 League Cup Final, losing to Manchester City. After four years at St James' Park Micky had a short spell at Cardiff City before returning to the North East to close out his career with Middlesbrough. Upon retiring Burns joined Middlesbrough's coaching staff. He later became the PFA's education officer. In this role he was instrumental in building up a formidable department that helped revolutionise the way young players were trained and educated. The moribund 'apprenticeship' system was replaced by a scheme that helped save many clubs youth teams. Micky also helped hundreds of ex-professionals rebuild their lives after their playing days were over. He was an innovative teacher and administrator who helped make the modern PFA the organisation it is today.

The Meltdown Report's figures were startling: on the opening weekend of the first Premier League season in 1992 there had been only 12 foreign players in the top division. At the start of December 2007 that figure had risen to 138. In addition, since the youth academy system had begun only 120 English players from academies had made debuts in the Premier League, while 617 overseas players had been introduced into the top flight over the same period. Other surveys told the same tale, one for the *Telegraph Sport* in 2007 revealed that of 532 Premier League players, only 182 were English – just 34.21 per cent. In the inaugural Premier League season, 1992–93, 71 per cent of players had been English.

Despite all this, for a union to be concerned or troubled about the nationality of its membership was deemed by many observers to be verging on racism, a harsh judgement on an organisation that had led the fight against discrimination on the pitch and the terraces for almost two decades when first establishing its KickItOut campaign. Taylor was sensitive to the charge: 'People will say it's all jingoism, that we're saying "it's all the fault of the foreigners" and so on, but that's not it at all. No one tries to be more socially integrative than myself, but for a country that is the richest in the football world, we are not achieving at international level.'

Meltdown stated the case clearly: 'The issue is balance. We have bought in foreign players in an unbalanced rush that has decimated the chances of home-grown players reaching the Premier League. We expect this shrinking pool of players to constantly produce world-beating [England] teams and are shocked when it fails to do so. It is our clubs' very power, based on foreign players, that has drained the England team of any realistic expectation of success.' The reason for that was because the existing pool of English players available for selection was shrinking. This was due to the shrinking numbers of English players coming through from youth ranks to play in the Premier League: 'What is at stake is not just the future of the England team, but the fundamental right of English players to rise as far as their talent will take them. That right is now denied. We have become a finishing school for the rest of the world, at the expense of our own players.'

Thus, the Meltdown Report appeared to be about the effectiveness of the English football 'industry' as a whole at grass roots level. It was an assertion that clubs should not be seen purely as businesses but also as part of the local communities where they are based and part of the identity of the nation to which they belong. It was also, albeit obliquely, calling into question some of the arguments used to transform the national game a decade or more before.

The original justification for the creation of the Premier League, an elite super league, was not just that it would reduce the number of games top players had to play and thus allow the England team to be less exhausted when tournaments came around; it was also asserted that top clubs would have more money to invest in top quality coaching facilities. The FA, benefitting from the increased wealth flowing into the game via the enhanced TV appeal of the newly structured game, would also be able to invest in a national coaching centre where top young English players could go to hone their skills. The benefits would spread down and help develop and enhance the game at all levels. That has not been how things have panned out. The National Football Centre had failed to materialise and a coherent coaching regime running from top to bottom in the English game has been disastrously shelved for years.

Following the creation of the Premier League, the education provision for young players had certainly undergone a transformation. In 1997 Howard Wilkinson, then FA Technical Director, as part of his 'Charter for Quality' had proposed an academy system to replace the existing football scholarships that all young apprentice players followed at that time.

A 'scholarship' lasted three years and was supposed to be tailored to the individual needs of young players. It involved 12 hours of academic study per week in a range of qualifications depending on the grades the 'scholar' had attained at secondary GCSE level. More academically gifted players were allowed to undertake A levels, while those with fewer GCSEs were able to take some A levels together with advanced GNVQs. Furthermore, the scholarships made it mandatory for players to receive funding for three years even if clubs decided to release players from their contracts after only two years.

Warren Barton Chairman 2003–04

After beginning his career with non-League Maidstone, Warren was transferred to Wimbledon in 1990 for £300,000, a UK record fee for a Third Division player. One of the most highly rated defenders in England at the time, in 1995 he also became the most expensive in English football when he moved to Newcastle United for £4 million. While at St James' Park he played in defence and midfield and was part of the England squad. He later played for Derby County, Queen's Park Rangers, Wimbledon and Dagenham & Redbridge. Warren Barton ended his playing days where he began, with Dagenham & Redbridge in the 2004–05 season. He coached the side during the week while working as a TV pundit at the weekend. In 2006 Warren was part of ITV4's World Cup team of pundits. He currently works for Fox Soccer Channel as a TV pundit and is also the Under-18 coach at LA Galaxy.

The problem was that the system was too closely tied to each club's management set-up. Rapid changes at the top in certain clubs – a manager being sacked and a new manager bringing in a completely new staff regime – often resulted in turmoil below, which in turn severely undermined the delivery of academic provision. Standards were inconsistent and difficult to assess.

Wilkinson's academy system by contrast was designed to be 'distinct from first-team management'. Under his proposals clubs would receive funding for an academy or centre of excellence which would exist apart from the parent club's management structure. The funding would follow as long as the academy fulfilled certain criteria ensuring 'that appropriate and adequate educational provision is available for each academy player, including primary, secondary, further and higher educational provision'. Similarly, for football clubs to have an associated centre of excellence, they were 'required to clearly outline the rules and guidelines concerning centres with regard to registration, welfare, educational needs, priority and objectives'.

When Wilkinson set up the charter for quality he estimated that there would be between 12 to 15 academies. However, when the programme was introduced virtually every club wanted one. There are now 41 academies and about 49 centres of excellence. It would seem, however, that providing young players with a three-year course in whatever subject they chose to study proved to be beyond the resources of both the football clubs and the funding bodies.

What eventually came to be offered was called an Apprenticeship in Sporting Excellence (ASE). Rather than allowing young players to select from a range of different qualifications, the ASE concentrated on helping them gain credentials in areas deemed to increase their chances of developing into professional footballers. The courses cover such subjects as nutrition, coaching and rehabilitation.

By 2005, however, the Premier League and Football League representatives conceded that a number of academies were not meeting the required standards. In December of that year, after much heated debate, the FA set up a monitoring group to visit the failing clubs to impress upon them that they needed to improve certain aspects of their operation. They had seven months to comply. It was then that the Premier League and Football League boards informed the FA that they believed that it did not have the power to pursue such a course of action.

Sir Trevor Brooking, the FA's head of youth development, explains: 'At this point our attempts to improve the development of young elite players more or less ground to a halt. We were at an impasse because there appeared to be no agreement on the required standards for academies, and so there was a clear vacuum of leadership. No one could impose sanctions on those clubs that were falling short of the required standards.'

The FA's technical control board, the committee dealing with the youth development system in England, has since gone almost two years without convening because of the tensions and disagreement between the FA, the Premier League and the Football League over who has the authority to oversee youth development. As Gordon Taylor put it: 'If the FA was an educational establishment and was asked to demonstrate its success in terms of its examination results it would probably find itself subject to "special measures". The millions of pounds poured into youth development via the academies and the centres of excellence have borne little fruit. It's not a pretty picture.'

Where the coaching of young players within the same academies was concerned, the PFA was similarly alarmed. Expenditure on the academies since the implementing of the charter had produced some of the best facilities for youth development in Europe, if not the world. However, it seemed that, with some notable exceptions, most academies were playing what one academy manager described as 'smash and grab football, where all that matters is the result.'

Jim Hicks, the current head of PFA coaching, noted crucial differences between young English elite players and young foreign players arriving in the top club academies. He explained, 'It appears that it is not a lack of technical ability that is the problem, but rather a lack of tactical awareness and the ability to play several positions and systems by the age of 14. Being "positional specific" from a young age places young English players at a disadvantage when compared with the greater all round knowledge of his world peers. Foreign players all have greater depth of knowledge of playing positions, something that must be correctly quickly on these shores.'

One coach at a Football League club admitted: 'My young lads watch Italian and Spanish football on TV and are fascinated by it. But if our lads started playing out from the back and interchanging positions the way any continental coach would want, they'd be smashed around the pitch and lose by a hatful of goals every week – and what would my chairman think of that? I'd be out of a job, for one thing.'

Young English players thus faced a double bind: their coaching from an early age was poor and therefore their progress was hindered. Increasingly, Premier League clubs, awash with millions from television and sponsorship money and demanding the most talented youngsters, were simply bypassing the home-grown product and scouring the world for ever-younger talent.

By 2007, where once only a handful of foreign players were being trained in English youth academies, almost half the academy 'scholars' at some clubs were foreign and more than a third at others. Manchester City led the field with 14 out of its 30 academy 'scholars' foreign. Liverpool had seven out of 15, Chelsea 10 out of 31, Blackburn and Bolton had eight out of 21 and Fulham had five out of 20. Some clubs were already setting up 'feeder' academies in countries as far away as China and Nigeria to discover young talent.

Ryan Giggs and Wayne Rooney with another Manchester United great, Billy Meredith, at the launch of the PFA Centenary year, January 2007.

Trevor Brooking, who came through the junior ranks at West Ham and went on to play for England, said the crisis was 'a serious concern'. 'Even a few years ago nobody foresaw this explosion of young foreign imports,' he said. 'We have got to invest in better quality coaches. Our youngsters have got to get there on merit.'

The second problem for young English players was that even when they did prove good enough to make a first-team squad they were liable to find their path blocked

Gordon Taylor receives his OBE from Prince Charles in 2008. He commented, 'This is a nice honour for me personally and it is also lovely recognition for the PFA in our centenary year.'

by a foreign international having been bought 'off-the-peg' as it were. For Taylor, the vast expenditure on the academies was thus a colossal waste of money: 'Having spent so much on developing young players, is it acceptable that most of the fruits of this expenditure have their path to the Premier League blocked by their clubs repeatedly buying older, ready-made players? Any good business invests in research and development. But our business has researched and developed young players – and then blocked their way to the top. Would we expect an IT company to spend a small fortune on researching and developing computers, but then spend the bulk of its income on importing computers from abroad? Would we expect a farmer to invest in crops, but then block the sale of his own produce by importing vast quantities of cheaper foreign food? Of course not. But behaviour we would find absurd in the rest of the world has become common practice in football.'

This was the real point of Meltdown: 'Somewhere out there is a lost generation of players. Worse – most of the British and Irish lads who are coming through the system are effectively already lost. Worse still, many of the generation behind them – that is boys who are now 16 and under – are going to be lost if the flow of foreign boys into academies keeps increasing, as every indication says it will. The fundamental right of home-grown boys to rise as far as their talent will take them is being denied. That cuts against the most basic concept of fairness and we should be ashamed that things have reached this stage. This is not sport. This is the free market gone absolutely mad.'

The Premier League, needless to say, saw things entirely differently, even down to the point of countering the stark figures Meltdown produced with figures of their own.

Arsenal, the club that had been the catalyst back in the 1930s for the original restrictions on foreign players, was the first club to announce a completely foreign 16-man squad for a match against Crystal Palace in February 2005. The manager responsible for this revolutionary move, Arsene Wenger, was adamant. 'For me it doesn't make any difference where people come from,' he said. 'You cannot want the most popular league in the world and have everybody come from one country. It doesn't work like that. That would be miraculous.'

Richard Scudamore, chief executive of the Premier League, was also forthright in defence of the status quo: 'Our responsibility is to put on the best possible show, with the best possible talent on the field and played in the best possible stadia. In our view, that sits very comfortably alongside what the England team are trying to achieve…we are producing a sufficient number of players for England.'

The Premier League thus resolutely blocks all attempts to alter the balance, whether these are suggested by FIFA or UEFA. When, in 2008, Sepp Blatter unveiled his so-called '6+5 plan'– a law forcing clubs to field a minimum of six home nationals in their starting line ups – Scudamore wasted no time in asserting that introducing limits on foreign players would only 'hinder the development of the game in England'. 'The problem with Blatter's logic is that you can get yourself into a difficult, jingoistic, almost racist debate about who can and who cannot play for your country,' he said.

In 2005 UEFA ruled that by the 2008 season clubs playing in European competitions must field at least eight 'home-grown' players in their 25-man squad. Of the eight, four would have had to be trained by the club's own academy and a further four trained within the same national association. 'Home-grown' was defined as a player who has been trained by his club or by another club in the same national association for at least three years between the age of 15 and 21 without any nationality conditions.

UEFA defined its sporting objectives in introducing the quota as aiming to promote training, to maintain competitive balance, to prevent player 'hoarding' and to enhance local identity and culture. It pressed for the ruling to be enforced in domestic competitions but it was clear that the FA, under pressure from the Premier League, who voted 16–4 against the idea, had no intention of doing so.

Ryan Giggs publicising a Children's Society online guide *Shaping Up* which features Manchester United players and details health and fitness tips for families, Summer 2008.

For the PFA the only realistic chance of success in encouraging grass roots youth development was by strengthening the UEFA proposal. In fact, its Meltdown Report called for a new rule whereby every team had at least three 'home-grown' players – of any nationality – on the pitch at any time in order to stop clubs bypassing their young players and bringing in cheap foreign internationals as a 'quick fix'.

Taylor said 'In Europe you cannot discriminate on the grounds of nationality so we have to really look at the UEFA proposal.' This, he felt, would 'encourage clubs to develop players for

David Beckham lends a hand to the PFA's children's hospital appeal, 2007.

the next generation. It may well be that clubs look at bringing in youngsters from abroad, but it would at least focus them on developing players and at the moment they haven't got the patience to be doing that. We would be very much in favour of the UEFA criteria being developed further because the European Commission has indicated they would go ahead with that because focus is on youth development, irrespective of nationality. That would give English youngsters at least the opportunities to succeed.'

Where the Premier League's response was concerned he was scathing: 'What worries me is the attitude of Arsenal vice-chairman David Dein. Here is a man, a prominent member of the FA's international committee, openly lobbying against UEFA's quota proposals. And I am also very disappointed that FA chairman Geoff Thompson under pressure from David Dein, is already trying to get that rule blocked. It is such a short-sighted, negative view.'

In fact, by late 2008 the future of the English professional game at all levels was the topic of intense, sometimes acrimonious, discussion. The immense debt being run up by various Premier League clubs, the proliferation of foreign owners and the lack of overall accountability were the key topics. The underlying theme was, however: who controls the game?

Sepp Blatter of FIFA felt that: 'We are now facing investment in football, particularly the [English] Premier League, that is out of control and this is where UEFA will have to do something with the licensing system.'

Lord Triesman, the new FA chairman, believed that a strong FA was necessary for the game to flourish. This view was endorsed by government culture secretary Andy Burnham, who insisted that the government was right to raise concerns concerning the game's 'relationship with money' because of football's importance to supporters, to the communities in which clubs are based and to the public at large: 'We need a strong, informed FA, that is responsible from grass roots level to the England game. They are the people who need to regulate the game in the interests of everybody.'

Richard Scudamore was inevitably unhappy with any interference with his organisation's commercial approach, which has reaped rich rewards for the clubs it represents. Defending the status quo as he understood it he opined, 'We should all pull together, we would be silly not to, but we all have slightly different virtues. The way it works best is tripartite, with the Football League and its incredible tentacles into communities, the Premier League with its different appeal and the FA working together. We have all got areas that we do well, but when you look at the areas of overlap, they are not that great.' In many respects it was a startling statement, suggesting that there was no organisation in complete control of the game in England. Why, he implied, should the Premier League yield to the whims of an organisation [the FA] that was in some ways its commercial rival? 'We are like competitors,' he said. 'We compete for sponsorship and for television rights and we are in the same space.'

With such a blatantly commercial interpretation of football life being mooted, it is no wonder that alternative visions have since been floated. For instance, the chief executive of the League Managers' Association, Richard Bevan, announced in October 2008 that he was mobilising the 'talent' of the game, including the PFA and the Professional Football Coaches Association, to form a collective capable of challenging the established order from UEFA to the Football Association: 'Together we have immense power, more than Michel Platini (UEFA), Lord Triesman (FA)

Great players both young and old gather at Manchester Town Hall to start the centenary celebrations, January 2007.

Dean Holdsworth Chairman 2004–05

Dean began his career with Watford before joining Brentford FC in September 1989 for £125,000 where he proved himself a prolific goalscorer, scoring 38 goals in the Third Division Championship winning season of 1991–92. He then joined the infamous 'Crazy Gang' at Wimbledon FC in 1992, playing alongside Vinnie Jones, John Fashanu and Dennis Wise. In October 1997 Dean signed for Bolton Wanderers for a Reebok record fee of £3.5 million. He subsequently joined Rushden & Diamonds, helping them to gain promotion. Dean is now manager at Newport County, playing in the Blue Square South. Dean has written a children's book about the exploits of two footballing brothers and has appeared on various celebrity television series.

and people running the game. You will see the PFA, PFCA and the LMA working closer together in driving the game in a more positive way, on the pitch and off it.'

Its unlikely that the PFA would seek to challenge the authority of the established governing body, however. With its crucial support for smaller clubs in financial trouble and its pioneering role in establishing such revolutionary measures as its Football In the Community schemes, the association has always striven to use its influence to protect the game's 'grass roots' and to counter any powerful centrifugal forces threatening to tear the game apart.

However, despite its relative affluence and increasing authority, it is still first and foremost a union, whose principal purpose is to defend its members and their interests, even if those interests would seem, at times, to run counter to those of the paying public. As Premier League clubs increasingly seek to 'globalise' their appeal and to claim ever more interest in far-flung continents, the eternally loyal 'home' supporters who turn up each Saturday could be excused for feeling that their main purpose is to provide the vocal backdrop for the 'brand' on sale. PFA members, whether they like it or not, form part of a football 'elite' that no longer recognises 'roots' nor local affiliations.

In a curious way, the association's purchase of L.S. Lowry's picture, *Going to the Match*, in December 1999, could be read as an attempt to cling on to some of the values that are fast disappearing from the national game. *Going to the Match* depicts fans flocking into Burnden Park, once the home of Bolton Wanderers (and, ironically, Gordon Taylor's main stamping ground when he was a player). Gordon Taylor said of it:

'It is the football picture. It's full of anticipation and movement at the start of a match which, as an ex-footballer, I know gets the adrenalin going. It captures all the atmosphere of the game and represents its heart and soul.'

Jack Charlton described it thus:

'This is just like it was in those days when I was young: all wooden open stands, cinders underfoot, terrible conditions in the toilets. It reminds me of Newcastle United years ago – everyone turning up 15 minutes before kick-off, seeing your Uncle Billy or your schoolmates in the crowd…there's so much in it, its fabulous.'

The painting cost close to £2 million and drew criticism from those who felt a union had no business dealing in such expensive artefacts. Taylor defended the purchase on two grounds. First, it was an investment (one that has since proved astute as the painting's value has risen steadily). At the same time, he suggested that he had been moved to save the painting 'for the nation', or rather, 'for football'. It would, he said, have been a tragedy had it gone abroad 'bought by an overseas collector'.

Millwall players participating in the National Literacy Trust's 'Playing with Words' campaign, a national reading initiative linked to football, Autumn 2008.

Chris Powell Chairman 2006

Chris began his career at Crystal Palace FC, moving to Southend United FC three years later where, as a very skilled, left-footed defender, he made 288 first-team appearances and was later voted the Southend United supporters' all-time cult hero! In January 1996 Chris moved to Derby County for £750,000 before being transferred to Charlton Athletic in 1998 for a fee of £825,000. While at Charlton he made 206 first-team appearances and was picked for the England team in 2001. In 2004–05 he played a major part in West Ham United's successful promotion campaign before returning to Charlton. In July 2006 he signed a one-year contract with Premiership newcomers Watford but returned to Charlton in 2007 as player-coach. He is currently under contract at Leicester City.

Burnden Park has long since gone the way of scores of other traditional inner city grounds, replaced by all-purpose, modern stadia that serve a different purpose to that of the old grounds. The game no longer has anything to do with 'matchstick' men flocking eternally into looming Burnden Park on a Saturday afternoon, and much more to do with satellite signals beaming a dazzling spectacle to billions of fans as far afield as the Middle East and China. The new venues are cash-generators and so, perhaps, *Going To The Match* could be said to represent the irretrievable past.

One senses that, for Taylor, buying the painting was something by way of a payback, that if he could not prevent the game itself being bought by foreigners, then he might secure its soul. Under his stewardship the PFA has become one of the biggest collectors of football-related 'treasures', be they medals, cups, statuettes, programmes or cigarette cards. Manchester's People's History Museum now has a dedicated section on the history of the game, giving the general public the opportunity to see many examples of the PFA's collection. In late 2008, at the Manchester Art Gallery, the association's pictures and posters were put on display in an exhibition called 'The Beautiful Game', with the Lowry painting as the centrepiece.

Collecting memorabilia has been portrayed as a typically English pastime, an obsession that fuels a nostalgia for 'the good old days'. Could the union's acquisition of so much ancient (predominantly British) ephemera be prompted by a subliminal sense of regret at what we, the public, have lost as against what so many of the union's own members have inherited?

Fanciful perhaps. Nevertheless, the association has remained physically close to its roots for a century now, resisting the temptation to relocate to the capital. If Billy Meredith and company were to wander back in time they would find the offices of the organisation they founded in 1907 just a few steps away from its original location above Meredith's outfitter's shop in St Peter's Square. There is, perhaps, some hope for the game in that.

APPENDICES

September 1955 TUC Congress at Southport

Wee Georgie Wood OBE seconded this motion:

'This Congress expresses its concern at the continued denial to professional footballers of proper and reasonable conditions of employment. It draws the attention of the Football Association to the fundamental rights of employees which have developed as a right of trade union insistence. It considers that professional footballers are entitled to enjoy the same rights as all other employees including freedom to make or terminate a contract of employment, freedom to earn as much as possible and freedom to take legal action on any matter affecting their welfare. Failure of the Football Association and of clubs in membership of the Football Association to acknowledge these rights has resulted in injustice and dissatisfaction among players. It has also led some clubs to use under-the-counter methods in securing players. Congress therefore calls upon the Football Association to arrange a conference of all interested parties to consider arrangements for a complete and comprehensive new deal for professional players.'

Jimmy Guthrie spoke as follows:

Mr Chairman and Delegates,

'I stand here as the representative of the last bonded men in Britain – the professional footballers. We seek your help to smash a system under which now, in this year of 1955, human beings are bought and sold like cattle. A system which, as in feudal times, binds a man to one master or, if he rebels, stops him getting another job. The conditions of the professional footballer's employment are akin to slavery. They smirch the name of British democracy. I have been accused by the Big Football bosses and in the press of exaggeration in talking about "slavery". Let the bitter facts speak for themselves.

'When a professional footballer signs a contract to play for a club the period of service ends on June 30th each year. At the end of that period the player may be retained and offered terms for a further 12 months. He may be placed on the Open-to-Transfer list or he may be given a free transfer. In the latter case he is unemployed and receives no wages but he is free to join a club of his own choice.

'Now, here is where the iniquity of British transfer system appears. Should a player who has been retained refuse to accept the terms offered, he can be prevented from ever earning his livelihood as that of a professional footballer. A player on the Open-to-Transfer list is prevented from joining a club of his own choice, until his former club, his ex-employer who does not pay him a penny, is paid a fee for his services.

'Take the recent case of Frank Brennan, the Newcastle United and Scottish centre-half. Brennan refused to accept Newcastle's offer of a basic wage of £8 a week which was a reduction of £7 a week under his previous contract.

'Newcastle could have stopped Brennan from getting another job as a professional footballer as he was retained. Meanwhile Brennan would have drawn no wages. It is quite true that Brennan could have followed the occupation of that of a barman or a street sweeper, but he could have been denied the right of following his chosen profession of that as a professional footballer. He had to knuckle under the system, or quit football. He resigned.

'It should be noted that each season 1/6th of footballers in the League are prevented from joining a club of their own choice. There are many others forced to accept reduced wages otherwise they must find other employment. The heartlessness of the clubs in the transfer market is hard to believe. A player and his family may starve while clubs chatter about what fee is to be paid for his services and the cut the selling manager will receive from the transfer. The clashes in which stars are involved make newspaper headlines, but thousands of players have suffered because of this system and their tragedies never get into the papers.

'Is there nothing to be said for the British transfer system? The Football Association and the Football League say this – "the system prevents the big, rich clubs getting all the best players." No mention, mark you, about whether or not the system is for the players' benefit. Just that it safeguards smaller clubs. This is not a feasible argument as the big, rich clubs get all the best players, anyway, by paying the biggest transfer fees.

'Linked with the transfer system as a method of shackling the professional footballer is the maximum wage limit of £15 a week. While on the one hand the football bosses say the transfer system is to prevent the richer clubs getting the best players – they get them anyway – the maximum wage is also claimed to prevent big clubs offering higher wages than the smaller clubs can afford. The dice is loaded in every way against the player ever being free to move or to earn anything like his real worth.

'Sweep away all the mealy-mouthed platitudes and this is what you are getting: while in every other industry or craft the worker is the one to benefit by his own special, personal skill or ability, the Football League system is designed to ensure that the cash benefits of a professional footballer's personal skill or ability will accrue only to the club having his signature (that club need not, in fact, be paying him a single penny in wages).

'Is that not a fantastic situation? Is that not like slavery? Does it not reek of the Dark Ages to claim that, whether paid or not, a man's working ability, his skill or flair, his services belong to a club which may not even have him under contract?

'Examine this much-publicised £15 a week which a footballer is said to be able to earn in the Football League. Less than 20 per cent of professional footballers earn the basic maximum wage. Even the great Trevor Ford gets £15 only when he plays for Cardiff City's first-team. Yet Trevor was worth £30,000 when Cardiff transferred him from Sunderland. Stars may cash in on their genius in other directions – and I don't blame them one little bit. Good luck to them.

'The majority of players, however, have no opportunity of cashing in on sidelines, and their pay and conditions are very seldom written about in the newspapers. It should be noted that the average wage for the profession is a paltry £8 a week (average wage for men in April, £10. 17s. 5d. – Ministry of Labour figures), and the average playing life approximately 7 years. Players can be retained for as little as £3 a week. They are so shackled and hamstrung by this iniquitous transfer system that they are rarely in a position to bargain. In fact no British footballer, whatever his status, can bargain to improve his lot. Contrast these two transfers in which British footballers were concerned.

'Notts County sold Jackie Sewell for £34,000. All Sewell got was a £10 signing-on fee and a weekly wage of up to £15. When Charlton sold Firmani for £35,000 to the Italian club Sampdoria, however, Firmani got a lump sum of £5,000, a salary of £100 a week, a luxury flat and other perquisites and his freedom to sign for who he likes after two years. Foreigners believe in paying to footballers themselves what they believe them to be worth. Yet here in Britain, home of democracy, clubs and not players get the benefit. Is it then so strange that foreign football flourishes while Britain lags behind?

'Some time ago, as the result of government advice, an organisation called the Standing Joint Committee was formed comprised of two representatives of the Football Association, two representatives of the Football League and four representatives of the union: "The functions of the Committee shall be to deal with all matters affecting the welfare of the players who are within its jurisdiction." Yet both the Football Association and the Football League continue to ignore the government directive by refusing to discuss the transfer system and pay. They refuse to allow a player union or legal representation on matters affecting his livelihood, the right of free speech, the right to work for whom he wants to work and the right to earn as much as he can.

'The Football Players' Union has done everything possible to reach agreement with the two bodies. We are reasonable men, who seek the same rights as all other Britons, the same rights as the men who control Association football. It is not a matter of "Who is right, but what is right."

'We have had enough of Human Bondage – we seek your assistance to unfetter the chains and set us free.'

BIBLIOGRAPHY

The Book of Football, Amalgamated Press, 1906.

Cameron, John, *Association Football and How To Play It*, Health and Strength, 1908.

Catton, J.H, *The Rise of the Leaguers*, Sporting Chronicle, 1897.

Chester, Sir Norman, *Report of the Committee on Football*, HMSO, 1968.

Coppell, Steve, *Touch and Go*, Willow, 1985.

Crampsey, Bob, *The Scottish Footballer*, Edinburgh, 1978.

Dougan, Derek, *How Not To Run Football*, All Seasons Publishing Ltd, 1981.

Douglas, Peter, *The Football Industry*, George Allen and Unwin, 1973.

Eastham, George, *Determined to Win*, Sports Book Club, 1964.

Fabian, A.H, and Green, G, *Association Football* (IV Vols), Caxton, 1960.

Fishwick, N. *Association Football and English Social Life,* Manchester University Press, 1989.

Ford, Trevor, *I Lead the Attack*, Stanley Paul, 1957.

Foul Book of Football No. 1 Best of Foul 1972–75, Foul Pubs, 1976.

Franklyn, Neil, *Soccer at Home and Abroad*, 1955.

Gibson, A, and Pickford, W. *Association Football and the Men Who Made It*, Caxton Publishing, 1906.

Guthrie, J, *Soccer Rebel*, Davis/Foster, 1976.

Hardaker, A, *Hardaker of the League*, Pelham Books, 1977.

Harding, J, *Football Wizard*, Breedon Books, 1985.

Harding, J, *Alex James*, Robson Books, 1968.

Harding, J, *Living To Play*, Robson Books, 2003.

Hill, J, *Striking for Soccer*, Sportsman's Book Club, 1961.

Imlach, Gary, *My Father and Other Working Class Heroes*, Yellow Jersey Press, 2005.

Inglis, S. *League Football and the Men Who Made It*, Collins/Willow, 1988.

Keeton, G.W, *The Football Revolution*, David & Charles, 1972.

Levine, P.A.G, *Spalding and the Rise of Baseball*, Oxford University Press, 1985.

Mason, Dr Tony, *Association Football and English Society*, Harvester Press, 1980.

PEP, *English Professional Football Planning*, XXII, 1966.

Redhead, S, *Sing When You're Winning*, Harvester Press, 1984.

Swann, Geron and Ward, Andrew, *The Boys From Up The Hill*, Crowberry, 1996.

Tischler, S, *Footballers and Businessmen*, New York, 1981.

VamPlew, Wray, *Pay Up and Play The Game*, Cambridge, 1988.

Wagg, S, *The Football World*, Harvester Press, 1984.

Winner, David, *Those Feet*, Bloomsbury, 2005.

Wright, Billy, *The World's My Football Pitch*, St Paul, 1953.

Articles and Reports

Burns, Michael, 'Working Together: Football and the Community' Projects Footballers Further Education and Vocational Training Society, PFA, 1985.

Canty, Edward and Bennett, Matthew, 'Webster CAS ruling can be of no surprise to football' *Football in Focus* Issue 10, Brabners Chaffe Street LLP, Manchester, March 2008.

Dabscheck, Braham
'International Unionism's Competitive Edge: FIFPro and the European Treaty', *Industrial Relations*, volume 58, no. 1 winter 2003, pp. 85–108
'Defensive, Manchester', in R. Cashman and M. McKenna (eds) *Sport in History*, St Lucia, 1979.
'A Man or A Puppet The FA's Attempt to Destroy the AFPU', School of Industrial Relations, University of New South Wales, Australia, 1990.

PFA AGM Reports and Minutes and the PFA website www.givemefootball.com

Groff, Joseph, 'The Andy Webster Case and the End of G-14' www.soccerlens.com, 2008.

Murphy, Patrick and Waddington, Ivan (eds) *Soccer Review* (various) Singer & Friedlander Football Review Produced in association with and hosted by The Centre for Research into Sport and Society at the University of Leicester and the PFA.

Lightbown, Chris et al. Meltdown Report, PFA, 2007.

Lowrey, James; Neatrour, Sam; and Williams, John, 'The Bosman Ruling, Football Transfers and Foreign Footballers Fact Sheet 16', Centre for the Sociology of Sport University of Leicester, 2002.

McArdle, David, 'One Hundred Years of Servitude: Contractual Conflict in English Professional Football before Bosman', Web Journal of Current Legal Issues in association with Blackstone Press Ltd, 2000.

McArdle, David, 'They're Playing R. Song. Football and the European Union after Bosman', *Football Studies*, vol. 3, no. 2, 2000.

Magee, Jonathan, 'When is a contract more than a contract? Professional football contracts and the pendulum of power', *Entertainment and Sports Law Journal*, October 2006.

European Commission White Paper on Sport, Seventh Report of Session 2007–08 Report, together with formal minutes, oral and written evidence. House of Commons Culture, Media and Sport Committee 8 May 2008.

Walters, G, 'The Professional Footballers Association: A Case-Study of Trade Union Growth', Birkbeck College Football Governance Research Centre, Research Paper No.1.

Redhead, Steve, 'The Legalisation of the Professional Footballer', PhD thesis submitted to School of Law, University of Warwick, 1984.

Newspapers/Magazines (pre-1945):

Soccer – Players' Union magazine (1940–50s)
Thomson's Weekly News
Lancashire Daily Post
Sporting Chronicle
Daily Dispatch
Athletic News
Bolton Cricket and Football Field
Saturday Post
Topical Times
Daily Sketch
Sports Pictures
Red Letter
Football Field

INDEX